PROGRAM
TEST METHODS

PROGRAM TEST METHODS

Edited by
William C. Hetzel

Computation Center
University of North Carolina
Chapel Hill

Based on the proceedings of the Computer Program Test Methods Symposium held at the University of North Carolina, Chapel Hill, June 21–23, 1972

PRENTICE-HALL, INC., Englewood Cliffs, New Jersey

Library of Congress Cataloging in Publication Data

Hetzel, William C.   1941–
    Program test methods.

    Bibliography: p.
    1. Computer programs—Testing.   I. Title.
QA76.H45   001.6′425   72-8657
ISBN 0-13-729624-X

© 1973
by Prentice-Hall, Inc.
Englewood Cliffs, N. J.

10   9   8   7   6   5   4   3   2   1

Printed in the United States of America

PRENTICE-HALL INTERNATIONAL, INC., *London*
PRENTICE-HALL OF AUSTRALIA, PTY. LTD., *Sydney*
PRENTICE-HALL OF CANADA, LTD., *Toronto*
PRENTICE-HALL OF INDIA PRIVATE LIMITED, *New Delhi*
PRENTICE-HALL OF JAPAN, INC., *Tokyo*

CONTENTS

CONTENTS

PREFACE

The Computer Program Test Methods Symposium was held at the University of North Carolina on June 21-23, 1972. Its primary purpose was to focus attention on the importance of the testing activity and establish a cross section of the current state of the art in program testing. The symposium was sponsored by the Association of Computing Machinery Special Interest Group on Programming Languages (ACM SIGPLAN) and the UNC Computation Center. The papers in this book are derived from the talks presented at the symposium.

Part I serves as an introduction to the other parts of the book, briefly summarizing and relating the chapters to each other as well as offering a definitional framework for the field of testing. Parts II to VIII form the core of the book and basically contain the edited papers of the symposium arranged in topical order. Part IX contains a large annotated bibliography of the testing literature. The bibliography is structured into subject areas and is referenced by all the chapters in the text.

Both the symposium and this book are the first devoted to computer program testing. That each has been needed for some time is now clear. The growth of a testing discipline has been painfully slow, despite the acknowledged need for better quality software. Even the scope of what is or is not a testing activity is not well defined. Terminology in the field is unclear and literature that would establish some foundations has not been written. Testing as an activity needs and requires more attention.

A sense of increasing urgency seems prevalent and much research is underway. In general, however, the methodology, techniques and theory of program testing are entirely inadequate. It is hoped that this book is a start toward the solutions needed.

ACKNOWLEDGEMENTS

Acknowledgements are due to the University of North Carolina Computation Center for providing the time and encouragement to work on the symposium and this book, to the National Science Foundation for financial support of my research in testing methods, to Don Kosy, Jim Cody and Edward Miller for their help with the bibliography and to Jean Sammet for her assistance as SIGPLAN liaison.

My special thanks go to Wayne Cowell for his work as Program Chairman and to my wife Nancy for her help and understanding.

PROGRAM
TEST METHODS

INTRODUCTION

I

It has frequently been said that the only error-free program is the one that will never be run again.

A.M. Pietrasanta

Everything of importance has been said before by somebody who did not discover it.

Alfred North Whitehead

OVERVIEW

William C. Hetzel

University of North Carolina Computation Center, Chapel Hill

PART I   Program Test Methods is organized into nine
                   parts. Part I serves as a preliminary to the
rest of the book. Chapter one and two by the editor provide an
overview of the later parts and offer a definitional framework
for the various testing activities. Chapter three by Fred
Gruenberger places program testing in historical perspective and
clarifies a few of the elementary testing ideas.

PART II   Part II explores some of the basic program
                   testing ideas and concepts. Chapter four,
also by the editor, discusses the principles of segmentation,
sampling, simulation, design for testability, standardization,
logical reduction and automation as the major principles of
testing reflected by our experience to date. The testing
literature is surveyed and grouped under each appropriate
principle. Chapter five by Jan Prokop considers the notions
of program correctness and the ideas of formal and informal
proofs of correctness as they relate to the broader testing
activity. The chapter covers a number of the various proof
techniques as well as the categories of languages susceptible
to each.

PART III   Part III is devoted to the very important
                   idea of designing and organizing programs
from the beginning so that testing is facilitated. Chapter
six by Victor Vyssotsky provides an overview of a variety
of techniques for designing software packages which ease the
burden of testing. Crucial factors considered are controlled
product design combined with early and continued emphasis
on test planning and test design. Simplified program struc-

ture and test repeatability are also emphasized. Chapter
seven by Peter Freeman reviews and examines the implications
of the ideas of functional (structured, hierarchical or top-
down) programming. An integrated programming environment to
support functional programming is proposed and two particular
features it should have are examined: effective top-level
execution control by the programmer himself and a continuous
context that preserves the effects of individual tests. Two
mechanisms, a type system and an extendable interpreter are
suggested as a basis for an implementation. Chapter eight
by Robert Snowdon is a description of a system called PEARL
that has been implemented to provide the type of program
writing environment proposed in chapter seven. Facilities are
provided in PEARL for the construction of assertions involving
abstract operations and data types. Partially completed
programs may be compiled and executed and then completed at
later points in the program writing process.

PART IV   Part IV explores the design of programming
                 languages to facilitate testing and proof
of correctness. Chapter nine by Don Kosy examines the relation between the language in which a program is written
and the ease and efficiency of assuring program correctness.
Some new language design strategies are suggested to improve
program reliability. Chapter ten by Donald Good and Larry
Ragland presents a programming language called NUCLEUS that
has been designed so that all programs written in the language can be subjected to rigorous proofs of correctness. The
techniques for formally defining the language as well as the
problem of the correctness of the verifier and compiler are
covered.

PART V   Part V is concerned with the specialized
                 testing techniques that are important for
the testing of mathematical software. Chapter eleven by Jim
Cody surveys the recent history and present status of activity
in the evaluation of mathematical software. A philisophy of
evaluation is discussed as well as some of the current and
projected evaluation projects. Chapter twelve by Edward Ng
is a description of testing methods and activities for elementary and special mathematical functions. Chapter thirteen by
Herb Bright and Isabella Cole discusses an automated method

for tracing numerical calculations in order to provide an
indication of the effects of finite precision arithmetic. The
process is one of test execution of user programs with actual
data. The data is used selectively and interpretively in an
error-indicating arithmetic in order to develop continuing
estimates of the current number of valid digits remaining.

PART VI   Part VI considers the specialized testing
                   techniques required for the testing of very
large software packages and systems. Chapter fourteen by
Alan Scherr presents an overview of the process used to design,
develop and test the Time Sharing Option of the operating
system for the System/360. The techniques used for the coordination of the system design, the building of the various versions
of the system and the testing done at each phase are described.
Chapter fifteen by John Brown et al, considers the development
of automated software verification tools for large systems.
The characteristics and utility of three particular tools are
discussed as case study examples. The examples are a program
to compare data bases, a system to measure test effectiveness
and a system to compare test results. Chapter sixteen by
Edward Youngberg proposes a design for a software testing control system called the Validation Control System. The system
assumes a set of pass/fail testing kernels and provides a
variety of services to assist in the testing of large component packages and operating systems.

PART VII   Part VII is concerned with a few of the
                   many models about program behavior that
have been suggested. The usefulness of models to program
testing derives from the power of a model to simplify the
testing required and reduce any necessary program analysis.
Chapter seventeen by Harlan Mills considers the complexity of
programs to be a "third dimension" in addition to the dimensions of storage and resource requirements. Some ideas for
measuring the complexity of a program in terms of the correspondence between static text and dynamic execution are formulated and the importance of the complexity of programs is
emphasized. Chapter eighteen by John Howard and William
Alexander discusses a system for converting the source code
of a program into a compressed state graph, manipulating the
graph to bring out distinctions between values of critical

variables, and matching the final graph against a prototype
of correct operation sequences. The approach has been implemented in an analysis program which has been used to test
selected parts of the operating system at the University of
Texas. Chapter nineteen by Jean-Claude Rault presents a
parallel between programs and digital circuits and considers
how methods originally intended for hardward fault diagnosis
may be extended to software fault diagnosis. In particular,
how methods originally intended for hardware fault diagnosis
may be extended to software fault diagnosis. In particular,
a testing scheme consisting of running random test cases for
two versions of the same program is proposed. One is written
in a very high level language, the other in a conventional
language more suited for efficient execution. Chapter twenty
by Grantham Holland distinguishes acceptance testing from
developer testing and provides some considerations towards
the formulation of a theoretical model which treats an
acceptance test as an empirical rather than analytical process.

PART VIII   Part VIII is concerned with standards and
                   measurements of program quality. Chapter
twenty-one by Walter Sadowski and Daniel Lozier proposes and
describes a system of standards for the validation of mathematical function algorithms. The system is modelled after the
physical standards techniques used by the Bureau of Standards
in other areas and consists of primary, transfer and working
standards. Chapter twenty-two by Ralph Keirstead and Donn
Parker explores the various quantitative software reliability
measures and the feasibility of formal software certification
based on these measures. The measure for program reliability
is developed as a function of the popularity, criticality and
reliability of the program modules, while module reliability
is considered as a function of the ration of the number of
tested module subdomains to the total number of domains.
Chapter twenty-three by Ruth Davis discusses the soft market
practices plaguing the software industry and proposes that
they by replaced by imposing quality control, demanding specifications and documentation, and utilizing validation and performance measurement services.

BIBLIOGRAPHY   Finally, Part IX contains a comprehensive
                   bibliography of the testing literature or-
ganized into sixteen topical areas. The bibliography is the
result of an extensive literature survey on computer program
testing, validation and certification.

A DEFINITIONAL FRAMEWORK

William C. Hetzel

University of North Carolina Computation Center, Chapel Hill

TESTING
ACTIVITIES AND
TERMINOLOGY

At the base of our testing problems is that there is currently no established discipline to act as a foundation. The literature is scrambled with little taxonomy to sort it out and few tutorial papers that would allow forgetting forever and the older references.

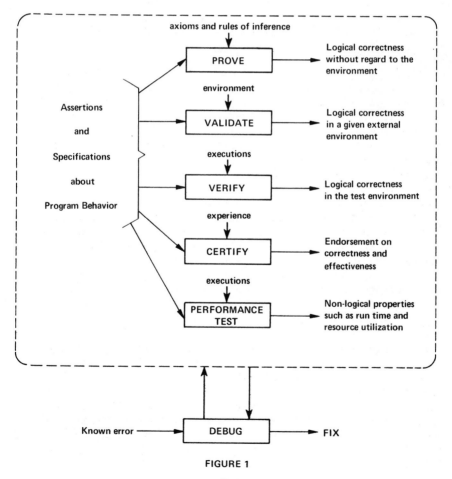

FIGURE 1

The diagram in Figure 1 is an attempt to establish a suitable definitional framework for the testing activity and to clarify some of the terminology that appears frequently in later chapters.

As applied to computer programs, the testing activity now encompasses an entire array of behavior, and many related words such as verify, validate, prove, certify and debug have become common in the literature. It is clear that these terms mean different things to different people. The figure tries to display what the editor believes are the consensus meanings in the belief that we need to better define our field and focus these terms in the literature.

The figure shows testing activities inside the dotted circle. This choice is based on defining any activity that increases our assurance or belief that a program performs "as it should" as a rightful *testing activity*. Some measure for defining a programs desired behavior is implied by this definition and we call such a measure a *specification*. The specification set or assertions describing the required behavior are shown as an input to all of the testing activities. *Debugging* does not meet this definition and is outside the circle. Historically, debugging and testing have been lumped together. They are actually quite distinct. Debugging starts with known errors and attempts corrections; testing measures how well the specifications are met. The two are related since testing uncovers debugging inputs (known errors) as an unhappy byproduct. Or as Gruenberger nicely puts it "When debugging is completed the program definitely solves some problem. Testing seeks to guarantee that it is the problem that was intended." The figure displays this interaction with arrows back and forth between the testing circle and debugging.

Inside the circle inputs to a box are suggestive of the information used by the process in the box while outputs on the right suggest the information obtained.

Distinguishing between the terms is admittedly a bit arbitrary. Verification, validation and certification are so synonymous that it is now difficult to separate them without offending someone. Validation is en vogue in the aerospace industry while certification seems to be the in-word for certain scientific and mathematical function codes. Verification has no particular bias and is used by everyone includ-

ing the designers of card punch verifiers. The dictionary
is of little or no help, as it tells us that certify is to
verify, verify is to prove to be true, and validate is to
test or prove the soundness of. Used in program testing,
however, there are some distinctions that are important enough
to make explicit.

Certification carries the connotation of an authoritative endorsement and seems to imply testifying in writing
that the program is of a certain standard or quality. Verification and proofs are usually only concerned with a program's logical correctness while validation connotes extending the testing to the program environment. Performance
tests and verification generally base their comparisons on
actual program executions, validation includes environment
information, certification generally requires authoritative
user experience, and proofs require a set of axioms and rules
of inference. Performance testing concentrates on the non-
logical properties such as resource utilization, run time,
I/O device requirements and various functional measures of
effectiveness.

All of the various testing activities tend to persuade
one that the program does in fact meet its specifications.
What is not generally recognized is that all of the processes
are subject to invalid conclusions. Many seem to be under
the delusion that proofs form some sort of exception. This
is not true. In mathematics axioms are given and certain
rules of inference are used to deduce or 'prove' theorems.
If the rules of inference are accepted and no deductive errors are made the theorems must follow from the axioms. To
apply to computer programs, the <u>axioms</u> as well as the rules
of inference must be true for the programming system in use.
In addition, the environment must be perfect. Even then the
worries are not over as described quite cleverly by Davis in
<u>Fidelity in Mathematical Discourse</u> [E11]. Davis references
a book called <u>Errors de Mathematique</u> by Lecat containing
over 130 pages of errors committed by mathematicians of the
first and second rank since antiquity. In the same article
he quotes a previous editor of the <u>Mathematical Reviews</u> as
estimating that one half of all published mathematical papers
contain errors and describes the several hundred errors that
were found in the <u>Handbook of Mathematical Functions</u>. These
remarks are not made to founder anyone's faith in mathematics
nor intended to upset any of the theorists, but rather to
place the proof of correctness activity in perspective

and hopefully to convince the reader that it is also a method, like all the other test methods, that can and does fail.

One final related term that appears quite often is *performance evaluation*. Strictly speaking, an evaluation does not compare actual against desired behavior but rather merely attempts to measure the actual behavior. Thus performance evaluation is not per se a testing activity and is not shown in the figure. Performance testing is suggested as the proper term when a "test" of the non-logical properties is appropriate.

Hopefully, these definitions will provide a basis for clarity and organization in looking at the testing activity. Although such a definitional framework is a prerequisite for improvement, defining terms does not solve our problems but merely aids in a better understanding of them.

PROGRAM TESTING: THE HISTORICAL PERSPECTIVE

Fred Gruenberger

Consultant, Woodland Hills, California

EARLY
HISTORY

To the best of my knowledge, the first time that program testing was distinguished from debugging was in 1957. Charles Baker, of RAND, wrote a lengthy review in Mathematical Tables and Other Aids to Computation of Dan McCracken's book Digital Computer Programming, and took Dan to task for not separating the two ideas. We don't want to be hard on Dan; his book was written in 1954, when only about a thousand people in the world could have called themselves programmers. But Baker's insight is applicable today, with program validation still confused with debugging, and an organized approach to the subject still lacking.

The distinction was first made vivid in an earlier note in the same journal in 1952, called "Adventures of a Blunder," by Brooker, Gill, and Wheeler at Cambridge. They described an error in the logic of a square root subroutine for the EDSAC. The subroutine, which had been tested, had been in use for some time before someone stumbled on to the pathological case for which it would not function properly.

TEXTBOOK
TREATMENTS

It seems to me that there are three clear divisions to the computing art:

1. What to compute--and for this we can state the criteria.
2. How to compute--the mechanics of the subject, and the only part to fill hundreds of textbooks.
3. Program testing--which is all art, and which demands a form of low cunning on the part of the programmer. It is during the testing phase of a problem solution that a programmer can really demonstrate that he is smarter than the machine.

F. GRUENBERGER

Our textbooks, starting with that early one of McCracken's, have been grossly lax on the subject of testing. The worst cases not only confuse it with debugging, but for the intermixed subject offer special rules that are patently ridiculous. For example, one of this year's texts suggests "rules" like these.

1. If an iterative loop will execute correctly 0, 1, 2, and 3 times, it can be expected to execute correctly any number of times.
2. If a given program will work on the first and last cases satisfactorily, it will work on the cases in between.

Such questionable advice will surely lead beginners into joining the hordes who grind out bad programs.

But other current books are not much better. Several of them recommend core dumps and trace routines as the proper (and only) tools to use for both debugging and testing. Others dismiss the subject nicely by simply stating that the programmer should take steps to insure correct answers. I have found only one text treatment that merits endorsement: the section of "Preliminary Testing," in Leeds and Weinberg's Computer Programming Fundamentals.

TEACHING TESTING IDEAS The computing industry is properly concerned with a large view of testing; that is, with system testing, and the testing of file manipulation packages, and the effects of programming languages on testing techniques. As a teacher, I am concerned with getting beginners indoctrinated into the concept of testing every routine. And this I find nearly impossible. I can teach the first two divisions of the art of computing to a significant fraction of my students. The concept of adequate testing of a program seems to register on about ten percent of the students, despite the use of every trick of teaching that I know. Maybe it's basically like the concept of a hot stove; ultimately you have to get your fingers burned to fully appreciate the theory.

Let me illustrate. Dr. Richard Hamming has a nice little problem in his book <u>Computers and Society</u>. Given input cards, each of which bears three integers, which are the lengths of the three sides of a triangle. For each card, print the lengths of the sides and an indication of whether the triangle is equilaterial, isosceles, or scalene. It's a dandy problem in logic and flowcharting for a beginning class. It also makes a nice exercise in program testing. How many test input cards would it take to validate the program adequately? Even the good students are astonished to find that it takes more than six cases to make a thorough test, and that the triplet (3,4,7) shouldn't be called a scalene triangle.

TESTING
GUIDELINES

Perhaps the main source of trouble in absorbing the notion of validating a program lies in the fact that there are no sure rules; that every program requires an original test procedure; that the intellectual effort to test a program is of the same order as that which created it. There are a few guidelines, though:

1. The test procedure must test the program and not some simpler variation of it. It is tempting, for a loop that is to run 1000 times, to change the loop test to 10, and test <u>that</u> loop. I put it to my students this way: You must arrange to test my program, and not some other program that you like better.

2. For most programs, the programmer is free to devise his test data. As a general rule, all-alike data is always weak for test purposes. Data that is all different is usually easily generated, and the results to be expected from systematic data can frequently be calculated by formula.

3. There must be positive feedback in every test procedure. This means printed results.

4. The results of the test procedure must be **not** only predictable but predicted. It never works to run a test procedure and <u>then</u> check to see that the results are correct, since printed output from computers will always appear to be correct. "Tell me what to expect as output before you get it."

5. The human eye is not a reliable device for checking numbers. No test procedure should rely on having more than a few numbers checked by human reading. Whatever it is that should be looked for, the computer can do it faster and better.

All that I've said is simple, obvious, and platitudinous. Good computing is like that: simple and obvious when it's done by masters. For most of us who are just average and who plug away at it, the simple and obvious guidelines have to be repeated every morning. We need something to cling to, like the accountant's "debits go toward the window; credits go toward the potted palm."

I'd guess that each programmer has had to go through the same cycle:

1. Who needs testing? I wrote the program myself and I know that it works perfectly.
2. Oops. My perfect program just blew up. I will not test my programs.
3. In fact, I won't commit any new program to production. I'll test and re-test.
4. There's a happy medium. Part of the art of testing is to know when to stop testing.

TESTING CONCEPTS

II

The art lies in knowing what to test for, how to devise adequate tests, and when to stop testing.

– F. Gruenberger

And diff'ring judgements serve but to declare that truth lies somewhere, if we knew but where.

– William Cowper

Men have become the tools of their tools

– Thoreau

PRINCIPLES OF COMPUTER PROGRAM TESTING

4

William C. Hetzel

University of North Carolina Computation Center, Chapel Hill

INTRODUCTION   Testing is an activity all of us have en-
dured many times. A fair amount has been
written about its problems, but as one studies it the first
impression is that we really know very little. However, looking at the literature collectively, there are important lessons and principles that are now becoming discernible. This
chapter surveys the testing literature by showing how it is
related to each of seven important testing principles. The
principles are discussed in the following sections and illustrated by appropriate references from the literature. The
reader is not expected to gain a full understanding of what
has been done in all the references, but rather an overall
appreciation for the testing activity as it is now practiced
and an understanding of some of the underlying forces behind
it.

SEGMENTATION   The first testing principle is the idea of
segmentation. The principle is based on
the classical problem solving scheme of separating a large
complex problem into a number of smaller sub-problems and
tackling each individually. In programming, this principle
has been stressed since as early as 1951 when Wilkes made
the subroutine the basis for programming on the EDSAC[1]. The
same principle accounted for the tremendous acceptance of
Fortran II with individual subroutine compilations in 1957
and since then has steadily become more engrained in programming design. The arguments for testing a small piece at a
time are much the same as for coding a small piece at a time.
Namely, conceptual clarity is greatly focused and test case
economies are realized from the knowledge that interfacing
units are already tested.

As the principle has been refined with time the term

-17-

modular programming has become popular. In modular programming, functional modules are coded and tested separately and then "plugged" together much like hardware is built. It is only now beginning to be recognized that seldom do the plugs match the receptacles. A number of package tools have appeared recently to facilitate module testing and improve plugability. Most such systems simulate a mainline program and permit specifying and checking module inputs and outputs. (See for example [D2] and [B8]).

An extension of the testing of program parts separately is that of successive "stages" of testing. The idea of "successively decreasing levels of subdivision during design, and of successively increasing levels of integration during testing" [J6] is fundamental and underlies the structuring of testing into 'stages'. Many references in the literature discuss appropriate testing stages for certain classes of programs. Ginzberg [J2] considers the stages for real time programs from individual subsystem test in a simulated environment up to entire system test in the real environment. Willmorth [J9] suggests a staged process of parameter testing, assembly testing and integration or system testing. Schlender [J7] uses the terms unit testing, interface testing and regression testing. The particular choice of the stages is not as significant as the understanding of the concept of attempting to examine and test new functions only after testing all sub-functions.

Overall, the segmentation testing principle is important because of the added conceptual clarity, the economy in test cases that is obtained and in being able to do more of the testing in parallel with program development.

DESIGN   The second idea in the literature that we
FOR   formulate as a basic testing principle is the
TESTABILITY   idea of designing in testability. Essential-
                ly, there is now an emerging recognition that
testing must be planned for throughout the entire design and coding process. It is illustrated in the literature in three quite different and important ways: a concern for testable problem specifications, designing in testing aids as a part of development and a concern for the structure of the program itself.

[1]The Preparation of Programs for Electronic Digital Computers, Wilkes, Wheeler, and Gill, Addison Wesley 1951.

First we consider the problem of testable specifications. The common practice now is of course to leave much to implicit understanding. The resulting problems are well known. Ambiguity and misunderstanding are the cause of almost as many errors as logical coding. Lack of automatic testability leads to subjective testing judgments and untested functions. Defensive programming begins to take up a significant fraction of the code as a guard against the unexpected input. Ideally, we would like the setting of specifications to be independent of the testing process. In actual practice the specification set is continually refined throughout program development and testing. Such feedback is simply forced by the imperfection of written specification methods.

Two alternatives have been proposed to eliminate implicit specification and its inherent problems. The first is to explicitly provide a full specification language independent of the code. This is basically an extension of the redundancy concept in coding theory and allows the testing process to become fully automatic to the degree that the specification language semantics are capable of representing the conditions to be tested. As examples, Worley [F21] discusses the concept of redundantly coded languages consisting of a code language and a dual language to specify assertions, specifications and behavior. King [I9] and others have suggested annotating a program to be compiled with propositions and the actual program is then verified by the compiler. The second alternative is to derive the code directly from the specifications instead of providing redundancy and checking the two against each other. This was first suggested by Dijkstra [B1] and if possible it permits obtaining a priori correct programs and eliminating testing altogether. This is true but assumes you have "tested" the representation of the problem in the specification language. Higher level language compilers which 'derive' lower level code are a partial step in this direction and they have certainly helped reduce the testing problem. Much more powerful specification languages are needed if further reduction is to be achieved. The power obtainable is however limited by the requirement that the executable code be practically derivable. Such a requirement probably means the method is already near its practical limit.

It is very difficult to avoid implicit specification. Languages are needed that are capable of specifying such items as subroutine entry and exit conditions, points at which data items are modified and the overall global flow of control. In addition, the language must be at such a level that the problem of insuring the specifications represent the respective abstract problem is kept small. Clearly, not enough emphasis has been given to such languages and work is only now underway that grapples with the specification language questions directly. Stark [F16,F17] for example has proposed a specification language for a class of mathematical problems that is designed to facilitate proofs of equivalence as well as translation into efficient machine programs. Much promise exists, and perhaps a proper specification language will make it possible to eliminate some of the distinctions between verification and performance testing.

Next under the design for testability principle, is the idea of putting testing aids in during development. Tobey [A24] and others have emphasized the need to design systems so the output required to enable verification of performance is available. The idea is a well established hardware design concept. Enslow [G6] for example in studying hardware testing concludes the most important factor is to consider the needs of the testing programs throughout the machine design stage. This is sort of a motherhood item. The prevalent opinion accepts the principle but doesn't act on it citing cost and deadlines as excuses. The author does not know personally of a single software system that really used testability as a design criterion. Perhaps some readers do, but I'm sure it hasn't happened often.

Finally, under the design for testability is the important and relatively recent idea of structuring the program logic to facilitate testing. The terms hierarchical, structired, functional, top-down and stepwise programming all convey this idea. Notable examples in the literature include:

1. Dijkstra [B2] discusses the designers responsibility to construct his mechanism in such a way, i.e., so effectively structured, that at each stage of the testing procedure the number of relevant test cases will be so small that he can test them all." Such a structure allows one to conclude correctness based on induction over the level of the structure of hierarchy.
2. Mills [B9] has proposed structuring the programming in an evolving tree structure of nested modules with no control branching between modules except for module calls defined in the structure. By limiting the size of the modules, unit testing can be done by systematic reading and the modules executed directly in a top down testing process.

3. Chapter seven by Freeman and eight by Snowdon expand further on these concepts.

In summary, the arguments for the importance of the principle of design for testability include:

1. Test new functions only after testing all subfunctions
2. Conclude correctness based on induction over the level of structure
3. Use structure, design and specification to achieve test case economies
4. Test in parallel with development
5. Avoid implicit specification

SIMULATION   The third principle is the idea of simulation. As systems have become more and more advanced, the development of simulation as a tool for controlling the test inputs has been almost a necessity. Simulation's main usefulness to testing is its ability to provide a controlled program environment. This permits delaying the testing of stochastic environment variables until later in the testing hierarchy and greatly simplifies the construction and interpretation of relevant tests.

Many examples of the principle are available. Simulation of mainline programs to test submodules is used almost everywhere in the field. Other special purpose packages facilitate the simulation of specific environments. TEST/360 and MUSE[L2,L5] are systems which simulate the user-communications environment to permit exercising a terminal system independent of multiplexing or terminal hardware. Supnik [A23] argues for the extensive use of machine simulation for testing of systems for small computers. In this scheme, the simulator provides the small computer environment in a larger system to allow room for testing aids. Another somewhat related automated aid is the hierarchical control program suggested by Keefe[L8]. The scheme proposes testing with another level of control program so that the regular control program can be run in problem state and be controlled and tested. Such examples are typical of the widespread application to testing that simulation has found.

Two difficulties arise. The first is the difficulty of insuring that the simulation environment is in complete

correspondence with the real environment. This forces the
testing organization into the 'stages' discussed earlier as
both the simulated and the real environments must be tested.
The second is that the problem of testing the simulation
program may be almost as difficult as testing the basic program. Such problems make the use of simulation quite expensive and may lead to its gradual disfavor as other testing
strategies become more refined.

Overall simulations main usefulness to testing is its
ability to:

1. Delay the testing of the stochastic environment variables
2. Simplify the construction and interpretation of relevant
   tests
3. Provide a controlled program environment

SAMPLING   The fourth principle is the idea of samp-
                ling. Based on the predominant role samp-
ling techniques play in industrial testing, it is a surprize
to see what little value sampling theory has had on software
testing. For many problems it is quite possible to have
several million potentially significant data cases. In such
situations most programmers simply try to find a reasonable
variety of cases for which their program seems to work and
then conclude it will always work. The key to the success
of such an approach is the ability to select tests that are
relevant and probe particularly sensitive program areas. Unfortunately, such selection is very difficult to do. Because
of the difficulty, many attempts have been made to use essentially random test data in a sampling oriented test process.
One form of this is the 'field test' where a program is 'randomly' tested by its own user population. Another is represented by the logic independent test data generators discussed earlier. It seems evident to this author that despite
its popularity such sampling by itself is quite inadequate as
a testing tool.

As an example, programs in the Biomedical Department
Series (BMD) from UCLA have been field tested by over 750 installations for more than 5 years and still found to contain
a number of undetected serious logical flows. Even more significant is to consider the record of OS/360 which probably
embodies the greatest field test in history. The cause of

such testing failures is basically that traditional sampling techniques do not apply to a product whose parts are highly interdependent such as a computer program. As such, no amount of sampling can replace the value of systematic orderly testing. The law of large numbers simply does not apply here. This is more or less true depending on the class of program under test. Compiler testing, for example, appears more amenable, and the Air Force Cobol Compiler Validation System [D6] is an example of a system somewhat based on the sampling principle that has reported considerable success.

Despite its problems in program verification, the sampling principle seems to have recently emerged with an important role in quality estimation. Rubey [G6] suggests that a way of circumventing detailed analysis of an entire program is to extrapolate the results obtained from analyzing only sample sections. Mills [G4] proposes a statistical test based on the introduction of intentional but random programming errors into a program before the testing process starts. Such techniques are still purely experimental and much more research is needed.

Overall the sampling principle is important because of the obvious test case economy as well as its simple, economic application.

LOGICAL REDUCTION   Our fifth principle is the important pursuit of logical simplification or reduction. The principle of logical reduction is to seek program transformations that make testing easier or more reliable. The transformations are required to preserve the logical properties under test. Typical transformations that are used convert programs to flowcharts and directed graphs or to some simpler reduced forms. Florentin [C4] suggests decomposing a program into intervals or program subunits having single entry points, multiple exits and all backward references coming into the entry point. The interval transformation is one that can be automated and simplifies both program proofs and other types of verification methods. Strong and Walker [C21] suggest an automated method to transform recursive programs to flowchart form. Nievergelt [C14] outlines a technique of generating higher level equations from lower level code for a very restricted class of machines. Prosser [C19] suggests the transformation of program graph connections to boolean matrices to permit easier automatic analysis. In all of the schemes, the success achieved so far has been very minimal. Often, even after the most extensive reductions, the space of independent data cases is too large to allow exhaustive testing, and the tester must still face the test case sampling and selection problem.

The only alternatives to test case selection that have been proposed are the proof oriented techniques in which the test conclusions are based not on execution but induction over a set of assertions. Here logical reduction can be quite powerful. Hoare, for example [E12] proposes an axiomatic basis for computer programming with logical reduction through established rules of inference.

As a summary it appears that most of the schemes applying the principle of logical reduction are far away from practical success in complex problems. The degree of automation and potential power of the principle remains to be seen.

STANDARDIZATION   Our sixth testing principle is that of standardization. Standardization facilitates the handling and automation of complex processes. Standardized code structure permits simplified program analysis as well as the easier application of proof techniques, etc. The principle like all others can of course be overused. A good guide is that the standard technqiues used must embody a technology that is better than the programmer devises for himself. That is, the price for standardization should not be an inferior program.

The most common instances of the standardizing principle to testing are in the module interface area. Jackson and Swanwick [B8] suggest the use of macros to enforce standard interfaces and testbeds. Talioferro [B16] proposes constraining programmers in implementation techniques so that tests may be prepared in parallel. Elmendorf [J1] and the Sadowski and Lozier chapter in this book suggest standardizing the test process itself. Finally, a number of programming groups have standardized a particular language subset so that only certain language features may be used.

In summary, standardization is important as a means for simplifying the testing problem and developing a widely used and accepted methodology.

AUTOMATION   Finally we consider the principle of auto-
                    mation. We can conveniently place most of
the remaining testing literature references under this principle. Being computer professionals it is natural that we
should seek automation of the test process. And in fact,
automation of various parts has been pursued quite relentless-
ly. Unfortunately, automation requires at least a semi-al-
gorithmic process to start with. The fact that testing is not
currently such a process has limited the possible success,
however a wide variety of special purpose tools are now in
use and many more seem imminent. The tools may conveniently
be grouped into the classes of test data generators, checkers,
testing estimators, transformers, and monitors and simulators.

Perhaps the earliest automatic test tools were the test
data generators. They can be grouped into two classes, those
independent of program logic and those related in some way
to the program logic.

The independent test data generators are typified by
parameter driven packages such as TDG-II, DATAMATICS, TEST-
CUBE and others. In these the user inserts parameter cards
to specify the test data he wants generated. Other automated
aids in this group are the function argument and value generators for the testing of mathematical routines as is discussed
in chapters eleven and twelve by Cody and Ng.

The test data generators that are sensitive to program
logic are much less common. Examples in the literature include the following:

1. Sauder [D1] suggests a Cobol language extension which
   adds a requirements division and a relations section to
   specify the logic of data relationships. A network
   analysis program then generates test data for different
   branches meeting the required relationships.
2. Hanford [B14] describes a syntax directed data generator
   for testing PL/1 compiler front ends that generates syntactically correct PL/1 statements.
3. Miller and Maloney [C13] suggest a procedure for simple
   programs to establish a test deck covering all possible
   paths based on an analysis of the program as a logical
   tree.
4. Scheff [D13] suggests the use of décision tables to perform any sequence of tests and choose the new sequence
   on the basis of the results.

A good summary of the test generator tools is provided by [H1] and [H2]. The basic problem in constructing all such test data tools is of course not the generation of data but rather the generation of relevant data. This point is discussed more fully under the sampling principle.

The second class of automated tools we describe is the checkers. These include the interface checkers such as MOD-TEST discussed earlier as well as a host of systems which permit program files as well as relations between program variables to be checked for various conditions such as the reasonableness of final program values.

An interesting type of checker the author has experimented with permits one to check on the variations in selected output variables as selected input variables move through designated ranges. Theorem provers can also be viewed as a tool in this class and many are now described in the literature.

A third group of automated test tools are the testing estimators. Testing estimator tools are in quite common use although very little is published about them. These tools attempt to measure or estimate the degree of testing coverage or thoroughness. A large group analyze program execution and report on branches tested or not tested, fraction of instructions not executed, modules or subroutines entered and so on. Gaines [G3] provides a good description of various plots of the instruction counter vs. time. Such plots depict graphically the dynamic execution of a program and display both the portion of the code tested and untested. Pietrasanta [E3] suggests basing the testing estimation on the use of a test case library and plotting the number of test cases coded, run and run successfully versus time. Tucker [E9] suggests yet another estimation based on the shape of the error accumulation versus testing effort curve. More research is needed on these various plots as well as a number of others not described to determine how successful they can expect to be.

Another class of automated tools comprises the various transformers which translate programs and program modules into various equivalent forms. The most common are the various flowchart programs which transform source programs into standard flowcharts or directed graphs. (Abrams surveyed these in [B10]).

The motivation for transformation is of course to achieve a simpler problem and thus all of the techniques discussed under the principle of logical reduction, if amenable to automation, can eventually become automated tools in this group.

Finally, as a last group of automated test tools we consider the class of monitors and simulators or tools that control the test environment. We have already discussed a number of simulators under the principle of simulation. A good example of a monitor for testing is given in chapter sixteen on a Validation Control System.

Overall, the arguments for automated tools can be summarized by:

1. Automation makes the test process more rigorous
2. Widespread use occurs only for automated processes
3. Savings in time and cost
4. We are biased towards automation

CONCLUSIONS   This completes our discussion of the principles of testing. We have tried to summarize the testing literature under the principles of segmentation, design for testability, sampling, standardization, logical reduction, simulation and automation. What can we now speculate about the future based on the perspective of what we view as the important testing principles? It seems inevitable to me that reliable software will demand automatic examination. This in turn means unambiguous testable specification languages must evolve to allow descriptions about program behavior and the environments in which they are to operate. To program this testability we must render explicit and processable those aspects of programming which today remain hidden.

Languages to facilitate and support testing should become increasingly widespread. As the complexity and cost of programming continues to spiral the cost trade-off is more and more in favor of including testing facilities. A testing facility as a language feature is seldom missed until a user has a program actually executing-- then there just is no substitute. Features must be provided to allow the user to specify the testing information he requires.

Sampling as a principle should decrease in importance and be replaced by hierarchical organization and logical reduction. Increasing use of levels of structure and standardized linkages will in the near future obsolete many of today's programming techniques. Testing procedures for simple problems should become more and more routine with the result that application to larger systems will become more natural and easy.

Today's limited programming technology and inadequate research must be replaced by new interests and developments. The teaching of testing and its principles as a part of the programming discipline must become widespread even in the beginning programming courses. Only then, will testing be recognized as an important and integral part of programming.

Many serious problems remain. A good scale for testing thoroughness seems far away. We seem to be stuck with either exhaustively testing or not knowing where we are. This leaves us with no answer to the question of when to stop testing or how to evaluate the impact of selected changes. (The uncertainty principle prevents us from achieving reliable measurements.) We can't seem to keep a system constant long enough to measure it, or be able to remove the test aparatus and be sure the same test results still hold. Unambiguous specification languages and new logical reduction schemes which might make the goal of practical exhaustive testing a reality are far from available. In general, the methodology, techniques, and theory of system testing are entirely inadequate. We can see improvement but much research is needed. A challenge for our work is clearly present.

ON PROVING THE CORRECTNESS OF COMPUTER PROGRAMS

5

J. S. Prokop

Office of the Assistant Secretary of Defense, Washington, D. C.

MOTIVATION   Our problem, or the motivation if you will,
is the very substantial waste in program-
ming effort which is devoted to correcting programs and to
correcting the damage which incorrect programs cause to data.
We have been approaching solutions to this problem on an
ad hoc basis for some time. For instance, the use of test
data by analysts, programmers and auditors is an attempt to
prove program correctness. The trap dump routines that programmers insert at strategic points in their programs and
then remove (almost always) when the program goes into production, are also an attempt to demonstrate program correctness.

The pragmatic approach to proving program correctness
also is seen in the emergence of automatic flow charting programs for some languages. While some of the motivation in
producing generalized flowchart routines was to reduce the
onerous documentation task associated with programming, these
routines are also very helpful in finding logical inconsistencies in the program structure. Somewhat the same sort of
comments can be made about decision-table languages. Another
popular ad hoc method for certifying programs is to have another programmer inspect the listing and desk-check it for
correctness. Outside of these approaches, the formal efforts
in proving the correctness of programs have been restricted
to quite trivial and essentially all numerical examples.

THE NOTION OF   In formulating systems to prove the correct-
CORRECTNESS   ness of computer programs, it is well to
clearly define the interest at hand and the
notion of correctness. We can reasonably assert that a program is correct if it functions with no unexpected results.
This notion has included in it the notion of an algorithm

[A12], but really encompasses much more. We can, for example, imagine an algorithm which is specified, for instance in Iverson's notation, and which is correct in every respect. If we now take this algorithm and prepare it for some standard programming language (e.g., FORTRAN), it is not unreasonable to anticipate an error in coding (such as subscripting on the wrong variable). In presenting the results of our coding to a computer we may encounter a number of problems such as an unusual syntactic interpretation, an unfamiliar but fatal default option in the compiler, a system routine which malfunctions at object time, or a transient in the hardware or power system which introduces an error in the program or the data. In speculating on this, we have allowed ourselves to consider the correctness of a computer program and its associated data at four different points in time: analysis, coding, compilation and object. Any of these may reasonably be interpreted as the real point in time of interest.

However, for completeness, we really should consider this problem domain to be defined from inception to solution. If we do this, we can claim to look at the problem and its analysis documentation apart from the programming of the solution. Although some programmers define their own problem, devise a solution, then code and test the resultant computer program, this is not so with most programmers or most problems. In particular, in the commercial environment, it is not unusual to have a requirement defined and documented by a functional manager, translated to ADP system terminology and documentation by an ADP analyst and then documented and interpreted further by a programmer. In such an environment, it would be quite reasonable to consider the notion of correctness of a computer program with reference to the specifications of the functional analyst's documentation, or the ADP analyst's documentation or the programmer's documentation (e.g., a program flow chart). For convenience, we will comment on the notion of correctness principally in regard to the coding of a computer program from the programmer's documentation. Of course, we can't stay completely within those bounds, but there are some things that we specifically are not interested in — for instance, are we solving the right problem; are we using the correct programming language [G8]; is the computer program measurably complex.[G5].

VALIDATION VS. CERTIFICATION
One interesting approach to proving the correctness of computer programs is in the Department of Defense COBOL compiler validation routines, under the aegis of Grace Hopper. Here the set of programs (some 126 programs, in all) test COBOL compilers against the ANSI COBOL syntax. The results of each of the tests (some 2,700 tests, in all) are printed for analysis and interpretation. A typical test of a COBOL compiler on a dedicated U1108 takes about 2 wall clock hours, and 20 cpu minutes. If a compiler passes a test, the test identification and the anticipated as well as the received results are printed. Now in the strict context of proving a computer program (in this case a compiler) to be correct, there are at least two things wrong with this approach. The first is that this is not a rigorous proof by any standard, since there is no way of knowing if all possible tests are made. In effect, this set of COBOL validation routines validates those and only those aspects which it directly tests and makes no claims for any other. In some respects it is akin to the auditor's test data mentioned earlier. The second limitation is that the set of routines not only can <u>not</u> assert the validity of the program, but additionally the results must be interpreted by analysts. We do not turn the machine on and have a binary pass-fail decision appear at the console. Now, these routines are in use and do work quite well within the limits of the claims made for them. Since I have great faith in things that work, I mention them to demonstrate the modest advances which have been made in actually proving the correctness of large computer programs in an operational environment. This lack of concrete proof of correctness, of course, is not a fatal defect. However, it does mean that we do not yet <u>certify</u> the correctness of large operational programs. At best we <u>validate</u> that the programs have passed only certain specified tests.

PROOF OF CORRECTNESS
One serious restriction on proving the correctness of computer programs is the obvious reflection that <u>programs simply are not written to be proved.</u> Computer programs are written to be efficient, to be easily read, to be transferable among different computing machines, and so on, but they certainly are not

written to be proved to be correct.

London [E12] quite correctly remarks that we need the following basic information in order to carry out a formal proof of correctness. We need to know:

1. the semantic properties of the programming language used,
2. the formal properties of the expressions, relations and operators of the inductive assertions (or debugging statements),
3. the semantics of the problem domain (the analysis documents),
4. a formal statement of the axioms and properties used (e.g., axioms of the first order predicate calculus) in order to develop the proof of correctness.

Additionally, we need to know that the verification procedure itself is error-free, which is a problem unto itself, and no small task to demonstrate.

Now, this sort of information requirement puts the proof of correctness in a somewhat different light. We are no longer asking that an arbitrary production program be proven to be error-free. We are now asking that the analyst and the programmer restructure their present analysis and coding procedures, and additionally that they be able to choose correctly a proof method; to choose, for example, the specific inductive assertions [E3] about the program, and then verify that the applicable assertion is true as each transition point is reached in the program execution. Good [I4] comments that the choice of inductive assertions is in itself a difficult problem, and that the construction of the verification conditions is an arduous task at best. The construction and recording in proofs, similar to theorem proving in the first order predicate calculus, seems amenable to automation [I9], however, as does the construction of verification conditions [I4], at least for naive conditions.

It is worthwhile noting at this point that we have made a transition in thought from the COBOL compiler validator approach which was mentioned earlier. That was a standard set of routines written in ANSI standard COBOL to test any COBOL compiler. The transition that has been made is to the consideration now of individual proofs of correctness for individual programs, not one proof for a whole class, such as COBOL compilers. It is easy to miss this kind of distinction, and quickly becomes enmired in the Universal Turing

Machine halting problem environment[1], or another UNCOL project[2]. We are talking now about a proof-of-correctness internal and integral to the individual computer program itself.

PROGRAMMING   While some programming languages would seem
LANGUAGE   to lend themselves more tractably to formal-
CONSIDERATIONS   ly proving the correctness of computer pro-
                      grams(e.g., ALGOL), others do not appear
to have this same surface respectability in regard to algorithmic style (e.g., COBOL). Whatever existing language is
used, there must be a conscious attempt to structure the program for proof-purposes. This emphatically means a reorien-
tation of our present programming practices, and perhaps some
thought as to the trade-offs to be considered. For example,
there may be a pronounced difference in execution efficiency
noticed for some class of program. We make these kinds of
trade-offs now when we choose a hopefully machine-transfer-
able language over a more efficient but machine-dependent
language. Analogous choices have to be made when considering
the cost and talent necessary to construct a proof and then
to prove a program to be correct vis a vis the current programming and debugging practices. If a new language is to be
designed specifically to facilitate proof of correctness, a
different consideration is raised, at least for systems of
computer programs. That consideration is imposed because we
are now faced with another dimension in an already fuzzy area,
that of the language mix to be permitted in a system of programs with the attendant problems of data structure compatibility, program efficiency, documentation, program transferability, programmer training and on and on. None of these
points is of **course** a barrier to such a language development
or use, but neither can these considerations be ignored by
the implementor, who cannot find himself entirely dissuaded
by assertions that proving a program to be correct should
require no more resources than conventional debugging. The
transfer of research into implementation too often is labeled

---

[1] Minsky, M.L., Computation: Finite and Infinite Machines,
  Prentice-Hall, Inc., Englewood Cliffs, N.J., 1967.
[2] Steel, T.B. Jr., "UNCOL: The Myth and the Fact," Annual
  Review in Automatic Programming, Vol.2 (R. Goodman, Ed.),
  Pergamon Press, New York, 1961, pp. 325-44.

as "implementation defined," when in fact that transfer may
be the largest problem of all.

A QUESTION   We should recognize that we are dealing
OF ECONOMICS   with at least two dimensions in this prob-
                      lem--the problem domain and the programming
language. Our degree of difficulty in solving the proof-of-
correctness problem progresses in somewhat this fashion for
the problem domain.

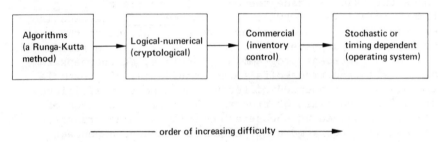

FIGURE 1

Similarly, for the programming language domain:

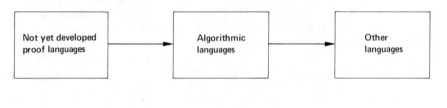

FIGURE 2

If we knew more about this proof-of-correctness area, we
might be able to draw up a matrix following the above description and fill in the matrix elements with a number to
indicate the degree of difficulty associated with each intersection of language versus problem domain. If we could fill
in this matrix authoritatively, we might be able to discuss
better the economics of trying to prove the correctness of
some class of programs. For instance, it may be that we can
write an operating system in a proof language, albeit inef-
ficiently, and prove its security within our resource limits,

but find that this is out of the question even for an algorithmic language. If we are still better informed about the proof-of-correctness area we could make a three-dimensional matrix by adding the dimension of proof techniques which are allowable under the several semantic properties of the several programming languages under consideration.

PROOF
TECHNIQUES

The proof-of-correctness by inductive assertions mentioned earlier is only one of several proof techniques [E12]. The technique involves inserting <u>assertions</u> between the lines of code in the program. The choice of assertions is comparable in difficulty to the choice of the induction statement in a proof by mathematical induction. These assertions can be binary decisions about the program state at transition points in the program. The correctness is proved by demonstrating that each of these assertions is true whenever the program is in that state, assuming that at each previous assertion-state a <u>true</u> value was encountered. Then, using induction on the lines of code, we can demonstrate that this produces an error-free verification procedure; [A12] (if all significant program states have been tested by the assertions, e.g., assertions to accompany each program statement.) While this technique is reminiscent of the practice of inserting debugging statements in the code, it is of course a much more rigorous procedure. It is not necessarily true that all programmers are producing programs at a level which requires that they understand the program so well that they can choose all the inductive assertions necessary. It may be these are the very programs which we are not really interested in proving to be correct. However, if we are, we have a significant personnel problem to resolve. This gets back again to the nagging question of implementation in an operational situation.

Another proof technique [E12] is to do a partitioned analysis of the cases to be covered. This is essentially what the auditor or the analyst tries to do in order to develop his test data, and differs here only in that we are not sampling input to test the computer program but are trying to be exhaustive to prove its correctness. If the input data can be partitioned into mutually exclusive classes, we can exhaust the possibilities by enumeration. Whereas the proof by assertion method was more of a programming technique, the partition analysis of the cases is really directed at the analysis more than the code, if we are permitted to make that kind of distinction. The trick is to be able to enumerate all the classes in order to see if they are covered. A hierarchical collection of data (e.g., a PL/1 Structure) is a useful device to use in the thought process when approaching this type of analysis. If we use this partitioned analysis, we still are faced with the question of the correctness of the computer program itself. This means that each of these cases must be traced through the program with a running commentary, or prose proof if you will, or that a proof by assertion is necessary.

It would seem to make good sense to construct proofs-of-correctness on both the analysis document and the code. In keeping with a distinction attributable to Blaau[3], we would be separately demonstrating the correctness of the logical structure (analysis) and the physical realization (code) of that logical structure. This division of labor takes due recognition of the many possible physical realizations of a logical structure, and makes the entire task a little less mind boggling than it appears at first encounter. Of course, nothing prevents us from dividing the code or the analysis into sections, and proving each one separately to make our task and our understanding of the task a little easier. However, this is more a question of tactic than one of strategy, and should not be viewed as a difference in basic proof procedures.

CONCLUSION   In conclusion, it would be fair to remark that we are not very much advanced in the art or science of proving computer programs to be correct. We notice a great effort to edit input for correctness (and then assume thereafter that the editing has been both correct and exhaustive), and almost no effort to prove that we will do the correct thing with the correct input, once we get it, or to provide for abnormalities generated by the program operating on correct input (or pathologic file conditions). The worst case examples of very large, very volatile (modification-wise) computer programs present special problems for proof of correctness, but the emphasis really should be

[3]Gruenberger, F. (Ed.), Fourth Generation Computers, Prentice-Hall, 1970, pp.155-168.

placed on the applicability and transference of proof techniques into a production environment for computer programs which are somewhere in the middle of the continuum from trivial to impossible.

DESIGNING PROGRAMS
FOR TESTING

III

I wanted certainty in the kind of way in which people want religious faith. I thought that certainty is more likely to be found in mathematics than elsewhere. But I discovered that many mathematical demonstrations, which my teachers expected me to accept, were full of fallacies, and that if certainty were indeed discoverable in mathematics, it would be in a new field of mathematics, with more solid foundations than those that had hitherto been thought secure. But as the work proceeded, I was continually reminded of the fable about the elephant and the tortoise. Having constructed an elephant upon which the mathematical world could rest, I found the elephant tottering, and proceeded to construct a tortoise to keep the elephant from falling, and after some twenty years of very arduous toil, I came to the conclusion that there was nothing more that I could do in the way of making mathematical knowledge indubitable.

— Bertrand Russell

Logic is neither a science nor an art, but a dodge.

— Benjamin Jowett
(1817–1893)

COMMON SENSE IN DESIGNING TESTABLE SOFTWARE

6

Victor A. Vyssotsky

Bell Laboratories, Madison, New Jersey

INTRODUCTION
AND
ASSUMPTIONS

Brian Randell observed at a symposium a
couple of years ago that precise design
methodologies work well for small systems,
but not for large systems, because large
systems are designed to do new problems for which there is
no experience on which to base the methodology. My interest
is mostly in large systems, and I agree with Randell. As
Randell also observed, there are a number of techniques
which, although too informal to be dignified as methodologies, do assist in building large systems.

I propose today to consider some techniques for designing large software packages which ease the burden of testing.
It seems to me that the crux of designing testable software
is to do a careful, controlled job of product design, emphasizing clarity and simplicity, and with constant attention to the question "If this were coded and in the machine,
how could I satisfy myself that it works as intended?" None
of what I shall say is novel. I am convinced that available, well known tools and techniques permit a much better
job of design for testability than is usually done.

My considerations will be limited to programs produced
for a customer. The customer may or may not be in the same
agency or company or university as the producer, but I assume that he is somehow paying for the software, and is
dealing with the producer at arm's length. Thus, I am ex-
cluding certain types of software from my considerations, as
for example, software produced as research. My customer has
some notion of what he expects in the way of a product; if it
does not do what he hoped, he will scream for me to fix it,
perhaps at my own expense. So I want the software to be
relatively free of errors when I deliver it.

V. VYSSOTSKY

An assumption which I will use throughout is that the planning and design of the tests which will be used both on the overall product and its various major parts is done by people within the producer organization who are separate from the product developers. I make this assumption partly because experience tells me that development and execution of tests will take me as much time and effort as product design and development. If I do not get started early on tests, the whole test effort will have to come at the end of my development cycle; this lengthens the cycle and costs more money in project carrying charges. Some other reasons why I want a separate test group will become apparent shortly.

For most sizeable software packages the only way to gain confidence that the product "works" is to test it. Now, given that the software has to function correctly for the customer at least most of the time, it is probably cheaper for me as a producer to do a good job of product design and implementation, and a good job of test design and test execution, than it is to do these poorly. Beyond some point, however, gaining additional confidence that the product is "correct" is going to cost me a lot of money. Since the customer is (hopefully) going to pay for the product, it is going to be expensive for him to get a product that has been tested past some level of assurance, and most customers place very definite limits on what they will pay for software. Hence, I will not design my product and my tests to give complete assurance that all the bugs are out; rather I will aim for some level of assurance that I determine more or less explicitly in view of the customer's needs. Given the desired level of assurance, what can I do in designing the software to help me get there?

IMPORTANCE OF SPECIFICATIONS First and most important, if I do not know what the program is supposed to do, no test can give me confidence that it is doing it. Curiously, the situation is asymetric; even if I do not know what it is supposed to do, I can sometimes be quite sure that what it is doing is not right. To some extent the testing of all large programs I am familiar with has been done without a good definition of what the program was intended to do. This means that comprehensive tests are difficult to devise, and that certain types of problems tend to be overlooked because of the uncertainty as to what is correct.

We want the best possible specification of what the product is supposed to do. We tend to fall short on this objective for some combination of three reasons. First, the producer and the customer both start with a rather fuzzy idea of what is desired; this is sharpened up slowly, and it may happen that it does not occur to anyone to consider some aspect of product specification until after delivery has been made. Among the cases where this shows up most clearly are cases in which the customer cannot start his big data base conversion until after you have provided the software, so that until then neither customer nor vendor realizes, for example, that waybills for shipments to St. Croix have to contain fields that are not provided for in the software. There are, of course, people in the customer organization who would have mentioned this if asked - but they were not asked. More important, the customer does not know what he wants the product to do until he tells you what he wants. This inevitably results in a long murky interaction during the design process.

Second, if the software deals with inputs from a physical environment, there are probably things the software producer does not know about the environment, or at least things that do not occur to him. For example, one tends to assume that traffic which goes in one end of a one-way vehicular tunnel has to come out the other end sooner or later. But I have watched a motorist turn around in the Sumner Tunnel in Boston and go out the wrong way, against the traffic stream. More serious, in many control applications nobody really understands the controlled process in detail; it is kept going be craftsmen of much experience who cannot (or will not) articulate the perceptual cues which guide their decisions.

Third, the developer naturally focusses on some nucleus of "well behaved cases", because those are the ones which are easy to think about and are also the ones which we consider central to the problem. The resulting programs tend to malfunction when confronted with the special cases we did not think about. One sees matrix packages which will not handle one by one matrices, routines for massaging networks in graph form which will not handle slings or loops or disconnected nodes, and so forth.

Fuzzy specifications are a chronic problem in the software business, and there is no easy way to remedy the situation. If one plans to test the program, however, it is worth devoting a lot of effort in the planning stages to looking for gaps in the specification, and plugging those gaps. Even on something as specifiable in principle as a compiler, it is very desirable to document in advance such questions as:

How large a source program is the compiler intended to handle; i.e., how many statements, labels, data names, external references, etc.? How much memory of various levels is the compiler to use? How fast is the compiler intended to run? What "efficiency" of object code is desired? How much checking for legality of input is to be done, and what is to be done when illegal input is discovered? What strategy is to be followed when the compiler encounters inconsistencies in its internal data base? And so forth.

For a real time program intended to provide high reliability, one has to think about and document the answers to similar questions. In addition, there is the problem of defining overload and specifying what the program is to do in an overload situation. One can design and code real time software, and even test it to some degree, without wrestling with the problem of what is the definition of design load for the system, how is overload to be recognized (if at all), and what is the system response intended to be when overload occurs. This problem is hard, because it is usually not easy at the outset even to define the traffic characteristics which will most influence internal loads in the system. The temptation is therefore to plunge ahead and implement something. However, there is no more unpleasant chore than trying to test a system thoroughly if the system has been designed without an explicit approach to overload. The same comments, of course, apply to the design of error response features.

UNDERSTANDING THE SPECIFICATIONS   Let us move on. We have a specification on the external characteristics of the product, and hopefully it is complete. The next question to ask is whether the test designers can understand the product specification, in the sense of being able to design a structure of tests for the product viewed as a black box. The first time the question

is asked the answer is apt to be no, and in this case the
only prudent approach is to redo the product specification.
If the test designers do not understand the product specification, the odds are very high that nobody else will either;
if one proceeds without an understandable specification, the
product designers will happily invent their way through the
gaps and obscurities, and the resulting product will be very
hard to test, use and maintain. Sometimes an attempt to redo the specification in more crisp and understandable form
will fail completely. This is a major warning signal. If
the problem is that poorly understood, all schedule and cost
estimates are likely to be badly mistaken, and a major re-
assessment is in order.

It takes real courage to pitch five hundred pages of
external specification in the trash and do it over; it takes
even more courage to chop out system features which are clut-
tering up the specification and making it incomprehensible.
It is usually not done, and it is not done for all sorts of
important reasons. Perhaps all that can be asked is that a
project which proceeds into implementation with a murky
specification should understand what lies ahead.

LEVELS   Supposing we have a specification for the
OF   externals of the product, what about the in-
SPECIFICATION   ternals. We obviously cannot afford to
                  limit our design for testing to the entire
product, so our product will have to be built as separately
testable pieces and subpieces. Each of these down to some
level deserves to be specified and tested in the same manner
as the overall product. This seems obvious, but failure to
do this contributes as much difficulty in test design as any
other factor I know of. I have seen many cases, including
some of my own programs, where a module had to be tested
with great effort after it was embedded in a larger package
because there was no adequate specification for the module
from which tests of the module itself could be designed.

When we get down to the lowest level of subdivision
worth considering as a separable design, some of the considerations in designing for test appear with a different aspect, and a few new facets emerge. The need for simplicity
is paramount, and bears on a number of aspects of detailed
design. For one thing, it helps a great deal to have the

product coded in a programming language which is well adapted to the problem since this permits tests which relate to the problem to match the structure of the code. This consideration may lead one to use GPSS or SNOBOL or LISP rather than, say, assembly language or PL/I. Of course there are cases where SNOBOL is a natural choice for one part of the job, LISP for another, and PL/I for the rest. My own intuition in such a case inclines toward using one language throughout, for consistency.

STRUCTURE
AND
SIMPLICITY

It is worth a large amount of effort to get simple, clear, understandable algorithms. I think programmers and their managers are usually far too tolerant of inexplicable algorithms. It may take considerable sophistication to understand a good algorithm, but it should not take a lot of grubbing around through special paths for lots of particular conditions. My own experience has invariably been that the great bulk of special cases can be subsumed back into general categories if I keep discarding algorithms until I come up with one that is clean. The difficulty with separate program paths for special cases from the point of view of test design lies not in the separate path itself, but rather in the certainty that the interaction of special case handling in other modules will not be completely thought out. If large numbers of special logic paths are present in each module, design of comprehensive tests becomes quite impossible.

Deliberate restrictions of coding technique and hardware capability are apt to be very helpful in improving testibility. GO-TO-free coding is becoming deservedly popular, largely because it reduces the combinatorics of program flow. Similarly, it is often desirable to place restrictions on address computations and storage allocation techniques; the reason is illustrated by the inordinate difficulty of designing adequate tests for programs which do paging on machines without paging hardware. A fine technique sometimes used in real time systems is to code in pure procedure and then, after the object program is loaded for execution, physically remove the store paths to program memory and the instruction fetch paths to data memory. In addition to its obvious effect in assuring that pure procedure is pure, it allows testers to verify by static inspection of code

as loaded that various other design standards and restrictions are adhered to, since they cannot be evaded by dynamic
computation during execution.

Subsetting of language and machine capabilities allowed
on a large programming job appears essential to the testability of the product. I cannot imagine any reasonable way of
testing a large PL/I program written by many people if the
implementation has made unrestricted use of base storage,
ON conditions, and multitasking. Any particular feature will
be mandatory for some job, but you cannot plan tests for a
given program if all features have been used on an ad hoc
basis. The test designer, after all, cannot desk check the
coding implementation; in fact, he should not have to read
the code. However, the use of such language features as the
PL/I ON statement will force special additional structure in
the tests, and the test designer can only take account of
this if such language features are used in a rigidly stylized
manner.

TEST   For a final observation let me jump out of
REPEATABILITY   the field of software per se, and remark on
                    an issue of system design. A problem which
can plague the testing of interactive or real time software
is unrepeatability of test runs. To some extent this may be
an unavoidable implication of the environment in which the
software executes, but much of its impact can be overcome by
a careful job of system design. Doing this involves attention to three design techniques. First, the data processor
hardware and software, including communications links between data processors, must be designed to minimize variation
of results introduced by asynchrony within this part of the
system. Second, driver hardware, or load boxes, which typically are themselves data processors, should be available to
provide repeatable test inputs that simulate the unrepeatable
inputs from the real world. Third, recording capability
should be designed to allow monitoring of execution without
perturbing execution timing. The provision of special load
boxes and recording facilities may sound expensive, and it
is; but if the customer expects your real time systems to
function day after day and month after month without crashes,
it is the only way I know of to get there. Without such facilities, even if you see the symptoms of an obscure bug during software checkout, you cannot make it hold still to be
swatted.

FUNCTIONAL PROGRAMMING TESTING AND MACHINE AIDS

7

Peter Freeman
University of California, Irvine

INTRODUCTION   The creation of large program systems has
been one of the major preoccupations of computing in recent years. The enormous difficulties such projects have often encountered have led to a consideration of
different[1] programming methodologies as one means of improvement. Functional (or top-down or structured) programming is
one of these that is gaining popularity.

The major emphasis of functional programming is on the
creation of correct programs so that much of the program
testing normally associated with building large systems will
not be necessary. No practical methods have yet been developed, however, that completely obviates all testing. Furthermore, this method encourages a system development sequence
that spreads testing out over time and intersperses it with
other activities. Thus, it is important to consider the implications of functional programming for program testing.

We will characterize two concerns: the need to explicitly describe the pieces of a system by the functions they perform and the importance of the programming environment in

[1]Although these methods are (rightfully) presented as improvements, they have been in common usage by list programmers for many years. For example, compare this partial
quote from the IPL-V Manual: "One programming strategy, often
called the "top-down" approach, is to divide each large process, no matter how complicated, into a small number of subprocesses. Each of these subprocesses is given a name, and
its function...is defined precisely by specifying exactly
what inputs it requires and what outputs it produces. How
this subprocess will carry out this processing does not matter
at this stage,..."

which a system is developed. The design for a programming system which will aid in the testing of systems produced in this way is sketched and an implementation basis for it is suggested. We begin with a brief review of the techniques we have subsumed under the term functional programming.

FUNCTIONAL PROGRAMMING There are three, not unrelated, ideas that typify what we will here call functional programming: Dijkstra's structured programming [B2], Parnas' software modules [F27] and Mills' top-down programming [B9]. The list programmer's concept of functional programming is nearly identical in intent and there are undoubtedly other equivalent formulations.

There are several aspects to what Dijkstra calls structured programming: correct generation of a program, proof of its correctness, and successive elaboration. Operationally, he suggests using program structures that are well suited to testing and a development strategy that permits a high degree of confidence in the correctness of the program logic. The first item is primarily a concern of language design, while the second is concerned with the order in which programs are designed, tested, and put together to form a larger system. The suggested strategy is basically the top-down method which has been elaborated by Mills.

Parnas' method is based on the observation that programmers get into trouble by implicitly assuming certain conditions to be true. His idea is to divide a system into modules and make explicit statements about their complete context. That is, each module is described by a function to be performed, a set of inputs and a set of outputs. The programmer has free reign to build it however he wants, providing he uses only the information explicitly given.

Mills' concept of top-down programming emphasizes the elaboration of control structures inherent in Dijkstra's ideas. His programming paradigm can be simply stated as follows: One first writes a completely rigorous program no longer than a page which satisfies the stated goals. Control enters at the top of the page and exits at the bottom. The program will primarily be the top-level of control, calling on subprograms to do the work. The inputs and outputs of each subprogram and what each is to accomplish, but nothing else, are clearly stated. The procedure is then repeated for each such subprogram, recursively if necessary, until no further expansion is needed.

This process is similar to the classical top-down design often done on paper. The critical difference, however, is that we write executable code at each step, not just paper designs. In fact, it is recommended that the programmer-designer actually debug the higher level routines before proceeding lower by using program stubs (minimal pieces of code to simulate the operation of a program) for the as yet unimplemented routines. Our primary concern here is the design of a programming environment to enhance this methodology.

MACHINE AIDS FOR FUNCTIONAL PROGRAMMING

There are many tools that can aid in the creation of program systems, ranging from compilers to "Do-what-I-mean" facilities [F18]. More important than individual tools, especially for functional programming, is the total environment in which the process takes place. An <u>integrated programming environment</u> is one in which all the tools needed to develop a program are immediately available at the same level of control: editors, filing systems, compilers, debugging systems, I/O facilities; such a system is usually interactive. Examples are: most APL systems, many Basic systems, and BBN Lisp. There are strong reasons for using an integrated environment in any situation: reduced system overhead in going from one phase to another, less conventions to be remembered, no mental swap time, etc. The blending of all aspects of program development into a continuous process in functional programming makes it essential. In what follows we assume that an integrated programming environment is used.

Keeping Track of Functional Specifications

Some of the power of functional programming stems from its insistence on clearly describing an object before it exists in final form. We can (and should) describe an object in functional terms as early in the design process as possible and then carry the description along as the object is further refined (by more detailed functional specification), coded, and finally tested.

It is possible to design using functions and their interconnections as the sole representation of the object being created [B7]. More important for our present purposes, however, are some simple facilities for keeping track of and using functional specifications. For example, if we define a structure to provide certain functions, we would like to know if such a structure (or a similar one) already exists. An integrated programming environment could be equipped with a language for stating functional specifications, a data base for keeping track of definitions and their interrelations, and mechanisms for automatically determining similarity of new structures to existing ones.

As the subpieces of a given structure are built, it is easy to forget one and/or build one whose functional definition differs from that required by the higher level routine. We could add checks which would automatically prompt the programmer for definitions of lower-level structures, check that all get defined, and compare test results (stated functionally) to requirements. If some coding regularity is enforced (e.g. standard ways of passing arguments and using temporary storage) then a certain amount of testing can be done automatically.

Functional programming requires a more explicit consideration of program descriptions (in the form of functional specifications) than is normally the case. This provides assistance to program creation and testing and provides an added bonus: a high level and understandable description of the system. The machine aids we have suggested should be viewed as advanced tools to aid this process. Now we turn to some more basic demands of a functional programming environment.

Elements of a System for Functional Programming

The type of testing proposed by Mills involves checking individual pieces of code (with a mocked-up context) before building the subroutines they use. The primary objective is to determine that a piece of code provides only the required functions. Other factors, such as execution time and memory usage, may also be checked at this stage. What is needed is an environment in which the proper test context can easily be built up, in which pieces of programs and dummy programs (stubs) can be pasted together, and most importantly, in which overall execution control is firmly held by the programmer.

There are two essential points. First, we are concerned
with the level of control. In most test situations the tester, the programmer, should be the top level. The system
should always return to a loop that asks him for more commands
(in the form of statements in a programming language); an attention button should permit control to be forced into this
loop if necessary.

Second, we are concerned with how this level of control
is used. The classical concept of program testing is primarily concerned with execution. The idea is to execute a program and inspect its output, make changes, and then iterate.
Construction of a large system consists of individual tests
followed by executions of assemblages in the same manner.
We are all familiar with some of the results of this methodology: each new increment of code added to a system requires
reexecuting all the procedures leading up to the new one,
large test data sets must be created, and program changes
must be entered in source files, new binary images compiled,
and a whole new module generated (if not an entire system).

Contrast this to what we call a continuous context mode
of testing. The idea is simple: the memory space in which
the system is evolving is preserved over time so that whatever changes occur in the programs or the data during an execution are not lost. There are variants of this idea (work-
spaces, save-for-restart files, checkpoint records) but all
foster the view that as we test pieces and build up a system
the main thing we are doing is changing data structures (programs, test data, checkout histories) in a memory that is
continuous over system creation time, not just system execution time.

When using functional programming we are more concerned
with the interconnections of parts of programs, inputs and
outputs, and the local effect of executing a small part of a
system. We are interested in the effect of execution on a
data structure, be it test scaffolding or part of the object
system being built. If we work in an environment restricting
us to an "execution" regimen then test drivers, data, and
instrumentation must be carefully built up so that a test run
will produce useful output. Their design and construction
will require considerable effort.

On the other hand, if we work with a continuous context,

integrated programming environment, much of the overhead of testing can be avoided. When the top level of control resides with the tester, we can view the testing process as a succession of short executions followed by ad hoc inspections of the context (memory) to determine if the execution had the desired effects. In most cases this will reduce the effort necessary to build a correct system.

Our purpose here has been only to sketch what we consider two major features a functional programming environment must have. There are clearly many others: the ability to create arbitrary data structures, the ability to have several different programming languages available to manipulate the continuous context, the ability of building up arbitrary notational systems and control structures, ways of producing final production versions of a system from the final result of the creation process, and the function tracking mechanisms discussed earlier.

A BASIS FOR IMPLEMENTATION   Providing a complete design for such a programming environment is beyond the scope of this paper and should respond to the demands of a specific set of goals. We will, however, propose two mechanisms that could serve as the basis for implementation.

First is a type mechanism that will allow blocks of memory to be differentiated. We assume that we can change the type of a given piece of memory, that the type can be obtained rapidly, and that the existence of a type does not change the actual storage (no special bits stored in a data word). This system overlays the name space comprising the continuous context and might be viewed as a form of segmentation of it. Although the types can be used by a language system (and probably will be by some of those operating in the context) they need not be. That is, arbitrary instructions can be laid down and executed by hardware in the name space without interference from the type system (or vice versa if proper conventions are followed).

The second mechanism is an extendible list interpreter which will interpret every symbol on a list by the type of the individual symbols. This permits us to paste together programs written in different languages. For example, we probably would have both an interpreter and a compiler for the main implementation language plus translators as appropriate for whatever other languages were being used. We could then paste together a number of programs using a simple list language; as the list is interpreted, the type of each symbol named will cause a different interpreter to be evoked, thus effecting the execution of the piece of code. In the case of machine code, the interpreter can be the hardware, of course, the only requirement being that a standard return of control be made to the main interpreter. (The system would have appropriate error traps so that if control is lost during interpretation of machine code, an attention key can be depressed and a recovery mode entered which will restart the top-level interpreter.)

These features permit the programmer to test pieces of code with an interpreter until he is satisfied they work properly. Then he can compile them and lay down the resulting machine code without changing the next-level-up of control which patches the routine together with others (some possibly stubs). As all of the subpieces of a given part are checked out and the overall control is shaped up, it too can be replaced by machine code. The top level language of the programming system, which is interpretative, is used as the scaffolding for pasting together pieces of the system. The fact that interpretation is done on the basis of types that are changeable provides the mechanism for easily changing the representation of a program without changing its lexical or syntactic connection to the rest of the evolving system.

For example, we might start with a program specification in the form of a data structure whose type would cause an interpreter to be evoked that would simply print the functional specifications on the programmers terminal. This might then be changed to a program (of a new type) which would return canned outputs whenever interpreted. A later version might be complete but be typed for interpretation rather than execution. Eventually we would compile the routine and hook the resulting machine code in so that it would be interpreted by the hardware. All of these changes would be effected without changing the name of the routine or any uses of it in the interpretative scaffolding.

We have briefly examined some implementation ideas for a system to aid functional programming. They are only part of a high-level design which must be further elaborated (by top-down programming, of course). Nevertheless, we hope that sufficient elaboration has been given to illustrate the basic ideas of testing in a functional programming environment.

CONCLUSION   Arguments can be made for and against a rich programming environment such as we have proposed. One argument commonly heard is that it is too expensive in terms of core usage and running time. This can be a problem with any system and we simply observe that the total cost of producing correct programs (including the cost of <u>not</u> producing correct ones) must be taken into account. Functional programming is aimed at reducing total costs and the ideas we have presented are aimed at making functional programming more effective, especially in the realm of testing and integration of system components.

Acknowledgements

Many of the underlying philosophies of program construction which led to the ideas presented here are due to Allen Newell. To him a special debt is owed. Some of the implementation ideas were developed for the L* system [B12] by a group composed of Allen Newell, Don McCracken, George Robertson, and the author. To the other members of that group, due thanks is expressed.

PEARL—A SYSTEM FOR THE PREPARATION AND VALIDATION OF STRUCTURED PROGRAMS

8

R. A. Snowdon
University of Newcastle Upon Tyne, England

INTRODUCTION   Underlying the whole PEARL system is the
basic philosophy of providing a programming
environment which will enable the programmer to construct programs in such a manner that he is able to verify their correctness and hence improve their reliability. The philosophy
behind the programming methodology owes much to the work of
Dijkstra [B4], Naur [B11], and Wirth [B17] on structured programming, while the ideas put forward by Naur [E5] and Floyd
[F19] and recently developed by King [I9] and Good [I4] on
program verification are relied upon in other parts of the
system.

The structural approach to program writing has been suggested by a number of authors, in particular Dijkstra [B4].
He submitted that the various levels could be constructed in
a top down manner such that the lower levels explain concepts
either of data type or of operation which have been introduced and used at a higher level. Each level is represented
by what Dijkstra calls a "pearl", the whole program being a
string of such pearls linking the various levels together.
Within each level the programmer may make use of some gross
concepts without being concerned over details of their implementation. The clarity thus gained makes comprehension of
the program that much better.

The program verification technique developed in recent
years consists of tagging the program at various points with
assertions about the state of the program variables at those
points. The program is then "verified" by proving that these
assertions will indeed hold true if the program is executed.
These ideas together with the structural approach to program
writing have been taken to form the basis of the PEARL system.
Within this framework, the ideas of multi-level modelling as
described by Zurcher and Randell [B18] and since expanded further [B19] are to be seen in the ability of PEARL to execute
incompletely specified programs. A programmer is allowed to
construct his program to some level of detail and get the com-

puter to execute it, means being provided to allow the use
of instances of abstract data types and operations.

Limitations

The actual system being implemented represents an initial exploration of the extent to which recent ideas on methods of programming can be made more practical by enlisting
the aid of the computer. Because of the tentative nature of
this work, there are shortcomings both from the human engineering point of view and in the facilities provided by the
system itself and in the programming language used. No consideration has been made concerning the problems of the cooperative design of a large program by a large group of programmers. Neither has there been any attempt to provide facilities for the writing of programs incorporating parallelism, rather a programmer is restricted to the writing of sequential programs.

MOTIVATION   In what follows the word "machine" is fre-
                   quently used. A machine is considered to
be an abstract entity, very similar to one of Dijkstra's
"pearls". It is capable of performing some action; a program
written for the machine indicating the sequence of operations
that define such action. It is also considered to possess
certain attributes and to operate in some environment. The
attributes are the various functions that the machine is
able to perform, while the environment consists of the various
types of object upon which it can apply these functions. It
is intended that the meaning of the word "machine" should be
taken as that given above, rather than to have its more
general implications.

A programmer has a problem to solve and a piece of equipment (i.e. the computer) to help him to solve it. He has to
consider his problem in terms that the computer understands
and then to write a program using such terms. In general
the computer will be pretty useless for his particular problem. (Unless his problem is to AND two bits together or to
LOAD a 32-bit general register). He should be able to decide
what sort of machine he would like by specifying the data
types and operations it understands. He then writes a program for his "ideal" machine to solve his particular problem.
These two distinct parts are called the specification and the

program of a machine.

This ideal machine does not exist and thus the programmer has now generated several more problems; i.e., how does he explain the concepts he has introduced for his ideal machine. Obviously he does it by introducing further "ideal" machines, each one explaining in more detail one of the concepts he has previously introduced. If we take this particularly simple view, we can imagine the machines linked together in a tree structure whose root is the ideal machine which solves the original problem. In practice, this tree structure is a special case of the more general directed graph with which we may represent the hierarchy of ideal machines [B15]. Furthermore, the construction of a program will involve more than a simple progression down the graph. Corrections and revisions will need to be made while construction may proceed in either direction. Thus the programmer must have some freedom to specify which concept he wishes to explain next or to link new explanations into an existing structure.

The process of introducing further ideal machines terminates when all of the desired concepts have been explained in terms recognizable to the actual computer. In the system being implemented this actual computer is as defined in the system programming language. It has two data types (integer and string) together with the normal operations upon instances of these data types.

One of the problems in programming is that of correctness. To this end the system programming language provides assert expressions which attach predicates to the program, while initial and final predicates may be expressed as part of the program for a given machine. These constructs act as aids towards obtaining a correct program for a particular machine and to ensure that the elaborations are done correctly.

REALIZATION   In order to provide a suitable environment
                 containing the features described in the
preceding sections, something more than a specially designed programming language is appropriate. Thus is born the broader idea of a programming system in which the programmer can not only write programs and have them syntactically checked

but also run them, check them and experiment with different realizations of particular concepts. The PEARL programming system contains (or is planned to contain) facilities to allow him to do all of these things based on the philosophies of structure and correctness. It has been designed primarily to be used in an interactive manner. The major facility provided is an ability to describe machines and link them together to provide a structured program. During this building process there is a requirement to maintain the correctness of the whole structure. At present, such checking is done with the assistance of the programmer, various language constructs being provided to give him the opportunity of expressing correctness criteria. Having partially constructed his program the programmer may wish to execute it to check whether his ideas are proceeding in a meaningful manner. Thus facilities are provided for him to do this, even though some of his concepts may be incompletely specified. He is able to alter the structure he has created by deleting or replacing particular machines. These alterations could invalidate the correctness of the whole structure and so further checking has to be done. Finally the system provides commands which enable him to list out details of his previous work such as lists of machines, data types or operations. A more detailed description of some of the facilities is given in succeeding sections.

Building the Program

Construction of the total program proceeds by specification of "ideal" machines together with programs for them. The system programming language is used for both of these purposes, thus enabling the syntax checker to check both machine specification and program. Each new machine is given a name. This serves to label both the specification and the program as a unit. Attached to each machine is a further character string. This is a comment to indicate what the machine is explaining and the method that is used. It can be considered as documentation for the machine and will be remembered as part of the machine. Following this is the machine specification which introduces types and operations. A new data type is specified by a <u>type</u> statement of the form:

<u>type</u> table

Operations are similarly introduced by an <u>operation</u> statement. The introduction of an operation takes the form of a procedure heading, as in ALGOLW for example:

<u>operation</u> construct (<u>table</u> a)

Having specified the machine, the programmer now must describe its action and indicate which concept the complete machine will explain. He writes a program and indicates a name for it. This will be the name of some concept previously introduced and enables the new machines to be linked into the existing hierarchy of machines. Thus if the operation "construct" had been introduced by the machine named M1, then some later machine, say M7, will be introduced to explain it. This link between M1 and M7 has to be exhibited.

We may continue the analogy with procedure declarations mentioned earlier. Whereas the introduction of an operation corresponded to the procedure heading, the elaboration of an operation corresponds to the procedure body. The link between the introduction (heading) and its elaboration (body) is made via the name of the operation. In fact the provision of just the simple name is not considered sufficient. A repetition of the operation name plus any parameter specification is required. (See first example at the end of the chapter). This is considered necessary as a reminder to the programmer of what he has already written. If the simple name alone is given, then the programmer will be provided with the original parameter specification. (See second example).

Having specified the machine and established the link to the operation he wishes to explain, the programmer now writes a program to perform this elaboration. To do this he uses the system programming language. This provides several sequencing primitives, an ability to create (declare) instances (or vectors of instances) of any data types understood by this machine, (this always includes <u>integer</u> and <u>string</u>) and to specify operations on declared data instances or on parameters.

The following are the basic sequencing constructs of the language.

1. S1; S2; ...; Sn
2. <u>if</u> E <u>then</u> S1 <u>else</u> S2
3. <u>while</u> E <u>do</u> S
4. <u>repeat</u> S1 <u>until</u> E
5. ability to perform an operation (including recursion).

where S1, S2, ... Sn are statements and E is a logical expression.

Most of these are as found in other high level languages. One feature normally found but missing is that of a procedure. However, most of the facilities provided by procedures are contained in the concept of an "operation" and thus provision of procedures was considered unnecessary.

The system programming language also serves to describe a machine that does exist in that it provides several basic concepts. This machine may be considered as the target machine for all elaborations such that when a concept is elaborated solely in terms of these basic concepts, it has then been fully explained and will be understood by the system's interpreter program. The basic concepts are available in all machines introduced by the programmer and are as follows.

1. Data types - <u>integer</u> and <u>string</u>
2. Operations
     between integers ...+,-,*,/,=,<,>,&,|,¬
     between strings ... || (catenate), substring se-
                             lection.
3. Selection of a particular element of a vector by sub-
     scription.
4. Assignment (:=) is available between instances of
     similar data types although in general this is an
     operation which will require elaboration.

If the syntax checker finds no errors in either the specification or the program of a machine, then the information supplied is added to that already present and the programmer can continue. In general the choice of what to elaborate next is entirely up to the programmer. However, if he refines a data type, then the system limits his choice to elaborating those operations which act upon instances of that data type. Until all of these have been elaborated, in terms of the structure given to the data type, his choice is limited. This restriction is essentially an implementation one, but can be supported for other reasons. When a data type is introduced into the environment as a concept, it is given no structure until such detail is considered necessary. At such a point in the construction process, the programmer will have no requirement for the concept as such, but rather will now be concerned with the internal structure he has given to the data type. The restriction of the programmers choice is

thus limited until he has elaborated all of his other concepts
to such a level of detail. This restriction only applies
when the programmer is proceeding purely "top down". If he
is replacing or inserting a machine at some later stage then
the relevant environment will apply.

The Correctness Problem

There are, nowadays, instances of automatic program
provers, or of programs that provide assistance towards this
end. (See [19] and [14]). These work by proving that, given
various assertions about the values of the variables of a
program at points within the program, then, given an initial
assertion, these assertions will be met as the program is
executed. This same principle can be applied to the programs
written for each new "ideal" machine. Thus the system language contains a special form of expression called the assert
expression. One of the requirements of such proof techniques
is that the meanings of the operations provided by the programming language are well understood. However, in PEARL,
further operations can be added as required. Thus a provision has been made for a meaning to be given to an operation when it is introduced.

As was noted in the introduction, there is a requirement
for a more explicit definition of the meaning of an operation
introduced in a conceptual manner during the construction
process. In this programming system, therefore, although a
basically top down philosophy is encouraged, operations are
required to have meanings so that precautions can be taken
against programmer error at all times during the construction
process.

The specification of a meaning takes the form of a pre-
condition and a post-condition described by assertions over
the parameters of the operation. Thus the syntax of an operation introduction takes the form:

> operation   <name> <parameters>
> provided   <pre-condition>
> yields   <post-condition> onexit

At present it is not possible to provide alternative
meanings dependent on the input parameters, but such an extension is clearly desirable.

e.g. <u>provided</u> cond 1 <u>yields</u> result 1
<u>or</u>   <u>provided</u> cond 2 <u>yields</u> result 2 <u>onexit</u>

To enable the provision of predicates over
any data type, a further concept is introduced, that of
'state'. A state is a predicate over a particular data type,
either programmer introduced or a basic type. It is a means
of indicating the condition in which an instance of that type
may be found.

States for a type may be introduced at any time that an
operation on that type can be introduced. Their introduction
is part of the machine specification phase and is similar in
form to an operation statement but without a meaning part.

e.g. <u>states</u> empty (<u>queue</u> a)

This example assumes that a data type, 'queue' has been
introduced and introduces the concept of a queue having no
entries in it. Thus the programmer may now test instances
of the type 'queue' for this condition by using the state as
as a predicate. He may also use it to give meaning to an
operation.

e.g. <u>operation</u> clear (<u>queue</u> a)
            <u>provided</u> <u>true</u>
            <u>yields</u> empty(a) <u>onexit</u>

Using this mechanism, assertions may be made about all
data types. The system programming language provides some
basic predicates for the integers (but none for strings) and
methods of combining basic predicates using & (and) and |(or).
From these assertions, the computer will be able to give assistance towards establishing the correctness of a program.

There is, however, a further dimension to the traditional
correctness problem. Although the program for a given machine
may be correct, it may be invalidated by the subsequent elaboration of a concept. Provision is made within the system to
overcome this problem.

When an operation is introduced it may be given pre- and
post- conditions. Similarly, when an operation is elaborated,
this elaboration may also be given pre- and post- conditions.
These latter conditions can be regarded as the meaning of the
implementation of an operation, whereas the former represent

the meaning the programmer has assumed. Checking between the
two sets of conditions is therefore provided an an aid
towards correct elaboration.

A further aid towards this end is provided via the parameter mechanism. As there are no global variables the only
means of communicating values between machines is by use of
parameters. These are considered as called by reference.
One of the problems of this technique is that of inadvertent
assignment. Thus a parameter of an operation must be specified as either variable or invariable. Only the former may
appear on the left side of an assignment. Specification of
parameters as variable or invariable occurs when an operation
is introduced. (The idea of separating parameters which may
be assigned to from those which may not, is also seen in a
paper by Hoare [F5]).

    e.g. An operation to copy one table to another might be
          introduced by:
          operation copy (table a vary, table b)

In any subsequent elaboration of "copy", only "a" may
appear on the left hand side of an assignment, while an error would be flagged for the statement,

    b:= ...

If the vary attribute is not applied to a parameter,
then it is considered invariate.

It should be noted that, despite the various analogies,
operations are not considered in the same way as procedures
in the traditional sense but more as being equivalent to the
basic instructions of some machine. Thus in keeping with this
viewpoint, there are restrictions both on parameters and on
the facilities normally supplied by the procedure concept.

Elaboration of Data Types

Instances of a data type are introduced by the declare
statement. Thus

          declare integer i

allocates a certain amount of storage which will be considered
as an integer and be referenced by the name 'i'.

Similarly

<u>declare</u> <u>table</u> t

should be considered in the same manner, allocating a certain amount of storage which will be considered as a table
and will be referenced by the name 't'. In both cases such
a statement has an effect on storage, allocating a certain
amount of space. How much space is a function of the data
type. If the type is not basic (i.e. <u>integer</u> or <u>string</u>) then
the amount of storage required will depend on the structure
that may be subsequently given to this data type.

The introduction of a data type is regarded as the introduction of an unexplained operation on storage. Two basic
operations are provided to introduce instances of type <u>integ-
er</u> and <u>string</u>. (An extension of the simple operations is
provided for <u>vector</u> declarations). Any other such operations
will need to be elaborated eventually in terms of these basic
operations. The introduction of an instance of a data type
by a declaration may be regarded as a call on the relevant
operation.

e.g. Introduce a type 'table' by machine A and give it
some structure in machine B.

A: 'introduce a table'
<u>begin</u> <u>type</u> table;
program: <u>declare</u> <u>table</u> t; ...
<u>end</u>
     .
     .
     .
B: 'structure a table into a title and 50 lines'
<u>begin</u> <u>type</u> line;
table: <u>declare</u> <u>string</u> title;
        <u>declare</u> <u>vector</u>(50) <u>line</u> body.
<u>end</u>

When the program of machine A is executed, <u>declare</u> <u>table</u>
will invoke the 'table' operation whose body is given in
machine B. This in turn will cause a call on the 'string'
operation followed by one for the 'line' operation which may
be elaborated by a further machine.

As noted previously, elaboration of a data type implies
a restriction on what the programmer can elaborate subsequently.

It is required that all operations which have parameters of such a data type be explained in terms of the new structure. Thus states are also elaborated in the same way as are operations and types. Given such explanations the correctness of the elaboration of an operation may still be checked despite any structure given to its parameters by elaboration of a data type.

USING THE   The programmer decides on the concepts he
PEARL SYSTEM   will require to solve his problem. He thus
                   has to "build" his ideal machine and write
a program for it to solve his problem. He then proceeds to
build further machines as necessary. Throughout this process
the computer will be checking the syntax of his programs,
assisting with the logic and correctness of his elaborations
and building the structure of the total program. The programmer issues commands to the system to indicate his wish
to build a further machine, to obtain details of previously
defined machines, to discover which concepts he has yet to
explain, or to run the total program as it stands or possibly
any portion of it.

After the programmer has correctly built a machine (i.e.,
no errors in either the specification or program parts), the
details are added to those previously entered. Interlinked
lists of machines, operations, types and states are kept in
a core, while the program part is sent to backing store
(disk). The program part is compiled into a reverse Polish
form so that it can be executed by a stack-oriented interpreter. The code emitted is such that a listing of the program can be easily recovered from the code using a symbol
table. Recovery of text is considered important for two purposes:

1. To enable the programmer easy reference to what he
   has previously written.
2. To provide a textual context for run-time error reporting.

Run Time Program Errors

The structural nature of the resultant program enables
the occurrence of any run time error to be meaningfully related to the original program text by the use of a simple

stack mechanism [B3]. In particular an error report can be made about the relevant machine rather than simply in the context of the total program. As aids to error detection, the various assertions that are made about programs when they are written are compiled as run-time checks and will cause error reporting if they are not satisfied.

Running Incompletely Specified Programs

It is possible to execute a program that requires some operation that has not been fully explained. When such an operation is encountered, the programmer will be asked to provide assistance, having been told the meaning that the operation should possess and the context of the call. By this technique a possible solution can be attempted without the need to program all the details.

Editing and Alterations

Because the total program is built of small pieces which are completely separate, alteration of parts of the whole does not imply a complete recompilation. A machine explaining some concept may be replaced by another without effect on other non-dependent machines. Certainly such replacement ought to have no effect on machines linked above in the hierarchical structure. (Above implies nearer the root). It may be possible to replace a machine without effect on lower machines. Checking of correctness will always take place to maintain the validity of the whole in the context of the new machine. Provision is made for various editing commands enabling the deletion, alteration, or insertion of machines. It should be noted that alteration of a machine refining some data concept will have a greater effect on other machines than will alteration of a machine explaining some operation or state.

Details of Implementation

PEARL is at present being implemented to run under the MTS operating system at Newcastle University. The core of the system is the interface with the user. This handles his requests and also acts as an overlay controller according to what function is required. This program is written PL360.

The compiler for the system is being developed by use of the XPL compiler writing system (McKeeman, 1970). At present error recovery is poor due to the parsing method, but it is hoped that later versions may be improved in this respect. The compiler generates code for the program part of each machine and also drives the routines which add new items to the various lists. These lists are built using the Newcastle File Handling System which enables linked data structures to be stored on disk.

Present Status

At the time of writing, the system does not exist in its entirety. A programmer may build complete programs, although checking of meanings is limited to calling upon the programmer to indicate whether a relationship is true or false, no attempt having been made to implement any form of logic checking system. At present all the assertions are compiled into checks which could cause an error report at run time. Facilities to enable the programmer to obtain information about the present state of his program, including listings, are provided, as are commands to allow the deletion and alteration of machines within the total structure. An interpreter for the code emitted by the compiler is largely written which will provide the run time facilities to give a reasonably complete system. The work was carried out in the Computing Laboratory of the University of Newcastle upon Tyne and supported by the Science Research Council.

CONCLUSION   In some respects there is a close resemblance to some of the features provided by an extensible programming language, although there are several features of such languages that are missing. Probably the most important restriction is that of a fixed control structure. The only sequencing allowed is that provided by the system and this has, by design, been kept simple. There would seem to be no reason, beyond that of complexity, for not allowing the user an ability to extend the control statements. In the present system however, the importance of introducing another dimension was not considered great enough to warrant inclusion.

The PEARL system is an attempt to provide an environment for writing structured programs together with the provision of some assistance towards ensuring their correctness. It also enables such programs to be executed whether completely specified or not, and to provide aids towards the location of errors. Only experience will show if such computer assistance and guidance may help in the problem of program writing.

EXAMPLE SESSION OF PEARL

This appendix shows a sample session using PEARL to construct a program to solve a relatively simple problem. The
scope of this example is of necessity, limited by the present
state of the implementation. The problem is given in Dijkstra [B20]and may be summarized as follows. We have to make
a program which will print 50 lines numbered from top to bottom by a y-co-ordinate running from 50 through to 1, the positions of characters on a line being numbered from left to
right by an x-co-ordinate running from 1 to 100. For each
of the 1000 positions given by

$$x = fx(j) \underline{\text{and}} \ y = fy(j) \text{ for } 1 \leq j \leq 1000$$

a mark has to be printed; all other positions are to remain
blank.

A comparison between the PEARL programs and the structured program subsequently developed by Dijkstra will show
how closely PEARL follows his ideas. In the sample session
the lower case text is entered by the user, while text in
upper case is written out by PEARL.

When the PEARL program system is initiated it will in-
vite the user to enter some command. This could be a request
by the user to run a program, or for details of the present
state of his program, or to initiate the building of another
machine. This last command is demonstrated at (1) and effects a call on the syntax checker routines. The programmer
then enters the relevant text to build a machine. This
starts with a name and a comment about the purpose of the machine, (2), and proceeds with the introduction of types,
operations and states for the machine (3). Notice the use of
states to give meanings to the operations as they are introduced. Having specified his ideal machine, the programmer
writes a program to solve his problem (4). The name 'program'
is provided in the system to get things started. When the
complete machine has been entered, the system provides several comments concerning errors and timing. The user is now
free to enter another command. He chooses to build again
and so the above process is repeated for a new machine. An
example of the assert expression occurs within the program

for the machine "jscanner", (5), while also in this machine is an example of how the meaning of an elaboration may be expressed (6). The session is terminated by the command "* quit", the next logical problem being to structure the data type "image".

```
             PEARL PROGRAM WRITING SYSTEM
             COMMANDS MAY BE ENTERED NOW
1)→    *build
2)→    compfirst:'store image of page before printing'
       begin type image;
          states built(image i), printed(image i);
3)→       operation
            build(image i vary)  provided true yields built(i) onexit,
            print(image i)       provided built(i) yields printed(i) onexit;
          program:
4)→          declare image page;
             build(page); print(page).
       end
       END OF CHECKING OCTOBER 22,1971.CLOCK TIME =10:29:43.30.
       11 CARDS WERE CHECKED.
       NO ERRORS WERE DETECTED.
       *build
       clearfirst:'expand build. Empty page first'
       begin states blank(image i);
             operation
               clear(image i vary)  provided true yields blank(i) onexit,
               setmarks(image i vary) provided blank(i) yields built(i) onexit;

       build(image i vary):
               clear(i); setmarks(i).
       end
       END OF CHECKING OCTOBER 22,1971.CLOCK TIME = 10:20:43.30.
       8 CARDS WERE CHECKED.
       NO ERRORS WERE DETECTED.



       *build
       jscanner:'setmarks.Put each of the 1000 marks on image'
       begin
             operation
               addmark(integer j,image i vary)
                 provided j>0 &  j<=1000 &  built(i) yields
                 (j<1000 &  built(i)) | (j=1000 & built (i)) onexit;

       setmarks(image i vary):
               declare integer j;
               j := 1;
               while j<=1000 do

5)→ assert  built(i) before


               ( addmark(j,i); j := j+1 ).

6)→ yields built(i) onexit


       end
       END OF CHECKING OCTOBER 22,1971.CLOCK TIME =10:40:49.87.
       18 CARDS WERE CHECKED.
       NO ERRORS WERE DETECTED.
```

FIGURE 1

-71-

```
*build
comppos:'calculate position of the jth mark'
begin states validx(integer x), validy(integer y);
     operation
        fx(integer x vary, integer j)
           provided j>0 & j<=1000 yields validx(x) onexit,
        fy(integer  y vary, integer j)
           provided j>0 & j<=1000 yields validy(y) onexit,
        markpos(integer (x,y), image i vary)
           provided  built(i) & validx(x) & validy(y)
           yields true onexit;

addmark(integer j,image i vary):
     declare integer (x,y);
     fx(x,j); fy(y,j);
     markpos(x,y,i).
end
END OF CHECKING OCTOBER 22,1971.CLOCK TIME = 11:11:22.34.
16 CARDS WERE CHECKED.
NO ERRORS WERE DETECTED.
*quit
```

FIGURE 1 (Cont.)

This shows a part of the first example. However, in the elaboration of "build" in the machine "clearfirst", the programmer uses just the simple name "build" rather than indicating the parameters of the operation as well. The example shows how PEARL provides him with those he had specified when "build" was introduced.

```
PEARL PROGRAM WRITING SYSTEM
COMMANDS MAY BE ENTERED NOW
*build
compfirst:'store image of page before printing'
begin type image;
      states built(image i), printed(image i);
      operation
         build(image i vary)     provided true yields built(i) onexit,
         print(image i)          provided built(i) yields printed(i) onexit;

program:
         declare image page;
         build(page); print(page).
end
END OF CHECKING OCTOBER 28,1971.CLOCK TIME = 13:46:10.07.
10 CARDS WERE CHECKED.
NO ERRORS WERE DETECTED.
*build
clearfirst:'expand build. Empty page first'
begin states blank(image i);
      operation
         clear(image i vary)     provided true yields blank(i) onexit,
         setmarks(image i vary) provided blank(i) yields built(i) onexit;

build:
*** ERROR, ORIGINAL HAD PARAMETERS
WILL USE ORIGINAL PARAMETERS AS FOLLOWS
IMAGE I VARY
clear(i); setmarks(i).
end
END OF CHECKING OCTOBER 28,1971.CLOCK TIME =13:53:54.75.
8 CARDS WERE CHECKED.
ONE ERROR WAS DETECTED.
THE LAST DETECTED ERROR WAS ON LINE 6.
*quit
```

FIGURE 2

DESIGNING LANGUAGES
FOR TESTING

IV

The errors of definitions multiply themselves according as the reckoning proceeds; and lead men into absurdities, which at last they see but cannot avoid, without reckoning anew from the beginning.

- Thomas Hobbes

A good notation has a subtlety and suggestiveness which at times make it seem almost like a live teacher.

- Bertrand Russell

APPROACHES TO IMPROVED PROGRAM VALIDATION
THROUGH PROGRAMMING LANGUAGE DESIGN

9

Donald K. Kosy
Rand Corporation, Santa Monica, California

That tendency to err that programmers have been noticed to share with other human beings has often been treated as if it were an awkwardness attendent upon programming's adolescence, which like acne would disappear with the craft's coming of age. It has proved otherwise.

Mark Halpern [A8]

INTRODUCTION   Program test and checkout for production quality software often consumes 40%-50% of the program development effort [A2]. Yet the languages in which most programs are written contain relatively few constructs to support this activity. Some even believe that certain language features are harmful and tend to promote errors, thereby greatly impacting the program test effort [B3]. Certainly the means available to express our intentions in computer programs has an effect on the nature and frequency of inaccuracies in our expression (if not in our intentions).

The purpose of this paper is to explore the relation between the language in which a program is written and the ease and efficiency of making sure that program is correct. First we provide working definitions for such overadaptive phrases as "validity", "testing," "language design," and the like. After a brief survey of features found in current language designs that assist in program checkout, we assess their utility in helping produce correct software. A new view of designing languages is proposed emphasizing the ability to help create correct programs. Some examples illustrating this approach are given and a measure of its utility is suggested. We conclude with directions for further research to expand and refine this concept.

DEFINITIONS <u>Validity, Specifications and Testing</u>
Programs that always perform as we intended
and never do what we don't intend them to are said to be
correct or *valid* programs. *Errors* are mismatches, e.g. a requirement not met, a boundary overstepped, a rule violated,
etc., between our intentions and program behavior. *Validation* is the process or act of demonstrating the validity of
a program, i.e. showing that there are no errors. This process aims at guaranteeing complete validity, including both
what the program should and should not do, but typically
this ideal is approached only asymptotically.

Our intentions are usually referred to as the *specification* of the program be it formal or informal, physically
written down or existing only mentally. Rephrasing the previous paragraph, *validation* attempts to show that a *program*
in its language, and a *specification*, in its language, functionally correspond one to one.

A program specification is generally not, however, as
solid as this statement would make it seem. Frequently our
idea of what we want the program to do, and hence its specification, is refined and changed by the process of writing
the program. Logical necessities are clarified, for example,
and augmentations usually suggest themselves. How can we
show that a program meets its specifications if these specifications keep changing?

For validation to have any meaning, we must assume that
our "ultimate intent," the mission a program is to fulfill,
does not change and provides the ultimate judge of whether
an error exists or not. Lying between our mental image of a
program's function and the computer's performance of that
function are really several levels of specification in several languages. Our validation procedures must, therefore, not
only encompass the correct movement of bits within the hardware, but also simultaneously evaluate how well each level
of specification encodes our real purposes.

Programs are tested to provide evidence that they satisfy their specification and to increase our confidence that
they will not misbehave. *Testing* consists of exercising
different modes of program operation through different combinations of input data (*test cases*) to identify errors.

Since part of a program's specification is that its form must follow the rules of the language in which it is written, detecting compile-time errors is as much a part of testing as finding errors at run-time.

Testing forms the backbone of program validation. We must have some evidence that a program is working properly in order to say we have demonstrated validity and testing is one way to supply that evidence.

Debugging is another essential part of producing valid programs and must be distinguished from testing. As stated by Elmendorf [J1], the function of *testing* is to show that an error exists while *debugging* then localizes the cause of error. Although debugging and testing are sometimes thought of as phases of program development (e.g., as part of the design-code-debug-test chain, Gruenberger [A7]), Elmendorf's definitions more clearly characterize the procedures and tools used to accomplish these functions. Debugging includes displaying the effects of program operation and the path of program operation to help us isolate and remove the cause of divergence from specification. Testing without debugging is a sterile exercise.

Language Design

Eliding any notion of rigor, completeness or comprehensiveness in the following, *programming language design* consists of specifying the vocabulary of symbols, the syntax of the statements and rules for combining statements, and the semantic meaning of statements and combinations of statements. (See Sammet[1] for a more complete treatment). The primary purpose of a programming language is to communicate to a machine a set of instructions to evoke computation, and the design of the language determines how one expresses what computation is to be done, and bounds the domain of computations that can be expressed.

Although languages are formally defined in specification documents or users' manuals, it is unrealistic not to realize that the real definition used by a programmer is provided by

[1] Sammet, Jean E., Programming Languages: History and Fundamentals, Prentice-Hall, Englewood Cliffs, N.J., 1969.

the compiler for that language. (Of course it is an old idea in formal language theory that a class of regular expressions is defined by an acceptor.) What is usually called the *implementation* of a language in practice turns out to be its most complete definition.

Implementation details can have just as great an effect on the utility of a language as its syntax and so should be considered part of the design of a particular language. Even though based on the same original language, different compilers define variant languages which are non-trivially different. The differences between these dialects can be crucial in many situations.

In particular, the handling of error-containing programs is one such situation where the definition of what computation to evoke as a result of a particular combination of statements has been left to the implementation phase. That a language is best defined by its processor holds not only for those features explicitly called out in the conventional language specification, but also for those expressly prohibited, and further for those not mentioned at all. Conventional language specifications give little attention to what to do with incorrect programs (e.g., specifications of ASA FORTRAN[2]) and so the compiler implementation is the only complete source of such definitions.

In discussing how a language affects program validation, the disposition of errors is of central concern. The syntax and semantics of error diagnostics, run-time checks, and debugging statements are all seen as valid and proper concerns for language designers regardless of whether they traditionally fall in the language "design" or "implementation" category.

CURRENT
VALIDATION-ORIENTED
LANGUAGE ELEMENTS

Debugging Tools
When asked what facilities a language provides for testing and validation, most programmers first think of the various kinds of debugging statements. These tools are the

[2]"FORTRAN vs. Basic FORTRAN," CACM, 7, 10, Oct. 1964, pp.592-675.

stethoscopes necessary to isolate the cause and location of
an error. A variety of techniques have been developed for
higher order languages in an attempt to recapture the efficiency and debug capability of first-generation hands-on programming. These techniques fall into three general classes:
dumps, the display of the contents of storage cells; *traces*,
the display of control flow during execution; and *debug control* essentially how to activate and deactivate dumps and
traces.

These basic tools have been considerably refined over
the years. In order to move from a machine orientation to
a problem orientation, for example, methods have been devised
to easily label and format a dumped segment of storage so it
appears as it was used in the program. To reduce the volume
of trace output, various levels of tracing selectivity have
been implemented including the variable trace (printing out
the value of a variable when it is set or referenced), the
subroutine trace (to monitor all CALL and RETURN statements),
and the run-time error trace (e.g., the type of error and the
statement in which it occurred). Debug control in higher
level languages has progressed from simply inserting TRACE
and DUMP cards, to the separate debug deck for specifying at
what points to record or report information, to on-line debuggers, such as Grishman's AIDS [M17], that provide the ability to interactively specify different monitoring conditions,
and finally to fully compatible interactive/non-interactive
debuggers, like Blair's PEBUG [M2], that give the user of a
higher level language all the break-point-setting and status-
interrogation power of on-line assembly-code debuggers in
ways completely oriented to that language. For fuller explanation of the above ideas, Gaines'thesis [M5] is a good
source. Kocher has compiled a fairly extensive (but somewhat
diffuse) survey of the literature [M6].

Testing Tools

Language elements that support testing tend to be less
conspicuous perhaps because they are more automatic (i.e.,
less subject to programmer control) than the debugging tools.
There are few examples of "testing commands" in any language.
Anything that helps to signal the existence of an error is
considered to be an aid to program testing, as defined previously. These tools operate either at compile-time or at
run-time.

Although not usually thought of as "test-tools," compile-time diagnostics signal errors that, if not caught would result in program failures. That a program conforms to the syntax of a language, that variables are used consistent with their declaration (e.g., arrays are used as arrays, scalars as scalars), that DO-loop and other statement blocks are properly nested, and so on, are essential to achieving a correct final program. The trend has been to provide more of these diagnostics and to make them more specific about the errors they are reporting. There are approximately 1000 of them (including warnings), for example, listed in the PL/I(F) Programmer's Guide.[3]

The run-time package associated with most higher order languages is the other major source of automatic error detection. Through a combination of internal tests and cooperation with the operating system, the language system can point out array subscript overruns, arithmetic overflow/underflow, wild control transfers, mismatched modes of formal and actual subroutine parameters and a variety of other errors that violate the rules of the language, or result from ill-formed algorithms. Since these typically involve run-time overhead, they have generally been employed more sparingly. There are 136 specific execution-time error types noted in the PL/I manual.

There is also a class of tools that are language-based but are extrinsic to the language and its compiler. Such things as cross-reference tables of program variables, flow charts, and certain kinds of test cases can be generated from the source code to provide different ways of viewing the program structure. These are of great help in testing, e.g.,by showing variables used but never set, or errors in logical branching, but are probably more economically handled by processors separate from the language system. Fallor [D5] gives a list of commercially available packages and we shall not consider them further.

THE UTILITY OF
CURRENT PROGRAMMING
LANGUAGES FOR
PROGRAM VALIDATION

The general characteristics of a programming language, as well as those features specifically oriented toward debugging, and those that aid testing,

[3] PL/I (F) Programmer's Guide, IBM Corporation, Form C28-6594-3, October 1967.

are all important in evaluating a language's assistance in program validation. A language providing generally higher level statements, e.g. statements that can do the work of three or four in another language, allows less chance for random mechanical errors to creep in when writing the program. Fewer potential errors per unit of code generated reduces the total amount of testing required by raising the probability that a test will be passed on the first try. Use of a large library of pre-written, pre-tested, error-free subroutines and functions has the same effect. Using a language well-suited to a problem allows better communication of the function and purpose of a program free of needless detail or circumlocution. This makes it easier to assess a program's correspondence with its specification and hence reduces the testing effort.

The special debugging commands have been useful in a different way. The trace and dump ideas have proven to be essential to locate and correct known errors, and the right tools for these jobs have greatly reduced the time and expense of doing them. The appearance of on-line debugging extensions to higher order languages, as exemplified by AIDS and PEBUG, has fulfilled most of our desires in the way of debugging displays, monitoring options, and debug control. Although there will undoubtedly be refinements, these kinds of tools will probably no longer be research subjects as they become engineered into production systems.

To correct an error, it must first be detected and the larger the program, the more vulnerable are the automatic test tools built into the language. Although the run-time facilities probably save the most consternation, compile-time checks may be even more important. By spotlighting certain classes of error before a program is even executed, compile-time diagnostics reduce the total number of possible errors which subsequent testing would have to discover. Moreover, errors detectable by the compiler are certain to be caught, since they don't depend on some special combination of input values, and consequently cannot lurk unsuspected to cause later program failure.

Current languages, even those including special debugging features, still impose too much of the validation burden on the programmer. Current techniques are overwhelmed by larger, more complex software. Such systems intensify the need for complete and economical testing and for strict interface compatibility. An enormous amount of effort is required to exercise all program options, and there is still always some doubt as to whether all cases have been tested thoroughly. Available language designs and debugging facilities do not directly address these kinds of problems. Increased flexibility and scope have exceeded advances in valiation assistance. There is simply too great a chance to make undetectable mistakes using currently available languages.

| IMPROVING PROGRAM VALIDATION | To improve program validation, and thereby improve the overall reliability of a software system, we must allow the machine to |

shoulder more of the validation burden. The design of the programming language is a uniquely suitable locus for this task, compared to changes to the hardware, the operating system, or other software, because the language and its compiler can "know" much more about the problem being solved. Thus they are in a much better position to assist the programmer in flagging errors, inconsistencies, or other suspicious circumstances, and in preventing erroneous code from being run. We may be able to reduce testing effort by suitable language design just as coding effort was reduced. There may be ways of communicating with the machine that are less prone to error and which allow more automatic and comprehensive error detection than are in use today. Some examples of this kind of language design follow.

Strictly Enforcing Language Specifications

One reason that many programs are incorrect is that they violate the specification of the language in which they are written, but the language system does not detect the violation. For example, it is all too easy to use an uninitialized variable in PL/I, branch into a DO-loop in FORTRAN, or pass a real argument to a subroutine requiring an integer in SIMSCRIPT, and never find out about it until sometime later, even though all these constructions are expressly prohibited in the user's manuals for these languages. Results of these operations are undefined and will usually show up elsewhere in some quite mysterious way. It is even more dangerous if they aren't noticed, however, since then the program will produce spurious output without giving any sign of it.

Explicitly enforcing every part of the language specification will tend to expose these kinds of errors quickly.

Languages at least partially employing this approach are WATFOR [M10] and DITRAN [M9], both FORTRAN dialects. This, in fact, was one of DITRAN's design goals, as stated in [M9]: "Any condition prohibited by the specification of the language or any condition prohibited by the machine implementation must be detected and not allowed to produce some undefined result." This includes checking for out-of-bounds array subscripts, use of undefined variables, mode conflicts in I/O operations, and many other violations. Similarly, WATFOR quite dramatically points out erroneous constructions where other FORTRAN compilers do not indicate any error and the programs execute to completion. Both WATFOR and DITRAN make very extensive checks on the program at compile-time and run-time to enforce their rules. While all languages enforce part of their ostensible specification, most don't include much run-time checking, apparently because of the difficulty or expense of detecting certain kinds of errors. We will comment on such efficiency questions later.

Eliminating Error-Causing Constructions

To err is human, and programming language designers might take greater notice of this aspect of human psychology. Our ability to communicate is limited by our propensity to make mistakes and we should construct our languages to help us overcome this difficulty. Some techniques can help programmers actually avoid error and others can at least move the error into that class detectable at compile time.

New primitives for common operations could reduce mechanical transcription errors. To augment a language like FORTRAN, Elspas, et.al. [F2], suggests such statements as

FILL A WITH 0

to take the place of a DO-loop initializing the array A and

BUMP K

to increment K by one. Only one error, for example, can be made undetected in BUMP K: the specification of the variable (assuming an error in BUMP would result in a syntax error). Compare this to

K = K+1

which allows all sorts of syntactically correct but erroneous permutations to enter a program:

$$K = K+I$$

$$K = J+1$$

$$K = R+1$$

and so on. By simply using fewer symbols, potential random errors per operation are reduced. This is simply an extension of the ability of a higher order language to reduce the number of random, undetected mechanical errors.

Requiring full and explicit declaration of all variables could reduce errors that occur by default. Such errors include the compiler mistaking a misspelled variable for a new variable, the programmer misunderstanding the attributes of a variable because of complicated background defaults, and the like. Requiring more extensive declarations might impact other classes of errors. Initialization errors could be avoided (with only small run-time efficiency penalties) by requiring all variables to be initialized when they are declared without exception. Requiring global declaration of the number and modes of subroutine arguments allows the compiler to flag interface mismatches involving these parameter lists (automatic conversion may mask deeper problems).

Certain features included in a language for "convenience" may actually cause more trouble than they are worth and should be eliminated. Automatic variable declaration, as mentioned above, may be one of these. Comments that can extend to multiple lines without punctuation (as in ALGOL-60 or PL/I) are another well-known source of strange and undetected errors. Although incorrect remote format lists are detected at run-time (e.g., in FORTRAN), if they were permanently bound to their READ or WRITE statements at compile-time, the compiler could test the appropriateness of the format-list for the variables it describes.

Many languages do not seem to help their users overcome the natural tendency to err. Although there are few statistics on the sources of programming error, and no systematic theory upon which to draw, the above suggestions represent some hunches about the means by which errors can contaminate programs. We might have more confidence in our program validation process if the above error entry points were closed

off. Weinberg [F19] is an excellent introduction to a more
scientific identification of error-causing language constructs.

Encouraging Validation-Oriented Programming Techniques

There are an infinite number of ways to write a program
to do a particular job, and the way it is written has an e-
normous effect on the difficulty of validating it. The control structure, the division of functions into subroutines,
the nature of the interface to the environment, even the way
the program listing appears on the page affects our ability
to master the complexity of the program and hence our ability
to validate it. A programming language can encourage or dis-
courage certain program structures by making things easier
or harder to express.

One of the most controversial proposals to encourage
(or in this case enforce) a particular program structure has
been made by Dijkstra [B4, B3]. He suggests eliminating
GO TO statements (unconditional branching) from programming
languages to achieve a more disciplined design and a more
readable and understandable final program. Instead of GO TO,
a programmer must rely on IF-THEN-ELSE, DO-WHILE, and basic
statement sequencing (and possibly the CASE statement) to
control sequencing. This scheme has already been implemented in one language (for the PDP-10) called BLISS [F23]. The
program structure which results tends to reduce the probability of undiscovered error by making clear at the beginning
of each block of code the logical reasons for its execution.

The unique modularity enforced by a GO-TO-free language
can be enhanced by other language-provided disciplines. Mills
[B9] recommends, for example, limiting the size of each subroutine to a single printed page and also controlling the
format of the listing of the program to emphasize the logic
(by suitable indentation) within the program. If these practices were shown to have significant impact on improving the
comprehensibility of programs, they might be incorporated into the language design and checked by the compiler.

While program structuring tools can improve our ability
to construct internally correct programs, other tools could
be devised to help test the validity of input data. Many
problems in validation arise from attempting to subject a
program to an input value it was not designed to handle. We

should probably look more carefully at our easy acceptance of that old maxim "garbage in, garbage out." Achieving a quicker and more accurate signal for "unreasonable" input data may be worth quite a bit in the same way that ounces of prevention can be worth more than pounds of cure.

On the theory that input validity checking is now not often done at least partially because it is cumbersome, the CHECK statement, below, might overcome such hesitation:

$$\text{CHECK} \{ \ \min \ \leq v \leq \ \max \}^{\text{C}}$$

where min and max are character or numeric constants, v is a variable, and $\{\}^{\text{C}}$ means the enclosed phrase may be repeated any number of times in a list, separated by commas. Such a statement would signal an error at run-time if the value of the variable were outside the specified range. In addition, such a statement could substitute the minimum or maximum value specified, depending on which boundary was violated, and continue executing the program, if such a strategy tended to detect more errors more quickly. Such a statement could be used not only to check values coming across an external interface, but also certain internal data, e.g., the values input to a subroutine.

Automating Program Validation

The greatest strides toward improving program validation can be made by implementing language designs that allow programs to be self-checking. That is, the machine can help evaluate program correctness if the language allows a more extensive statement of what the program is trying to accomplish. By incorporating more of the specification of the program into the body of the code, we might expect to improve reliability by taking advantage of *redundancy* in the software analagous to the way we can exploit redundancy in hardware.

At least one rudimentary example of this has already been presented. Use of the CHECK statement begins to provide an implicit and machine-testable representation of the territory a program covers and some of the relationships between its variables, i.e., parts of the program specification. The application of CHECK can be extended to include testing the reasonableness of intermediate results, much the way check sums (see [A7]) can provide some confidence that a procedure has processed all the data we intended it to. The values

specifying the ranges in CHECK statements also serve as
convenient guides to designing test cases. Although employing such statements may appear to be expensive, machine
checks on implicit assumptions may be much cheaper than re-
lying on "programming virtuosity" in the long run.

Knuth [A12] and others have described a different way to
monitor a program during execution. By augmenting the basic
code with data collection instructions, a compiler could direct that counts be kept of the frequencies of execution of
each statement in a program. (Knuth used a separate pre-com-
piler to add such data collection instructions, however.)
For use in testing, a statement executed with zero frequency,
i.e., never, indicates an untested section of code. A list
of such statements then provides a very good basis for constructing test cases that cover the entire program. Although
execution of each statement in a program during testing is
not sufficient to guarantee a program's validity (since there
may be any number of paths through a particular statement),
it seems reasonable that executing every statement at least
once is necessary to fully test a program.

Redundancy at run-time, and its expense, may not be necessary if sufficient redundancy can be designed into the
language itself. We have already seen how improving the
match between the primitives in a language and the tasks to
be programmed, and the introduction of more extensive declarations can establish and maintain constraints on a program
that are testable at compile-time . If additional semantic
classes of variables and operations can be defined by the programmer to identify particular purposes for particular variables, these purposes can then be verified by the compiler.

A number of examples of exploiting such semantic declarations are given by Lowry [F9]. Specifically, he describes a
new class of data categories called *ranges* used to indicate
permissible values, operations, and interactions for program
variables. Ranges and their attributes are declared, and
variables are in turn declared to be in those ranges:

```
RANGE   RDOLLAR LEGIT  (RDOLLAR+RDOLLAR, -, < ,
            RPAYRATE*RHOURS), RHOURS VALUES (0 TO
            168), RPAYRATE;
DECLARE OVERTIME IN (RHOURS), PAY IN (RDOLLARS);
DECLARE PAYRATE IN (RPAYRATE);
```

D. KOSY

The LEGIT attribute specifies the legitimate operations on the variables in those ranges and the VALUES attribute defines permitted values. For example, the variable PAY in the range RDOLLAR can be added, subtracted, or compared to other variables in the RDOLLAR range. Using these declarations, the compiler could detect the following inconsistencies:

IF OVERTIME > 200 THEN GO TO E;

OVERTIME = PAY;

PAY = PAYRATE+OVERTIME;

It is interesting to note that general dimensional analysis of engineering and scientific formulae could be performed within this framework using a few additional range attributes.

The most ambitious conception of this approach has been given by Floyd [12]. He envisions a language in which not only the algorithm can be specified, but all the logical elements of the purpose of the program as well. The machine is then expected to demonstrate the correctness of whatever program, or partial program, has been constructed to satisfy this specification. The machine is further expected to provide counter-examples to show the defects in incorrect programs. Paraphrasing Floyd's paper, we might see the following program in this language:

BEGIN

INVARIANTS A, N, X;   INTEGER B, C, D;

(ASSERT $N \geq 1$, FOR $1 \leq I \leq J \leq N$ THEN $A[I] \leq A[J]$);

(ASSERT FOR $1 \leq K \leq N$ THEN $A[K] = X$);

B:= 1; C:= N;

ITERATE (ASSERT $1 \leq B \leq C \leq N$, FOR $B \leq K \leq C$ THEN
$A[K] = X$);

UNTIL B = C

```
BEGIN

D:= (B+C) DIV 2;

IF   X ≤ A[D]   THEN C:= D

              ELSE B:= D+1

END

L:= B;

(ASSERT 1 ≤ L ≤ N, A[L] = X);

END.
```

The first two ASSERT statements indicate the initial assumptions, that A is a sorted array of length N and that X is one value in the table. The others indicate intermediate and final relations that must always hold at those points in the program. The above is sufficient for the compiler to verify that the procedure locates the symbol X in a sorted table of known size. The specification is provided explicitly by the ASSERT declarations. Through redundancy, the language has become a very powerful assistant and since Floyd's language is also interactive, correctness can be verified at each step in program development.

CAN LANGUAGE DESIGN Too often language design reflects
REALLY AFFECT   merely speculation upon a user's needs.
PROGRAM VALIDITY   Are the things proposed in this paper
                     only additional examples of such specu-
lation?

We are fortunate, in this case, to have one very good collection of objective data on certain kinds of programs that can help us evaluate some of these proposals. A study by Rubey, et al. [A21], to empirically evaluate PL/I through the coding and checkout of benchmark programs provides a very rich and detailed source of quantitative information, especially on aspects of debugging and testing programs of interest in this chapter. These benchmarks were used to compare PL/I to other programming languages (FORTRAN, COBOL and JO-VIAL) by implementing representative application problems in both PL/I and in another higher level language appropriate to the application. Seven application program specifications were used resulting in fourteen programs being written. This netted 7300 lines of code (7627 statements) and consumed about 180 man-days in program design, coding and debugging. Debugging and checkout required about 70% of the total effort. The average size of each program was 521 lines (545 statements).

A record was kept of all the language-related errors found in these programs including both those found at compile-time, and at run-time. A total of 354 errors were recorded, 261 caught during compilation and 93 run-time errors. The cause of each error was also tabulated in fairly great detail.

From the full record of these errors, we have estimated the effectiveness of some of the language elements described in the previous section.* Although it is impossible to determine if any errors could have been avoided by using certain programming techniques or the availability of error-reducing statement forms, the data permit a rough measure of the worth of eliminating error-causing statements and strictly enforcing the language definition.

Recall that an error detected at compile time removes the potential of that error contaminating the execution of that program. An error that can be detected by the compiler will certainly be flagged and then removed.

The more errors we can move into the class detectable at compile-time, therefore, the greater confidence we can have in our program validation.

The measure of effectiveness to be used, then, is the number of errors found at run-time in the Rubey study that could have been caught àt compile time through a differently designed language. We will assume the mistakes are still made but that they are caught earlier and with greater certainty.

*The tables are not reproduced here since to present them in full would require too much space and to aggregate them in generic categories removes enough detail to completely wash out their meaning for our purposes.

The results are:

1) requiring full and explicit declaration
   of variables, arrays and functions   - 26 errors found
2) requiring full initialization   - 9 errors found
3) using less error-prone syntax   - 14 errors found
4) strict enforcement of language
   definition   -   3 errors found

                                 Total   52 errors found

More than half (56%) of the 93 execution errors could probably have been caught earlier given a more validation-oriented
language design.

CONCLUSIONS   We have suggested that a programming language
                       can have a significant effect on program
testing and validation efforts, and have described several
approaches to improve the validation process through improved language design. However, many questions remain. The
most apparent is that of efficiency. Although most of the
checking features seem feasible and straightforward, how can
we afford all that extra execution time and space? We certainly should be able to turn off any high-overhead feature
we didn't need. Are special "debug compilers" a good way to
achieve validation capability while maintaining the possibility of later re-compiling efficient "*production*" code? Some
features may not be implementable at all under certain operating systems or on certain types of machines. On the other
hand, many have suggested that microprograms be used to implement more run-time testing tools. Burroughs has for some
time built dynamic array subscript-checking into its hardware.

     Other problems may also exist. For example, a language
incorporating the philosophy of this paper may be very cumbersome, requiring many declarations and other lengthy and
tedious statements. Does the gain in reliability justify the
inconvenience and longer program coding time? Or, perhaps
these techniques will be too restrictive and the lack of
flexibility turn out to be a very severe limit on the power
of the language. But most fundamental, since many of the
constructs have not been systematically evaluated, we have
no hard evidence that they really do impact the validation
problem for real programming jobs.

D. KOSY

It is evident that many interesting tradeoffs need to be studied in this area. Now that computer technology provides fairly fast machines and powerful compilation techniques, we should investigate the effects of different language designs on program production and particularly on program validation. In the future we would expect programming languages to be our assistants as well as our servants.

NUCLEUS—A LANGUAGE OF PROVABLE PROGRAMS

10

D. I. Good and L. C. Ragland

University of Texas, Austin

INTRODUCTION   Nucleus is a language designed specifically for producing computer programs that run correctly. In designing Nucleus we have strived to attain a number of goals.

1. It must be possible to subject any Nucleus program to a rigorous proof of correctness by the inductive assertion method. Thus the language may contain only those constructs for which verification conditions can be constructed, and must also have a way of stating inductive assertions within a program.
2. The structure of Nucleus should facilitate the actual construction of correct programs. Toward this end, we have used a rather high-level, Algol-like syntax because of our belief that the smaller the barrier between the abstract steps required to solve a problem and the encoding of these steps in a specific programming language, the greater the probability of constructing an error-free program. Also, the language has a simple procedure mechanism so that one can apply, at least in a primitive way, the ideas of structured programming (Dijkstra [B4] Wirth [B17].
3. Nucleus programs must be easily compilable into almost any machine language. If we can, in fact, produce useful Nucleus programs that actually run correctly then we most certainly will want to make Nucleus easily available on a wide range of machines.
4. It must be possible to prove the correctness of at least a semi-automatic inductive assertion verifier for Nucleus programs. "Semi-automatic" implies that the verifier need not contain an automatic theorem prover. In order to apply the inductive assertion method to nontrivial programs, it is almost a necessity to use the mechanical assistance of a verifier simply because of the sheer volume of work and detail that must be dealt

with. If we are to construct valid proofs of correctness about Nucleus programs using this mechanical assistant, we also need to know that it operates correctly.
5. It must be possible to prove the correctness of a Nucleus compiler. Unfortunately, even a valid proof of
correctness of a given program is not sufficient to
prove that it always will execute correctly when actually run on a computer. The reasons for this are clear.
The Nucleus program must be compiled into some machine
language, and then run on that actual machine, and all
of this takes place in the environment of some operating
system. Any of these components may malfunction causing the program to execute incorrectly in spite of a
correctness proof. We will stop short of requiring ab-
solutely correct machine hardware and a correct operating system, but we will insist on a correct compiler.
6. All aspects of Nucleus, both syntactic and semantic,
must be defined rigorously. This goal is induced by the
previous goals of proving the correctness of a verifier
and a compiler. These proofs will require a precise and
rigorous specification of all aspects of the language.
7. Last, but by no means least, it must be possible to express useful and significant programs in Nucleus such
as its own, and other compilers and verifiers. We want
to be able actually to use this language in practice to
begin the long overdue process of upgrading the quality
of computer software. We are not necessarily advocating
the rewriting of large amounts of existing software in
Nucleus. What we can do, and this is one of the important reasons for developing Nucleus, is write compilers
and verifiers for other programming languages. In this
way we can begin a process of bootstrapping more and
more sophisticated and correct software in more and more
programming languages. This bootstrapping process with
Nucleus as the base language is discussed in detail in
Good[1] and is the motivation for the name "Nucleus".

The first two sections present an informal description
of the Nucleus language. The third section covers the method
of formal definition. This formal definition generally follows the axiomatic approach of Burstall [E9] and has been influenced strongly by the goals of proving a Nucleus verifier

[1]Good, D.I., Developing Correct Software, In Proceedings of
the First Texas Symposium on Computer Systems, To Appear,
1972.

and compiler. Basically, this method uses transition networks to define syntax and axioms to define semantics. The
combination of these two techniques has led to a unique approach to defining a programming language. Another feature
of the definition of Nucleus is the use of "implementation
parameters". These parameters are quantities that must be
specified to complete the definition of the language, but
whose actual definition is left open. For example, the definition states precisely <u>where</u> tests for integer overflow are
required, but do not specify <u>what</u> this test must be. The
final section summarizes the current status relative to the
aforementioned goals.

NUCLEUS, AN   Nucleus resembles the languages used by the
INFORMAL   program verification systems of King [19]
DESCRIPTION   and Good [14], both of which are based on
                     subsets of Algol 60. Also we have borrowed
some features of Pascal[2] and some of the syntactic devices of
Algol 68.

<u>Basic Elements.</u>

        The basic character set of Nucleus consists of 64 char-
acters,

{blank A B C D E F G H I J K L M N Ø P Q R S T U V W X Y Z
0 1 2 3 4 5 6 7 8 9 ([ ]) ↑ * / ↓ + - < ≤ ≥ > = ≠ ¬ ∧ ∨ →
≡ , ; : . $ # }

These characters are grouped into tokens which are the basic
symbols that may be used in writing Nucleus programs.

        Each of the characters in the basic character set, with
the exception of blank, letters, digits, :, ↑, and $ is a
token. A : also is a token provided it is not followed immediately by =. := forms a separate token.

        Each of the following sequences of letters constitute a
reserved word:

[2]Wirth, N. The Programming Language Pascal, Acta Informatica,
1, 1971.

ARRAY, BØØLEAN, CASE, CHARACTER, DØ, ELIHW, ELSE,
ENTER, ESAC, EXIT, FALSE, FI, GØ, HALT, IF, INTEGER,
NØP, ØF, PRØCEDURE, READ, RETURN, START, THEN, TØ,
TRUE, WHILE, and WRITE.

Each reserved word is a single token.

An ASSERTION token has the form

ASSERT text;

where text is any sequence of characters not containing a
semicolon, except for semicolons immediately preceded by the
character ↑. The assertion tokens provide a means of stating
inductive assertions in the program. This form allows the
use of free-form assertions such as those used by Good [14]
as well as more formal ones such as those used by King [19].

An IDENTIFIER token is a letter followed by any number
of letters and digits, with the exception of the reserved
words and ASSERT.

A NUMBER token is any sequence of digits.

A character sequence of the form ↑c is a CHARACTERCON-
STANT token where c is any element of the basic character set.
The ↑ serves to quote the single character immediately follow-
ing it.

A character sequence of the form

$ text $

may appear between any adjacent pair of tokens and is treated
as a comment. The text must not contain $.

Tokens may be separated by any number of blanks, and except for the text of an ASSERTION token, no token can contain
embedded blanks.

Programs.

A Nucleus program has the form

declarations procedures START IDENTIFIER.

The declarations define the global data variables of the

-96-

program. Nucleus has no concept of a local data variable, the only variables available are the global variables speci- fied in the declarations. The declarations are followed by a set of procedures and the two tokens, START and IDENTIFIER. IDENTIFIER is the name of the procedure where execution of the program is to begin, and hence, must be the name of some procedure in the set of procedures defined prior to START.

Declarations.

The declarations of the program define simple variables and arrays. A declaration of simple variables has the form

    type IDENTIFIER,...,IDENTIFIER;

where type is either INTEGER, BOOLEAN or CHARACTER. A varia- ble of type INTEGER may take on any integer value x that satisfies inrange(x). The function inrange is an implemen- tation parameter and evaluates true iff x is an integer repre- sentable on the machine supporting a particular implementa- tion of Nucleus. Type boolean variables may take on the logical values true or false, and the value of a type char- acter variable may be any single character in the basic character set.

A declaration of arrays has the form

    type ARRAY IDENTIFIER[NUMBER],...,IDENTIFIER[NUMBER];

Arrays may have only one subscript with an assumed lower bound of zero and an upper bound of NUMBER.

Every IDENTIFIER that is declared must be declared uniquely to be either a simple variable, an array name, or a procedure name.

Procedures.

The form of a Nucleus procedure is

    PROCEDURE IDENTIFIER; body EXIT;

IDENTIFIER is the name of the procedure, and the body defines the statements and assertions associated with it. Procedures have neither parameters nor local variables. Parameterless procedures are a certain, but admittedly rather drastic solu- tion to the problems that can arise when verifying procedures with parameters (see Hoare [E15]).

Bodies.

A body is any sequence of statements and/or assertions
that is followed by one of the tokens EXIT, ELSE, FI, ELIHW,
NUMBER or ESAC. The body includes just the sequence of
statements and assertions. It does not include the terminating symbol.

Statements.

The various kinds of statements are described individually in the sections that follow. Any of these statements may
be preceded by a list of labels of the form

    IDENTIFIER:...IDENTIFIER:

and must be terminated by a;. Any IDENTIFIER may be used as
a label provided it is used only once in any given procedure.
Labels are local to the procedure in which they appear.

Assignment Statements.

An assignment statement has the form

    leftside := expression

where the leftside is either a simple variable or an array
reference. The types of the expression and the leftside must
agree. If either the leftside or the expression is undefined,
execution terminates.

Go To Statements.

A go to statement has the form

    GO TO IDENTIFIER

where IDENTIFIER must appear as a label on some statement in
the same procedure as the go to statement. A go to cannot
jump across a procedure boundary.

Return Statement.

The return statement has the form

    RETURN

and is a jump to the end of the procedure in which it appears.

Null Statement.

The null statement has the form

NOP

and causes a jump to the next statement in sequence.

If Statements.

There are two kinds of if statements

IF expression THEN body FI
IF expression THEN body ELSE body FI

In both cases the expression must be of type boolean. These statements have their usual interpretation with the addition that if the expression is undefined, execution terminates.

Case Statement.

The case statement is adapted from Pascal and provides a mechanism for doing computed multi-way branches. It has two forms

CASE expression OF alternative sequence ESAC
CASE expression OF alternative sequence ELSE body ESAC

In both forms the expression must be of type integer and if the expression is undefined, execution terminates.

Before completing the description of the case statement, we must describe the alternative sequence. This is a sequence of bodies each of which is preceded by a sequence of NUMBER labels. The label sequence has the form

NUMBER: ... NUMBER:

Thus, an alternative sequence has the form

numericlabels body numericlabels body ...

A given NUMBER may appear only once as a label in any given alternative sequence.

In the simple case statement, the expression is evaluated and control flows to the beginning of the body in the alternative sequence having the label equal to the value of the expression. If no such label exists, control flows to the end of the case statement. Also if control flows to the end of any body in the alternative sequence, control flows next to the end of the case statement.

The CASE-ELSE construction is similar except that if the expression does not equal a label on some body in the alternative sequence, control flows to the body following the ELSE.

While Statement.

A while statement has the form

    WHILE expression DO body ELIHW

with the usual interpretation. The expression must be of type boolean, and if the expression is undefined execution terminates.

Enter Statement.

The enter statement has the form

    ENTER IDENTIFIER

This is a recursive call of the procedure named IDENTIFIER. Before entering the procedure, the point following the enter statement is saved on the return point stack. When a procedure exits, control flows to the point on top of the return point stack provided the stack is not empty. If the stack is empty, execution terminates. The upper bound on this stack size is an implementation parameter, and any attempt to exceed the stack limit causes program termination.

Halt Statement.

The form of the halt statement is

    HALT

and causes execution of the entire program to terminate immediately.

Read Statement.

The read statement has the form

READ IDENTIFIER

where IDENTIFIER is the name of some array of type character.
The read statement accesses the standard input file. This
file is structured as a sequence of <u>records</u> numbered 1,2,...
Each of these records either is or is not an end-of-file
record. If a record is not an end-of-file record, it consists of a sequence of n elements of the basic character set.
The record size, n, is the same for all records and is one
of the implementation parameters.

At the beginning of program execution an input file
record pointer is set to zero. The execution of a read statement then proceeds as follows:·

1. The input pointer is increased by 1 to a value of, say,
   p.
2. If record p is an eof record, the character T is placed
   in IDENTIFIER[0] and the rest of the elements in the array are unchanged.
3. If record p is not an eof record, the character F is
   placed into IDENTIFIER[0]. Then character i of record
   p is placed into IDENTIFIER[i] for all i such that
   $1 \leq i \leq$ min (upper bound of IDENTIFIER, record size).
   The remainder of the array, if any, is left unchanged.

Write Statement.

The write statement has the form

WRITE IDENTIFIER

where IDENTIFIER is the name of some array of type character.
The write statement accesses a standard output file whose
structure is similar to the input file, the only difference
being the record size. The size of the records on the output
file is also an implementation parameter and need not be the
same as the record size of the input file.

At the beginning of program execution, an output record
pointer is set to zero. Execution of a write statement then
proceeds as follows:

1. The output pointer is increased by 1 to a value of, say, q.
2. If IDENTIFIER[0] contains the character T, record q becomes an eof record.
3. If IDENTIFIER[0] does not contain the character T, characters 1,...,m of record q become the characters contained in IDENTIFIER[1],...,IDENTIFIER[m] where m = min (upper bound of IDENTIFIER, record size). The rest of the characters in the record, if any, become blanks.

Expressions.

Expressions are built from primaries in the usual way. The operators that are available are given in Figure 1 and each operator may be applied only to operands of the appropriate type.

Operator	Priority	Operand Type
unary $+$, $-$	1	INTEGER
$*$, $/$, $\downarrow$ (modulo)	2	INTEGER
binary $+$, $-$	3	INTEGER
$<, \leqslant, =, \neq, \geqslant, >$	4	See below
$\neg$	5	BOOLEAN
$\wedge$	6	BOOLEAN
$\vee$	7	BOOLEAN

FIGURE 1

The relational operations may be applied to operands of any type, provided both operands are of the same type. If operands of type boolean or character are used, the transfer function to type integer is applied automatically.

If an expression would evaluate to a value v such that the implementation parameter inrange(v) = false, then the value of the expression becomes undefined. The expression also becomes undefined upon divide (or modulo) by zero.

Primaries

A primary may be a constant (a NUMBER, TRUE, FALSE, or CHARACTERCONSTANT token), a simple variable or an array reference. In an array reference, IDENTIFIER [expression], the expression must be of type integer. If the value of the expression falls outside the array bounds, the value of the array reference is undefined. A primary also may be the application of one of the type transfer functions.

Transfer Functions.

Any one of the type transfer functions, INTEGER, BOOLEAN, or CHARACTER, may be applied to an expression of any type. If the type of the expression is different from the name of the transfer function, the appropriate one of the following six functions is applied.

```
boolofchar(x) = boolofint(intofchar(x))
boolofint(x) = false  if abs(x) mod 2 = 0
             = true   if abs(x) mod 2 = 1
charofbool(x) = charofint(intofbool(x))
charofint(x) = " "  if abs(x) mod 64 = 0
             = "A"  if abs(x) mod 64 = 1
                .
                .
                .
             = "#"  if abs(x) mod 64 = 63
             (The order above is the same as the order
             of appearance in the basic character set
             exhibited in the section on tokens.)
intofbool(x) = 0  if x = false
             = 1  if x = true
intofchar(x) = 0  if x = " "
             = 1  if x = "A"
                .
                .
                .
             = 63  if x = "#"
             (The order is the same as above.)
```

EXAMPLE   Two examples of Nucleus procedures are
NUCLEUS   given as Figures 2 and 3. Figure 2 is a
PROCEDURES   simple binary search routine. The Figure 3
                   routine reads the input file and stores
the integer value in the first five columns of each successive

record in successive elements of the array A. This process
continues until the next eof record is reached or until 500
records have been read whichever comes first.

```
PROCEDURE BINARYSEARCH;
$ SEARCH ARRAY A FOR X $
ASSERT 0 ≤ N ≤ 100;
ASSERT A[I] ≤ A[I+1] for I = 0,...,N-1;

FOUND :=FALSE:
FIRST :=0; LAST :=N;

ASSERT ¬ FOUND:
ASSERT IF A [0] ≤ X ≤ A[N] THEN A [FIRST] ≤ X ≤ A[LAST];
ASSERT X = X.O, N = N.O; A = A.O;
WHILE FIRST ≤ LAST DO

     MIDDLE:= (FIRST + LAST) /2;

     IF X < A[MIDDLE]
     THEN LAST := MIDDLE-1;
     ELSE IF X = A[MIDDLE]
          THEN FOUND := TRUE; RETURN;
          ELSE FIRST := MIDDLE+1;
          FI;

     FI;
ELIHW:
ASSERT IF FOUND THEN X.O - A.O MIDDLE AND 1 ≤ MIDDLE ≤ N.O;
ASSERT IF ¬ FOUND THEN X.O IS NOT IN A.O;

EXIT;
```

FIGURE 2

```
PROCEDURE INPUT;
ASSERT : RDHD ≤ J<K→ ¬:REOF(J)∧[↑0≤ :RDFL(J,C)≤↑9 FOR C=1,...,5];
ASSERT : REOF(K);

N:= -1;   CODEOFZERO:=INTEGER(?O);

WHILE N ≤ 500 DO

     READ BUFFER;
     IF BUFFER[0]= ↑T THEN RETURN; FI;
     VALUE :=  INTEGER(BUFFER[1]) - CODEOFZERO;
     COLUMN := 2;
ASSERT   : RDHD.O ≤ J ≤ (:RDHD.O)+N→A[J] = NUMERICVALUE[:RDFL(J,1),...,
                                                      :RDFL(J,5)];
ASSERT VALUE = NUMERICVALUE[:RDFL(J,1),...,:RDFL(J,COLUMN-1)];
     WHILE COLUMN ≤ 5 DO
          VALUE := VALUE *10 + INTEGER(BUFFER[COLUMN])-CODEOFZERO;
          COLUMN :=COLUMN + 1;
     ELIHW;
     N := N + 1;
     A[N] :=VALUE;
ELIHW;
ASSERT N = MIN(K,500)
ASSERT :RDHD.O≤J≤(:RDHD.O)+N→A[J] = NUMERICVALUE [:RDFL(J,1),...,
                                                  :RDFL(J,5)]:
EXIT;
```

FIGURE 3

THE FORMAL   The definition of Nucleus consists of two
DEFINITION   components. The *syntax* of Nucleus is a set
                    of rules that determine whether or not any
given character string is a Nucleus program. For any string
of characters that is a program the *semantics* of Nucleus
specify the execution of that program. The basic tools chosen
to define the syntax and semantics are due to Woods[3] and Burstall [F1], this choice being influenced strongly by the goals
of proving the Nucleus verifier and compiler.

The syntax of Nucleus is stated in terms of transition
networks. The networks used are a modification of the "augmented transition network grammars" described by Woods for
dealing with natural languages. These networks are based on
finite state transition diagrams, and hence, the language
defined by the grammar is the set of strings accepted by the
network. In essence, what this amounts to is defining the
language by defining its recognizer. This provides several
advantages in proving the Nucleus verifier and compiler,
both of which must contain recognizer components. First of
all the complete syntax can be defined using just transition
networks, including such restrictions as no identifier may be
declared more than once, and + may only be applied to expressions of type integer. The correctness of the recognizer
components of the verifier and compiler then can be stated
solely in terms of an equivalence with the transition networks.

The semantics of Nucleus are defined by the axiomatic
method described by Burstall [F1]. First, we define a transformation from programs into sentences in the predicate calculus. This transformation we will call the *semantic mapping*
and the set of sentences produced the *reduced program*. In
defining Nucleus we have used the same transition network
that defines the syntax to define the semantic mapping. Then
we also define a set of axioms such that given a reduced program, the execution of that program can be deduced from the
axioms. The value of the axiomatic approach in proving things
about Nucleus programs is obvious.

Syntax.

The definition of the Nucleus syntax consists of two

[3]Woods, W.A., Transition Network Grammars for Natural Language
Analysis, Communications of the ACM, 13, 10, October, 1970

distinct transition networks, one a parsing network and the
other a scanning network. The scanning network reads the input string of basic characters and groups these together to
form the input string of tokens for the parsing network. We
will first describe the way a transition network operates, and
then the precise interface between the parser and scanner.
The networks that are described below are simpler in operation
than the ones described by Woods primarily for two reasons.
First, we do not need all the features that are necessary to
cope with natural languages. In particular, these networks
have no backtracking mechanism. Second, these networks are
sufficiently simple so that their operation can be defined
axiomatically. These axioms are another important advantage
in proving the recognizer components of the verifier and compiler. Although the operation of the networks can be described
completely and precisely by axioms, here we present only an informal description.

A transition network is a directed graph consisting of
labelled states and arcs. One state is designated as the
initial state, and some set of states is specified as recognition states. The network also has associated with it a
stack for saving arcs, an input string, an input pointer, and
a set of registers. The input string is the string of characters that is the candidate for membership in the language defined by the network, and the input pointer can point to any
individual character in the string. The registers contain
values that can be manipulated and tested by the network.
Each arc in the network is labelled with either an input string
character, nil, or the name of some state. Each arc also has
associated with it a test, a set of actions and a scan flag.
The test is a condition defined on the registers, and the actions are sequences of assignment operations on the registers.

The operation of the network begins at the initial state
with the input pointer pointing to the first character of the
input string and the arc stack empty. For any state that is
attained, the operation of the network proceeds in the following way. First the arcs leaving the state are examined to
find a traversable arc. To determine a traversable arc, all
arcs labelled with input string characters are considered
first. If the character labelling the arc matches the character pointed to by the input pointer and the test associated
with the arc is satisfied, then the arc is traversable. If
there are no traversable character labelled arcs, we next
consider arcs labelled with nil. A nil labelled arc is

traversable if its test is satisfied. If still no traversable arcs have been found, then we consider the arc labelled with a state name. (We allow each state to have at most one such arc leaving the state.) This arc is saved on the arc stack and the next state attained is the state used to label the arc. If the network proceeds from that state to a recognition state, the arc on the top of the stack is reconsidered and is traversable if its associated test is satisfied. If so, it is popped from the stack. In order to ensure that each state can have at most one traversable arc we also impose the following additional conditions on the network:

1. Any two arcs leaving a state may have the same character label only if their associated tests can never be satisfied simultaneously.
2. No two nil labelled arcs leaving a state may have tests that can be satisfied simultaneously.
3. A state may have at most one state labelled arc leaving that state.

Once the traversable arc for the state is determined, the actions associated with that arc are performed; if the scan flag for the arc is set, the input pointer is advanced to the next character on the input string and the next state attained is the state entered by the traversable arc. If a state has no traversable arc and is also a recognition state, then the arc on the top of the arc stack is reconsidered as indicated above. An empty stack determines acceptance in the language of the part of the input string preceding the input pointer. If a state has no traversable arc and that state is not a recognition state, then the input string is rejected as a sentence in the language.

One additional condition is imposed on the network.

4. A recognition state may not have a state labelled arc leaving that state.

With this condition, and the fact that every state has at most one traversable arc, we can always make the proper transition or termination decision without any further scanning, either looking ahead or backtracking, of the input string.

A character labelled arc leaving a state requires that the input pointer be pointing to that character in the input string. A nil labelled arc makes no specific requirement

about the character pointed to by the input pointer. A state
labelled arc can be thought of as requiring that the input
pointer point to the first character of a phrase (zero or more
characters) that is acceptable to the network when the network
is continued in the state corresponding to the label of the
arc.

As an example, consider the opening segment of the parsing network given by Figure 4.

```
PROGRAM:

    FIND    NIL
    DO      DEFINED.SIMPLE.SET := [ ]
            DEFINED.ARRAY.SET := [ ]
            TYPE.FUNCTION : [ ]
            DEFINED.PROCEDURE.SET :=[ ]
            REFERENCED.PROCEDURE.SET := [ ]
            DEFINED.IDENTIFIES.SET := [ ]
    NOSCAN 1
 1: PHRASE DECLARATION.SEQUENCE
    NOSCAN 2

 2: PHRASE PROCEDURE.SEQUENCE
    TEST   REFERENCED.PROCEDURE.SET SUBSETOF DEFINED.PROCEDURE.SET

    NOSCAN 3

 3: FIND    START
    SCAN    4

 4: FIND    IDENTIFIER
    TEST    TOKEN.STRING IN DEFINED.PROCEDURE.SET
    DO      SENTENCE(↑INITIALPROCEDURE=↑ TOKEN.STRING)
    NOSCAN 5

 5[RECOGNITION]:
```

FIGURE 4

This represents a graph with states and arcs labelled as in
Figure 5.

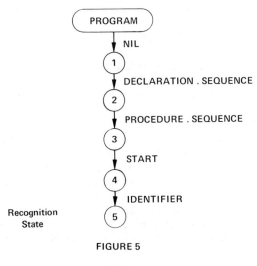

Recognition
State

FIGURE 5

The word FIND is used to specify character and nil labelled
arcs, and PHRASE is used for state labelled arcs. TEST and
DO denote the tests and actions associated with an arc. The
scanning is specified by SCAN or NOSCAN and the symbol appearing to the right of the scan flag is the name of the state
entered by the arc. For states having more than one exiting
arc, the arcs are listed sequentially following the state
name, If an arc does not have a TEST, it is assumed to have
the test condition that is universally satisfied, or equiv-
alently no test . Similarly for an arc with no DO, the identity transformation is assumed. Every arc will always have
either FIND or PHRASE and also either SCAN state name or
NOSCAN state name.

Operation of the parsing network begins at the state
labelled PROGRAM. The only arc leaving this state is nil
labelled with no test, and hence this arc is always traversable. The actions on the arc initialize a number of set-valued
registers. DEFINED.PROCEDURE.SET, for example, will be constructed (by further actions in other parts of the network)
to be the set of all IDENTIFIER tokens declared as procedures,
and REFERENCED.PROCEDURE.SET will be constructed as the set
of all IDENTIFIER tokens mentioned in ENTER statements.
The actions are performed, the input pointer is not advanced,
and we proceed to state 1. At state 1 we encounter an arc
labelled with the state named DECLARATION.SEQUENCE (which
appears further on in the network). At this point the arc
from state 1 to state 2 is stacked and the network proceeds
to determine if the input string is headed by a phrase that
is acceptable by continuing its operation at the DECLARATION.
SEQUENCE state. If so, the network resumes operation with
the arc from states 1 to 2, and the intervening operation
of the network will have advanced the input pointer to the
character just beyond the DECLARATION.SEQUENCE phrase. Since
the arc from 1 to 2 has no test, the next state attained is
2. At this point, the network tries to find a PROCEDURE.SE-
QUENCE phrase. The recognition of this phrase determines
values for the REFERENCED.PROCEDURE.SET and DEFINED.PROCEDURE.
SET registers. The test on the arc from 2 to 3 introduces
the requirement that every IDENTIFIER mentioned in an ENTER
statement must be defined as a procedure. The network then
proceeds from this point to look for the characters START and
IDENTIFIER following the PROCEDURE.SEQUENCE phrase with the
additional condition that the IDENTIFIER token must be defined as a procedure (The SENTENCE action is described in the
section on the semantic mapping.) Finally the network goes
to recognition state 5.

The definition of Nucleus contains two separate networks, the parsing network and the scanning network. The input string for the scanner is the actual string of characters in the basic character set of Nucleus that comprise the program. The scanning network also can read an additional "end-of-file" character. Thus, character labelled arcs in the scanner are labelled with members of the basic Nucleus character set or end-of-file and the scan flag controls the advance of the input string of basic characters.

The operation of the scanner defines and leaves values in two special registers, TOKEN and TOKEN.STRING. The value of TOKEN specifies the type of token recognized and TOKEN. STRING contains the actual string of characters comprising that token. These two registers also are accessible to the parser on a read only basis. There is no input string as such for the parser. But instead the TOKEN register always contains the character of the input string (of the parser) pointed to by the input pointer. The scan flag of the parser controls the initiation of the scanner. When the parser does a SCAN, the scanner is initiated to define new values for the TOKEN and TOKEN.STRING registers. The Nucleus scanner is defined so that it will recognize any string of basic characters as some kind of token.

Semantic Mapping.

The semantic mapping of Nucleus transforms any Nucleus program into its corresponding reduced program. The Nucleus program is a character string, and the semantic mapping also regards each predicate calculus sentence in the reduced program as a character string. Thus, the transformation is from one string into a set of strings. Also most of the functions in the reduced program take character strings as arguments. The Nucleus parsing network is used to define the semantic mapping through the use of a special action called SENTENCE. The action SENTENCE(x) defines the character string x to be a sentence in the reduced program. Thus, the parsing network not only defines the reduced program, but also gives a procedure for constructing it. The example in Figure 6 below shows the reduced program that corresponds to a simple Nucleus program. The sentences in the reduced program are listed in the order in which they are defined by the parsing network. The numbers in brackets at the left of the reduced program are the state numbers where the sentences are defined.

Nucleus Program	Reduced Program
INTEGER J,K,N;	[7]SIMPLE("J")
	[7]SIMPLE("K")
	[7]SIMPLE("N")
PROCEDURE POWER;	
(0) J := 0;	[25]ASSIGN("POWER:0","J","0")
(1) K :=1;	[25]ASSIGN("POWER:1","K","1")
(2) WHILE J < N DO	
(3) K :=2*K;	[25]ASSIGN("POWER:3","K","(2)*(K)")
(4) J :=J + 1;	[25]ASSIGN("POWER:3","J","(J)+(1)")
(5) ELIHW;	[47]JUMPTO("POWER:5","2")
	[47]IF("POWER:2","(J)<(N)","3","6")
(6) EXIT;	[17]EXIT("POWER:6")
	[17]EXITPOINT("POWER")="6"
START POWER	[4]INITIALPROCEDURE="POWER"

FIGURE 6

The numbers in parenthesis at the left of the Nucleus program
are not a part of the program. These numbers serve effectively as labels (local to the procedure) for key points in the
programs. These points then are referred to in stating the
reduced program. For example, the points "2", "3", and "6"
are referred to in the sentence IF("POWER:2","(J)<(N)","3",
"6"). The meaning of this sentence (which is established by
the axioms), is that point "2" in procedure POWER has a two
way branch. If the expression "(J)<(N)" is true at point "2",
control goes next to point "3", otherwise to point "6". The
values of these points are controlled in the parsing network
by the register POINT. The placement of the numbers (n)
above, indicates the value of POINT at the time the parser
begins scanning the respective line. In order to refer
uniquely to a point in any one of a set of procedures we
simply prefix the procedure name and a colon onto the numeric
label. For example, the label "POWER:2" is viewed simply as
a character string that uniquely identifies point "2" in procedure POWER.

Semantic Axioms.

Most of the semantic features of Nucleus are included in
the subset of Algol 60 axiomatized by Burstall [E9], the notable exceptions being the CASE statement and the input/output
statements. In spite of this, however, we have used a quite
different set of functions in stating the reduced programs
and a different set of axioms. Although we will not go into

detail, the example program in Figure 6 is a Nucleus version of an example given by Burstall for computing 2**N and illustrates some of these differences. The motivation for a different approach again is the provability of the Nucleus verifier. The axioms are structured so as to facilitate a proof that the verifier produces valid verification conditions.

The Nucleus axioms are based directly on the concept of state vectors. A <u>state vector</u> S is a function from some name space N into some value space V. Each member (n,v) of S we call a cell, n being the name of the cell and v its value. Thus S(n) is the value of cell n in state vector S. In the axioms we make extensive use of the conventional operation A[n,v,S] on state vectors that produces a state vector identical to state vector S except that the value of cell n is changed to v. A[n,v,S] is defined explicitly by Axiom 47,

$$A[n,v,S](x) = \text{if } x = n \text{ then } v \text{ else } S(x)$$

In Nucleus we take the view that the execution of a program is a sequence of state vectors $S_0, S_1, S_2, \ldots$. This sequence itself can be regarded as a function, E, from the non-negative integers into state vectors ($E[i] = S_i$). Thus $E[i](x)$ is the value of cell x in the ith state vector in the execution of the program. The execution of a program is defined by defining the function E. Taking this view, the Nucleus axioms fall into three classes, declaratives, evaluatives, and imperatives. The declarative axioms define the name space of the state vectors in the execution of a program, and the evaluative axioms describe the evaluation with respect to an arbitrary state vector $E[i]$ of expressions required in the imperatives. Ultimately the imperatives define the execution by specifying $E[I+1]$ in terms of $E[I]$, and they define the conditions under which the program terminates.

In Nucleus there is a unique value space that is the same for every state vector $E[I]$ of every program. This value space consists of the union of a number of disjoint sets: the set of integers, the set of boolean values, true and false, the basic character set of Nucleus, and the set of character strings of the form 1:d where 1 is a string such that 1 is an IDENTIFIER token and d is a non-empty string of digits. The value space also contains an undefined element U which is distinguishable from every other element in the set. Since the value space is the same for all programs, it is not defined by the axioms.

-112-

NUCLEUS - A LANGUAGE OF PROVABLE PROGRAMS

Every Nucleus program has an associated name space which
serves as the name space for every state vector E[I] in the
execution of that program. The elements of this name space
are character strings defined by the declarative axioms. For
example, if the reduced program has the sentence
ARRAY("BUFFER","1"), then from axioms

7   array(a,b)→ bound(a)=b
and 8   0≤i≤ integervalue(bound(a))→
        innamespace(a "[" digits(i) "]")

we can deduce that the character strings "BUFFER[0]" and
"BUFFER[1]" are in the name space of the program.

In addition to an undefined element U, the name space of
every program contains the elements ":LOC", ":LVL", ":RDHD",
":WTHD", and ":RTNPT[0]", ":RTNPT[1]", ... , ":RTNPT[maxstack-
size]". The quantity maxstacksize is an implementation parameter. We do not specify in the axioms what the value of
this parameter must be, that is left open to vary from one
implementation of the language to another, or even from one
run of a given program to the next. The names above that are
defined for all programs identify special cells in the state
vectors E[I]. ":LOC" serves as a location counter. This
cell takes on the l:d string values in the value space. These
values are the names of points in the various procedures as
described in the section on the semantic mapping. The cells
":RTNPT[0]" , ... , ":RTNPT[maxstacksize]", together with
the cell ":LVL",function as a return point stack for handling
the recursive procedure calls. Each of the :RTNPT cells may
take on the same kind of values as cell ":LOC", and ":LVL"
takes on machine representable integer values between -1 and
maxstacksize.

The other two components of Nucleus that exist for all
programs are the standard input and output files. These
files are not treated as components of the state vectors, but
rather as functions. However, the cells ":RDHD" and ":WTHD"
which serve as the record pointers to these files are in the
state vectors. The input file is described by the two functions :REOF and :RDFL. The file is viewed as a potentially
infinite sequence of records numbered 1,2,3,.... The function
:REOF(x) is true if record x is an end-of-file record, and
false otherwise. Each record consists of positions ("columns")
numbered 1,2,..., readsize where readsize is an implementation parameter. The function :RDFL(x,y) associates some

-113-

element in the basic character set of Nucleus with position y of record x, for all records x such that :REOF(x) is false, that is for records that are not end-of-file records. If :REOF(x) is true, :RDFL(x,y) is undefined for all positions y. For example, if ¬:REOF(1),:RDFL(1,1) = "A", :RDFL(1,2) = "4", :RDFL(1,j) = " " for 3≤ j≤80 = readsize and :REOF(2), the first two records of the input file contain

"A" "4" ... 78 blanks ...
end-of-file

The input record pointer is cell ":RDHD" in the state vectors of the program. The value of this cell always begins at zero and is increased by one just <u>before</u> the reading of each new record by a read operation. Thus, ":RDHD" always points to the record just read. Since this cell must be capable of pointing to any one of a potentially infinite number of records, it may take on any arbitrarily large, but finite, values. This does not, however, present any insurmountable problem in actually implementing Nucleus. Thinking in terms of a card input file, the :RDFL and :REOF functions would define the position of the read head of the card reader with respect to the first record on the file. ":RDHD" would not necessarily be implemented as a cell in the core memory of the machine.

The output file is viewed in a similar way through the functions :WEOF and :WTFL and the output record pointer :WTHD. The basic difference is that the axioms take the input file as given prior to execution and make no attempt to redefine it, whereas the output file is totally defined by the execution of the program. Thus given the functions that define the input file, one can deduce from the axioms the values of the functions that define the output file.

As an example of how the axioms define an execution, consider the sentences

    simple("J")
    simple("N")
    if("POWER:2","(J)<(N)","3","6")

taken from the example program. Suppose that we have deduced already that

    E[2](":LOC") = "POWER:2"
    E[2]("J") = 0
    E[2]("N") = 4

By axioms

    3   simple (":LOC")
    2   simple(x)→innamespace(x)
    16 innamespace(x)→x.i=if x=U then U else E[i](x)

we can deduce that ":LOC".2 = POWER:2". Thus we can use axiom

    53 if(":LOC".i,x,p,q)→
            [x.i=U→ termination(i)]∧
            [x.i≠U→E[i+1] = A[":LOC",pname(":LOC".i) ":"
                                if x.i=true then p else q,E[i]]]

to deduce that

    IF("POWER:2","(J)<(N)","3","6")→
        ["(J)<(N)".2 = U → TERMINATION(I)]
     ∧ ["(J)<(N)".2 ≠ U →
            E[3] = A[":LOC", PNAME(":LOC".2)":"
                        (IF "(J)<(N)".2 THEN "3" ELSE "6",E[2]]]

Now from the sentence in the reduced program, one can deduce
the consequent of the implication above. Then
one can use the sentences simple ("J") and simple ("N") and
axioms

    28 (x "<" y).i = if x.i=U ∨ y.i=U then U else x.i<y.i
    44 ("(" x ")").i = x.i

16, and 2 (given previously) to deduce that "(J)<(N)".2 is
true and thus also not equal to U, the undefined value. From
that we can deduce by axiom

    45 pname(x ":" y) = x

that E[3] = A[":LOC","POWER 3",E[2]], and then by axiom 47
(given previously) that

    E[3](":LOC") = "POWER:3"
    E[3]("J") = 0
    E[3]("N") = 4

CONCLUSION   Sufficient work has not yet been completed
                    to allow us to say definitely whether or
not Nucleus satisfies all of its design constraints. However,
considerable work has been completed with quite favorable in-

dictations and certain statements can be made.

1. Any program in the language can be subjected to a proof by inductive assertions. Assertions can be placed in the program, and verification conditions can be constructed for all features of the language by methods described either by King [19] or Good [14], with the exception of the read and write statements. It is straightforward however, to develop from the axioms verification conditions for these that are stated in terms of the standard input and output functions. A Snobol IV program that constructs these verification conditions has been successfully completed.

2. Does the structure of Nucleus facilitate the construction of correct programs? The best answer seems to be, yes, more so than some languages and no, less so than others. The only real progress toward this goal seems to be in terms of the use of a high level syntax and the inclusion of at least a primitive procedure mechanism. The progress toward this goal seems discernible only when one considers what programming in Nucleus would be like without these features.

3. Although no compiler has yet been written for Nucleus, the language contains only simple operational ideas for which compiling techniques are well known. The only possible exception is the CASE statement, but even this can be handled by a simple run time search through the set of defined case labels.

4. Work is currently well advanced on writing and proving the correctness of a Nucleus program that constructs verification conditions for Nucleus programs. Although this proof is not yet completed, no insurmountable obstacles are foreseen, and in fact, much of Nucleus has been designed to make this proof possible.

5. A proof of correctness of a Nucleus compiler has not yet been examined in detail. However, because of the great similarities between a verification condition generator (we could just as well say verification condition compiler) and a compiler, a successful proof of the Nucleus verifier above would strongly indicate the feasibility of proving the compiler.

6. A complete formal definition of Nucleus has been developed by the method described in this paper.

7. It is possible to express Nucleus compilers and verifiers in Nucleus.

NUCLEUS - A LANGUAGE OF PROVABLE PROGRAMS

The ultimate goal of Nucleus is to serve as a starting point, a point around which we can begin to construct actual computer programs that really do run correctly. From this point we can move on to build an ever increasing quantity of high quality software. This can be done directly by expressing programs in Nucleus, but even more important, it can be done indirectly by writing in Nucleus correct processors for other more usable and sophisticated languages.

TESTING
MATHEMATICAL SOFTWARE

V

It is reasonable to assume that the writer of a library program subjected it to a thorough test. It is folly for any user to use such a program without thoroughly testing it himself.

- F. Gruenberger

Round numbers are always false.

- Samuel Johnson

Since modern experimental physical science started with the work of Bacon, no one who published quantitative results without a credible estimate of accuracy would have been taken seriously. In computing work, much of what we do amounts to numerical experiments . . . yet it has become commonplace for computer users who are otherwise competent scientists to generate and even to publish computational results without even a gesture toward quantification of their numerical accuracy.

- N. Metropolis

THE EVALUATION OF MATHEMATICAL SOFTWARE

11

W. J. Cody
Argonne National Labs, Argonne, Illinois

"... it is an order of magnitude easier to write two sophisticated quadrature routines than to determine which of the two is better." --

J. Lyness at IFIP '71

INTRODUCTION   The evaluation of mathematical software is an art and not a science. Its importance is evidenced by the attention it received at the Mathematical Software Symposium held at Purdue in April, 1970, and by the recent volume of technical papers. The development of the art has been slow and chaotic, partially because software evaluation is difficult and partially because it has not been a professionally recognized activity attracting large numbers of talented people. There does not yet exist an over-all methodology for evaluation except in the special case of software for the calculation of functions. Despite these handicaps some very good work is being done and progress is being made.

The present paper is an attempt to bring some order into the chaos. We are not yet ready to turn the art into a science, but we can survey and attempt to classify some of the more important current techniques and projects for software evaluation.

PRELIMINARIES   As a first step we must eliminate confusion due to terminology. Mathematical software is a relatively new term denoting computer programs implementing mathematical algorithms. In most cases the algorithms involved are numerical procedures for solving specific types

of problems, such as the evaluation of a particular function
or the solution of a particular type of differential equation. It is common to identify such an algorithm with a
computer program as is done in the algorithms section of the
Communications of the ACM. But we must draw a careful distinction between the mathematical algorithm and the corresponding software, for an algorithm can be embedded in many
different computer programs. As host to the algorithm each
program manages the flow of information to and from the algorithm and performs certain ancillary services such as detecting and processing error conditions. Different programs
may contain, for example, different convergence criteria and
may offer the user varying degrees of control over the solution of his problem. A good algorithm is therefore a necessary, but not a sufficient condition for a good subroutine.

A second primary distinction between an algorithm and
mathematical software is in documentation. The documentation for an algorithm consists mainly of a description of
the problem solving process together with assumptions about
the variables and a summary of the results to be expected.
Software documentation must include all of this information
in addition to information on such things as the proper interface with other computer programs and the remedial action
taken when improper data or other errors are encountered.

An item of mathematical software thus consists of a
computer program and its documentation. The overall quality
of the software is to be judged by the quality of each of its
component parts.

The evaluation of mathematical software is frequently
referred to as certification. Unfortunately, this term has
several meanings. To certify can mean either to give reliable information about, or to guarantee. The interpretation
given to the term "certified software" by the individual
using the software is probably entirely different from the
interpretation given by the individual doing the certification work. For this reason we prefer to use the term software evaluation here, and to use the term certification only
when it has been carefully defined as in the NATS project
[K1].

In the evaluation of mathematical software we are faced
with all of the problems involved in the evaluation of other
types of software, though possibly not on the same scale

(it is difficult to imagine a quadrature routine as complicated as a compiler, for example). In addition, we have the
somewhat unique problem of evaluating the numerical performance of the program. The ideal evaluation effort for an
item of mathematical software might therefore address the
following questions:

1. What are the numerical properties (accuracy, etc.)
   and speed of the program?
2. Precisely what problems does the program solve, i.e.,
   what is the domain of the program?
3. Is the coding correct?
4. Is the program easy to use?
5. Is the documentation appropriate?

In a sense, the whole evaluation effort is aimed at the
last question, for good documentation should make it possible to obtain detailed answers to the previous questions.
To obtain such answers the author of a program must go through
an exacting evaluation process himself. This is seldom done,
but even when it is done further evaluation by a disinterest-
ed party is necessary to verify that the author has not overlooked something.

NON-NUMERICAL There are two distinct levels of program eval-
ASPECTS OF   uation. The first, which we will call per-
EVALUATION   formance evaluation, primarily seeks answers
               to the first two questions in our list, al-
though the third question is of incidental interest. The
emphasis at this level is on technical questions relating to
the underlying mathematical algorithm and the ability of the
program to solve problems. Since the questions can be ad-
dressed in an objective scientific manner, they are most
likely to appeal to the professional numerical analyst. The
second level, a complete program evaluation, must also specifically address the last three questions. Answers to these
questions are frequently non-technical, subjective and difficult. The professional numerical analyst frequently finds
such questions repulsive. Consequently, most of the evaluation activity for mathematical software is of the performance evaluation kind.

We will postpone our discussion of performance evaluation for the moment and consider the last three questions

in our list. The term correct coding in the third question refers to the absence of both inadvertent programming errors, commonly called bugs, and design errors, or mistakes. One way to check a program for bugs is to provide tests which cause every logical path in the program to be executed at least once. Both Fosdick [A5] and Ingalls [C25] describe schemes for partially automating the tedious task of verifying that a particular path has been traversed, but the provision of appropriate test cases is still left to the ingenuity of the evaluator.

The detection of design errors is a much more difficult problem, for it may not be clear what possibilities exist until a program is examined. The only common denominator appears to be the association of design errors with error detection or the lack of it. A square root routine which does not do something special when it encounters a negative argument clearly has a design error. Similarly, a routine for the solution of ordinary differential equations has a design error if it objects (or malfunctions) when the independent variable is stepped in a negative direction. The difference between these errors is essentially the degree of foresight required of the evaluator to check for them. We have often heard it suggested that the best way to detect design errors is to hand the program to a completely naive user. There is some truth in that, for he is more likely to try a complicated polynomial root finder, complete with all conceivable diagnostics and sophisticated error estimates, on a linear polynomial than is a sophisticated user.

The question of ease of usage concerns the robustness and accessibility of the program. By robustness we mean its ability to recover from abnormal situations without unnecessary termination of the computer run. The appropriateness of any diagnostic information and of the default numerical responses to abnormal conditions are included here. Proper evaluation includes test cases with illegal arguments and cases most likely to lead to underflow or overflow conditions, for example. The accessibility of the program refers to its calling sequence. Potential users may be repelled by long and complicated calling sequences, while calling sequences that are too short may not provide the user with sufficient control over the solution of his problem. Obviously the question of program accessibility is largely a matter of personal taste and proper evaluation calls for a certain tolerance on the part of the evaluator.

The evaluation of documentation is intended to determine how well the documentation provides the answers to the other questions in our list. Good documentation is neither too conservative nor too extravagant in its claims for the program. It is concise and accurate in describing such things as calling sequences, error monitoring facilities, and the advantages and limitations of the program. Proper evaluation includes, at the very least, verification of each of the claims made.

The discussion of the three questions just considered points up the fact that evaluation is an art and not a science. Only broad trivial philosophical statements can be made about seeking answers to each of these questions. The degree to which the questions are answered in any particular situation is a reflection of the ingenuity, patience and conscience of the evaluator.

PERFORMANCE   Error Analysis
EVALUATION

       There are three primary sources of error in any numerical result. The first, transmitted error, is the result of inherited error, that is, error in the original data. The second, analytic truncation error, is the result of replacing essentially infinite mathematical processes by finite processes in the mathematical algorithm. And the third, roundoff error, is the result of using a finite precision arithmetic. If a computer is involved, this third error reflects not only the method of rounding but also such design characteristics as the base of representation of the number system and the number of guard characters used [K26]. For mathematical software the latter two errors are collectively called the generated error, since their sum represents the error generated within the computer program assuming exact data.

The particular approach taken to determine the accuracy of a computer program depends partially upon the ease with which the other errors can be isolated from the transmitted error, and the importance of doing so. We will not go into the philosophical questions concerning the isolation of transmitted error ([K24] [K25]) but merely state that there are valid arguments for and against the practice. In some contexts it is appropriate, and in others it is not.

The first, and most obvious, approach to evaluation of

accuracy is based on forward error analysis. The computer program is simply checked on problems with known solutions, the performance being judged on how well the computational result agrees with the known result. In this approach, unintentional inclusion of inherited error is common, the most frequent source of such error being the provision of data in decimal form. Since terminating decimal fractions are seldom represented by terminating binary fractions, the data given to the computer program involves rounding errors unless a conscious effort has been made to choose data which is exactly representable in the computer. By the same token, errors made in converting binary results may completely mask the accuracy achieved by some routines. With a little care both of these sources of error can be eliminated and the direct comparison of results can give meaningful and useful measures of the generated error [K5].

Direct comparison of results is not always appropriate, however. For example, when the solution to a problem involves an array of numbers, the correlation of errors between the individual elements of the array becomes important. In such cases it is more appropriate to show that the computed solution is the exact solution to a problem which is a perturbation of the original problem. Instead of measuring the differences between the computed solution and the mathematical solution of the problem posed, the difference between the problem posed and the problem solved is measured. This "backward error analysis" [K50] can be applied to any computation but is especially useful for ill-conditioned problems. The usual application is in the form of consistency checks involving theoretical identities. One of the advantages of this approach is that the consistency checks can be made an integral part of the program being checked, thus supplying each user with information about the performance of the program on his problem.

Domain Analysis

An entirely separate question is the determination of the domain for the program. The best mathematical software may falter when applied to problems it is not designed to solve. The numerical solution of ordinary differential equations, for example, becomes more difficult as the equations become stiffer. (Stiffness is a technical term whose meaning need not concern us here. For a precise definition and discussion see [K36] and references cited there.) Methods

not specifically designed for stiff equations frequently
malfunction on such equations, while methods designed to
solve stiff equations may be horribly inefficient on non-
stiff equations. Some knowledge as to how stiff an equation
can be before a program malfunctions or becomes inefficient
is important if the program is to be properly used.

There are corresponding distinctions in most broad
classes of problems. For example, quadrature problems can
be classified according to properties of the integrand such
as continuity, continuity of higher derivatives, existence
of peaks, and oscillatory behavior [K33]. Unfortunately,
we don't always know what properties are the most important
for distinguishing the difficulties of numerical solution,
nor do we know how to describe these properties in parametric
form. The future parametric classification and codification
of problems in much the same way fingerprints are now classified is an intriguing possibility. We will return to this
idea a little later. For the moment we can say that determination of the domain of a program is important, but difficult.

Timing Analysis

We have so far ignored the question of timing a program.
Timing is perhaps one of the oldest measures of program performance, and it is still important. But not in the same
sense as previously. Precise time measurements down to the
millisecond have little meaning when programs are being run
in time-sharing environments or under huge operating systems.
In fact, it is almost impossible to determine precise timings
under such conditions, for timing at that level of precision
is a function of the transitory computer environment as well
as of the program being timed. For simple programs such as
function subroutines, reasonable estimates of execution time
are still possible and are useful. But for more complicated
programs the most useful estimates are those which are, for
example, based on the number of function evaluations required
in a quadrature program or related to the order of the matrix
in an eigenvalue program.

Performance Profile

All of the previous discussion of performance evaluation
has set the stage for what J. Lyness calls the performance

profile of a program.[1] Basically, the performance profile
is a set of statistics and parameters describing the performance of a given program on a standard set of problems. The
scheme involves continuous evolution of the problem set to
reflect new sources of difficulty as they are identified.
The problems and statistics used would ideally serve to define the domain of the program as well as to give detailed
information on its speed and accuracy. A quadrature routine,
for example, might be tried on a standard integrand in which
the sharpness of a peak could be specified by a parameter,
certain standard timing and accuracy statistics being gathered for particular values of the parameter. But, in addition, the value of the parameter which first caused a malfunction of the routine would become a part of the performance profile. It is this last item which distinguishes
the performance profile idea from previous ideas such as
those of Witte [K51]. Clearly, the development of a meaningful performance profile scheme for even one type of problem
would be a long term activity. Realization of this activity
is obviously still in the future, yet in a few moments we
will describe certain contemporary evaluation projects which
bear remarkable resemblances to Lyness' proposal.

We believe that performance profiles are the ultimate
goal of performance evaluation. They include the determination of accuracy using forward error analysis or backward
error analysis, whichever is appropriate, and the measurement
of speed. They also include the specification of the problem
domain, something that probably cannot be meaningfully done
without the previously mentioned idea of parametrization and
codification of problems. From this vantage point it seems
natural that the future realization of either a performance
profile scheme or a problem classification scheme will necessarily mean the realization of both.

PRESENT   We now consider in more detail the evaluation
TECHNOLOGY   of certain specific classes of mathematical
              software by surveying recent literature and
contemporary projects. Despite the fact that our list of
topics and projects is incomplete and our discussion of each
item is brief, we hope to present an accurate picture of the

[1]
Lyness, J.N., Private communication

present state of affairs.

Function Subroutines

Here, both theory and practice are in a most satisfactory state of affairs. The most widely exploited technique for accuracy evaluation is a Monte Carlo approach based on forward error analysis [K5] although techniques based on backward error analysis have also been proposed [K14, K37]. In the first approach, the accuracy of a particular program is determined by direct comparison against "correct" function values for exact arguments chosen in an appropriate random manner. Properly implemented, the test procedure measures only the generated error. Statistics frequently gathered include the frequency of error in units of the least significant bit of the machine representation of the result, the maximum relative (or absolute) error, and the root mean square error.

Many of the elementary function libraries supplied by computer manufacturers with their Fortran compilers have been evaluated either by the manufacturers themselves [K35] or by concerned users [K6, K9, K18, K31, K38, K52]. In at least one case a manufacturer has modified his library based on adverse evaluations of it [K9, K38]. Some of the work in this latter effort is described in more detail in the paper by Ng later on in the book.

Current activities include a project at the University of Minnesota to evaluate and upgrade the Fortran elementary function library on the CDC 6000 series of computers,[2] a project at the National Bureau of Standards for supplying standard test material for function programs (described in detail in the Sadowski and Lozier paper), and the NATS project [K1]. This latter effort is NSF sponsored, and is intended to provide tested and "certified" (in a carefully stated sense) software for certain special functions of mathematical physics and for certain matrix eigenvalue problems.

Although in some isolated cases, notably in the work of

---

[2] Frankowski, K. S. and Liddiard, L.A. private communication.

Kahan[3] and Turner[4], function subroutines have been checked
for preservation of mathematical properties such as weak
monotonicity, such checks are not made as often as they
should be. To our knowledge Kahan3 is the only one who has
succeeded in mathematically proving, as opposed to experimentally verifying, the accuracy of a function routine.

Differential Equations Subroutines

Next to special functions, subroutines for the solution
of ordinary differential equations (ODE's) are probably subjected to performance evaluation more frequently than any
other class of subroutine. For the past few years, T. Hull
at the University of Toronto has been particularly active in
this area. In 1966 at a SIAM meeting in Iowa, Hull outlined
a systematic approach which he intended to follow [K19]. He
proposed that problems and methods of solution be classified,
and that well-defined measures of goodness be developed. His
goal was to permit the selection of a best method from a
given class of methods relative to a given class of problems
and to the specified measure of goodness. It is difficult
to say just how these proposals influenced the ideas of a
performance profile and the parametric classification of
problems, but Hull's ideas definitely came first.

Recently Hull and his colleagues published a progress
report setting forth in some detail a set of standard problems and measures of goodness for non-stiff ODE's [K20].
The report includes a discussion of several of the better
contemporary ODE programs and concludes with a detailed performance evaluation of each. A subsequent memorandum contains a proposed set of problems and methods to be evaluated
for the stiff case.

We cannot summarize all of the work in this field, but
we would like to point out the work done by Crane and Fox
[K8] at Bell Laboratories, and the work of Krogh [K22] at
JPL. In particular, Krogh has recently undertaken a poll of
fellow workers soliciting opinions and comments on matters related to performance evaluation of ODE programs [K23]. He
expects to publish the results.

---

[3]Kahan, W. Private communication, Univ. of California, Berkeley.
[4]Turner, R.L. Private communication, NASA Lewis Research Center, Cleveland, Ohio

Quadrature Programs

Although there have been some isolated evaluation efforts and proposals incorporating parametrization and codification of integrands [K17, K33], the recent emphasis has been on establishing a standard set of test problems and statistics without systematic codification. The best known collections are probably those of Casaletto et al [K2] and of Kahaner [K21], the latter collection being used by de Boor [K10], and perhaps others.

The overall situation appears to be favorable for a major advance in evaluation technique for quadrature routines in the near future. Lyness' interest and insight into the parametrization and codification of quadrature problems is one important ingredient. A second is that meaningful codification appears most feasible in this case. Such an advance, if it should come, would necessarily modify the approach to evaluation of other types of software.

Other Classes of Subroutines

The situation for other broad classes of mathematical software is confused. As with quadrature routines, the present emphasis is on standardizing problem sets and performance statistics. One of the earliest such collections was given by Witte for polynomial root finders [K51]. Witte's careful description of how the collection was to be used and how it was intended to grow has served as a model for subsequent collections in other problem areas. Unfortunately, except for a study made at Purdue [K11], the collection has not been extensively used and has not grown.

Similar problem collections exist for nonlinear equations solvers [K42], linear equations solvers [K15], least squares problems [K49], and matrix eigenvalue problems [K12, K13, K41], among others. Except for the essay by Hanson on evaluation of linear equations solvers [K15], little guidance is given toward the use of these collections. No significant steps have been taken towards problem parametrization or a true performance profile.

In the case of matrix eigenvalue programs, the previously mentioned NATS project [K1] has undertaken an extensive and careful testing of eigenvalue routines as a part of its documentation and "certification" process. The tests apply

W.J. CODY

Wilkinson's backward error analysis to the situation for which it was originally developed. On the basis of these tests, the software is believed by the originators to be of exceptionally high quality. But systematic testing independent of those tests designed by the project's investigators has not been as great as they would have liked. Certainly, performance profiles for these routines have not been attempted.

LITERATURE AND SIGNUM, the Special Interest Group on Numeri-
BIBLIOGRAPHIES cal Mathematics, has been interested from its conception in the software evaluation problem. The unrefereed SIGNUM Newsletter contains frequent articles and reports on the subject. In addition, a working group under the direction of Karl Usow is collecting an informal bibliography, parts of which have already appeared [K41, K43]. Additional specialized bibliographies are found in the works of Hull [K20] for ODE's, and of Cody [K5, K6] for elementary functions. Section K of the bibliography at the end of the book is not to be regarded as complete, but it does contain all recent papers known to the author.

The book Mathematical Software edited by J.R. Rice [K43] contains the proceedings of a special symposium held at Purdue University in April, 1970. The papers collected there largely concern the problems we have been discussing here.

CONCLUSION The evaluation of mathematical software is an activity which is constantly growing in importance. The techniques are still relatively primitive and ad hoc in nature, yet significant progress is being made in specific areas. The basic methodology for special functions is now widely accepted and used, and recent work with ODE's appears promising. The ideas of parametrization and codification of problems, and of a performance profile for software may be applied to quadrature routines in the near future. We still have a long way to go, but the day is coming when software evaluation will be a professionally recognized scientific activity, and no longer an art.

THE EVALUATION OF MATHEMATICAL SOFTWARE

Acknowledgements

The author is indebted to W.R. Cowell, B.S. Garbow, B.T. Smith and H.C. Thacher, Jr., for their constructive criticism of this manuscript, and to colleagues too numerous to mention whose views have helped shape those of the author.

MATHEMATICAL SOFTWARE TESTING ACTIVITIES

12

Edward W. Ng

Jet Propulsion Laboratory, Pasadena, California

INTRODUCTION   In recent years there have been a number of *library certification projects* which were carried out for the evaluation and validation of mathematical function subprograms of various FORTRAN libraries. Examples among these are the evaluation of the IBM 360 library at the Argonne National Laboratory [K3, K18], that of the UNIVAC 1108 library at the National Bureau of Standards [K31] and at this laboratory [K4]. Most of these projects were briefly reviewed by W.J. Cody [K6].

In the context of mathematical function subprograms, the term certification usually means the critical evaluation of the performance characteristics of the subprogram, such as reliability, efficiency, storage requirements and documentation. In this sense all the projects mentioned above attend to only one or two aspects of the overall certification effort. Naturally all the investigators in this area consider the reliability characteristics first and foremost. In this presentation we describe in some detail the efforts that have been carried out at this laboratory, where we are exclusively concerned with testing the reliability of the subprograms. This effort was initiated as early as 1963 when C. Lawson [K27] first studied the accuracy of the Double Precision Arithmetic on the IBM 7094 computer. Subsequently, in the period 1965-1967, approximations for the elementary functions were generated and tested for the book "Computer Approximations" [K16]. More recently our testing results have caused Sperry Rand to improve the UNIVAC 1108 FORTRAN library [K35].

METHODOLOGY OF   Methods of certifying subroutines may be di-
TESTING   vided into two broad classes: logical vali-
                 dation and statistical testing. The former
method treats a subroutine like a theorem. Given certain

-135-

input (hypotheses), it is implicitly asserted that the subroutine will produce a set of determined output (consequen-
ces). This implicit assertion is then tested logically to
see if it can be affirmed or negated. It is probably fair
to assess that it will be quite some time before library
functions can be certified deductively, if it is at all practical to do so. The statistical approach basically involves
a comparison against some standard reference of a set of output computed by the subroutine. Inherent in this method is
the assumption that one can find a standard reference that
is itself reliable. Cody [K5] recently discussed the merits
and demerits of three types of such testing commonly used,
viz., comparison against published tables, identity checks
(e.g., sin3x- 3sinx + 4sin^{3}x = 0) and automatic tabular comparisons. Though all the certifications mentioned above
were based on the last type of testing, they differ in implementation and emphasis, naturally being constrained by
different environments and philosophies. Our implementation
is 'user oriented', in the sense that we depend on a package
constituted of a hierarchy of FORTRAN callable subroutines.
In fact this 'user oriented' structure has been proved useful in a number of ways. First, it was conveniently portable to others for testing library function subprograms on
IBM 7094 and UNIVAC 1108 computers. In fact, as described
subsequently, the package is very simple to use for this purpose. Second, some modules of our implementation have been
transported to other installations and machines for computations totally unrelated to subroutine certification (e.g.,
Laplace Transform Computation and Astrophysical Calculations,
[K46]. Third, our implementation is readily adaptable to
other types of subroutine testing and in fact as described
in a subsequent section, has been applied to the certification of algorithms submitted to the Communications of ACM.
For the moment we shall restrict our discussion to FORTRAN
library functions.

A typical Fortran library contains three function subprograms for each elementary mathematical function (trigon-
metric and inverse trigonometric, exponential and hyperbolic,
logarithm, and square and cube roots). The three function
subprograms are for single precision real, double precision
real and single precision complex arguments. The first logical priority is to establish the validity of the double precision function subprograms that may in turn be used as standard reference against which the other subprograms are compared. To this end there must be established for each funct-

MATHEMATICAL SOFTWARE TESTING ACTIVITIES

ion a reference routine which computes the function more accurately than double precision, and which is itself validated by some independent means.

ORGANIZATION OF   This section describes the organization of
TESTING   the testing procedure carried out at this
                 laboratory. There are four basic aspects of
the package of testing programs. They are the extended precision arithmetic, the reference routines, the comparison
driver programs and the organization of output statistics.

Extended-Precision Arithmetic

     For the execution of high precision extended range float-
ing point arithmetic, we have constructed a set of FORTRAN-
callable subroutines. This set allows arithmetic operations
in 3 levels of precision (70,.105 and 140 significant bits)
and is generically referred to as the "Q-precision arithmetic package" [K28-K30]. It consists of six FORTRAN subroutines and one Assembly language subroutine. A Q-precision
number is represented as an array of 3 to 5 words, the first
containing the signed exponent, the second containing the
sign of the number and first 35 bits of the fraction part,
and the rest each containing 35 additional bits of the mantissa. Precision higher than 140 bits may be achieved by extending certain storage arrays beyond 5 words. This package
is then used for two-way conversions between double precision
and Q-precision numbers, the basic arithmetic operations (addition, subtraction, multiplication, and division), and the
input and output of Q-precision numbers. At this laboratory
two versions of the package exist, for the use of the IBM
7094 and the UNIVAC 1108. A third version, for the IBM
360 O/S, has been constructed at the University of Southern
California.[1]

The Reference Routines

     We have constructed Q-precision reference routines for
the functions square root, sine, cosine, exponential and
logarithm (with base e, 2 and 10), hyperbolic sine, arcsine
and arctangent. Other reference routines, such as tangent,

[1]Tooper, R.F., Private communication.

cube root, etc., may be readily built up from these basic
ones. The following considerations are taken into account
in the construction of the reference routines. First, efficiency is in general of minimal concern, because the testing of double precision subroutines need be done only occasionally, for example, every time a new FORTRAN library is
supplied. Second, with efficiency not a constraint, the
methods that require the least complications in algorithmic
and code design are most appealing, as with such methods the
performance of the reference routine is better understood and
well under control. For the elementary functions in question
the choice of the classical Taylor series or its Pade rational
form is appropriate for this purpose. Third, the reference
routine is not required to yield last-bit accuracy. It follows that identity checks are quite satisfactory as long as
the identity used is not part of the computational algorithm
for the reference routine. With these considerations the
reference routines are constructed with two types of relative
truncation error bound, viz., less than 10^{-21} for 70-bit arithmetic and 10^{-35} for 140-bit arithmetic. The current versions
do not make provisions for 105-bit arithmetic but it is a
simple matter to modify the reference routines to include
those.

The Comparison Program

There are two sets of comparison programs, one for testing single-precision functions and the other for double precision. Each set contains three components: (1) a data element, (2) a driver program, and (3) a comparison subroutine.
The package is mainly set up for testing a scalar function
of one or two arguments. For a 2-vector function (e.g., a
complex function) one may either test the function norm or
the components separately.

The data element contains sets of parameters. Each set
specifies the function to be tested, a closed interval of
the argument or a closed rectangle for two arguments or one
complex argument, and the number of test values (typically
3000) for this interval or rectangle. Thus for a particular
function there may typically be four to six intervals chosen
to cover all the major computational paths in the function
subprogram and certain critical subintervals of the independent variable where the function is known to have extraordin-
ary behavior. For example, for the function cos(x), the
choice of the interval [0, $\pi/2$] tests the primary range of

approximation, the choice $[\pi/2,\pi]$ and $[-\pi,0]$ tests respectively the usage of reflection formulae about the axes $x=\pi/2$ and $x=0$, the choice $[\pi,8\pi]$ tests the range reduction and the choice $[\pi/2-10^{-4},\pi/2+10^{-4}]$ tests a critical range where the relative error is expected to be substantial.

The driver program basically reads in the above parameters and invokes the appropriate subroutines to compute the function values in the test and reference precisions. The simplicity of usage of the package is underscored by the fact that a user only needs to communicate with the driver program through a NAMELIST input. For example, if he chooses to test the double precision cosine function in the interval [0.5,1], with 1000 test arguments, all he need to do is to supply the following data:

```
$INPUT
X1 = 0.5D0, X2 = 1.D0, N = 1000, KFUN = 2, NPLØT = 50, NARG =1
$END
```

Here X1, X2 and N are obvious user-defined parameters. KFUN, NARG, and NPLØT are parameters specifying respectively the the function in question (cosine), the number of arguments and the desired number of points for the output error plot.

The comparison program accepts the interval from the driver and subdivides it into a number of subintervals, from each of which a uniform pseudorandom number is generated. These test arguments are then conveyed to the driver for the computation of the function values. This program in turn utilizes these values to compute statistics of interest, as described next. We parenthetically note that the argument is generated in the test precision and then converted to the reference precision by appending zeros, thus producing identical arguments. Furthermore, the function values are compared in the reference precision, in contrast to the practice of some authors [K5] to convert the reference value to the test precision and then to compare via fixed point subtraction.

Performance Statistics

Basically three types of errors are computed. They are the absolute and relative errors and the error in units of the last bit position of the test value. The last type of error is useful for a precise interpretation of the number

-139-

E. NG

of correct bits that the test value has. Various statistics
about these errors are presented in the form of histograms,
tables and a plot. For example, the mean, root mean square,
and maximum of each are tabulated. So are the ten largest
errors of each, along with the associated arguments and function values in both decimal and octal. On the next page is
a portion of the performance statistics output for the single
precision sine function with argument in the interval
$[-\pi/2, 0]$.

CONCLUSION   In summary the usage of the package of testing programs has produced a number of visible
results. It has provided us a study of the quality of the
IBM 7094 and UNIVAC 1108 FORTRAN library mathematical functions. Such study has led to the discovery that some library
functions are based on poor algorithmic or code design and
others contain blunders [K9]. The performance statistics
have caused Sperry Rand to improve the UNIVAC 1108 FORTRAN
library [K7]. In fact the testing performed at Sperry Rand
was based on this particular package.

We have also applied this package to the certification
of other types of mathematical software. For example, we
have certified our library subroutines for gamma and error
functions, exponential and elliptic integrals, and Bessel
function. Certain algorithms published in Communications of
the ACM have been certified here [e.g.,K39], and in addition
the entire testing procedure has been applied to various scientific computations such as astronomical calculations.

Acknowledgement

The basic package of computer programs described in the
text has been developed by Dr. C. Lawson, with the assistance
of D. Campbell, C. Devine, and E. Ng. All of these persons
have applied the package to the various testings as mentioned. The present author is indebted to C. Lawson and C.
Devine for reading this manuscript and for making helpful
suggestions. This paper presents the results of one phase
of research carried out at the Jet Propulsion Laboratory,
California Institute of Technology, under Contract No. NAS 7-
100, sponsored by the National Aeronautics and Space Adminis-
tration.

EXAMPLE STATISTICS OUTPUT

Single Precision Sine Function with argument in the interval $[-\pi/2, 0]$.

```
         TESTING THE  UNIVAC 1108 LIBRARY SUBROUTINE OF THE    TRIGONOMETRIC SINE   FUNCTION.  INTERVAL IS .-PI/2.+0.

SE         3000  RANDOM ARGUMENTS UNIFORMLY DISTRIBUTED BETWEEN      -.15707963+01    AND       .00000000

UNIT* =      .7450581-08

    D = YSNGL-YDBLE
    A = D/AUNIT
    E = D IN UNITS OF THE LAST BIT POSITION OF YSNGL
  REL = D/ABS(YDBLE)
    R = REL*12**27)
```

NO. OF GOOD BITS	CLASSIFICATION INTERVALS FOR E, R, AND A	E COUNT	E PER-CENT	/E/ COUNT PER-CENT	/E/ CUMULATIVE COUNT PER-CENT	R COUNT PER-CENT	/R/ COUNT PER-CENT	/R/ CUMULATIVE COUNT PER-CENT	A COUNT PER-CENT	/A/ COUNT PER-CENT	/A/ CUMULATIVE COUNT PER-CENT
	BELOW -2**10	0	.0			0	.0		0	.0	
16	-2**10 TO -2**9	0	.0			0	.0		0	.0	
17	-2**9 TO -2**8	0	.0			0	.0		0	.0	
18	-2**8 TO -2**7	0	.0			0	.0		0	.0	
19	-2**7 TO -2**6	0	.0			0	.0		0	.0	
20	-2**6 TO -2**5	0	.0			0	.0		0	.0	
21	-2**5 TO -2**4	0	.0			0	.0		0	.0	
22	-2**4 TO -2**3	0	.0			0	.0		0	.0	
23	-2**3 TO -2**2	0	.0			0	.0		0	.0	
24	-2**2 TO -2**1	0	.0			0	.0		0	.0	
25	-2**1 TO -1.0	0	.0			0	.0		0	.0	
26	-1.0 TO -0.5	31	1.0			346	11.5		31	1.0	
27	-0.5 TO -0.0	1499	50.0			1184	39.5		1499	50.0	
27	0.0 TO 0.5	1457	48.6	2956	98.5	119C	39.7	2374	79.1	1470	49.0	2969	99.0
26	0.5 TO 1.0	13	.4	44	1.5	280	9.3	626	20.9	31	1.0	3000	100.0
25	1.0 TO 2**1	0	.0	0	.0	0	.0	0	.0	0	.0	3000	100.0
24	2**1 TO 2**2	0	.0	0	.0	0	.0	0	.0	0	.0	3000	100.0
23	2**2 TO 2**3	0	.0	0	.0	0	.0	0	.0	0	.0	3000	100.0
22	2**3 TO 2**4	0	.0	0	.0	0	.0	0	.0	0	.0	3000	100.0
21	2**4 TO 2**5	0	.0	0	.0	0	.0	0	.0	0	.0	3000	100.0
20	2**5 TO 2**6	0	.0	0	.0	0	.0	0	.0	0	.0	3000	100.0
19	2**6 TO 2**7	0	.0	0	.0	0	.0	0	.0	0	.0	3000	100.0
18	2**7 TO 2**8	0	.0	0	.0	0	.0	0	.0	0	.0	3000	100.0
17	2**8 TO 2**9	0	.0	0	.0	0	.0	0	.0	0	.0	3000	100.0
16	2**9 TO 2**10	0	.0	0	.0	0	.0	0	.0	0	.0	3000	100.0
	ABOVE 2**10	0	.0	0	.0	0	.0	0	.0	0	.0	3000	100.0

	E	/E/	R	/R/	A	/A/	ME	/MEL/	D	/D/
MEAN	-.01	.25	-.01	.32	-.01	.20	-.8157-10	.2413-08	-.997-10	.1454-08
STD. DEV.	.24	.15	.38	.21	.24	.15	.2855-08	.1528-08	.1823-08	.1103-08
MAX POS. VALUE	.63	.63	.97	.97	.50	.53	.7201-08	.7201-08	.3694-08	.3937-08
MAX NEG. VALUE	-.53	.00	-.94	.00	-.53	.00	-.4994-08	.0000	-.3937-08	.00n0

```
THE TEN LARGEST POSITIVE VALUES OF E

          X                      X                  YAPPROX                    YTRUE                         E

    -.11284409+00       602061624617          60206261255L       60020626L255  1376231.2163        .5033
    -.54184079-02       606234714314          606234715224       600.23471522  437510707522        .5056
    -.21255299+00       601115542024          601117754365       60011775543A  537464631531        .5062
    -.76904943-01       602304776511          602305235447       600230523544  73742076.2672        .5073
    -.25440747-01       604137133926          604137162441       60041371624A  136600326117        .5195
    -.38386587-01       603305422270          603305472414       60033054724I  436407700205        .5232
    -.95869364-02       605305665712          605305670270       60053056702L  035737444715        .5322
    -.18636445-01       604316520374          604316531426       60043165314I  634504455477        .5526
    -.22338718-01       604222001200          60422202065A       60042220208L  434213142540        .5583
    -.11765006-01       605176367753          605176374407       600517637990  727751623233        .6257

THE TEN LARGEST NEGATIVE VALUES OF E
```

A METHOD OF TESTING PROGRAMS FOR DATA SENSITIVITY

13

H. S. Bright and I. J. Cole

Computation Planning Inc., Washington, D. C. and
NASA Goddard Space Center, Greenbelt, Maryland

INTRODUCTION   This chapter introduces a machine method
for testing to provide explicit indication
of the effects of the finite precision of machine arithmetic
on the accuracy of results.

In human-controlled calculation, especially using fixed-
point arithmetic procedures, whether by hand or by machine,
all data transfers are subject to inspection. Certain major
arithmetic faults (e.g., loss of almost all significance
when two almost-equal numbers are subtracted) which are due
to chosen precision limits in hand calculation or desk calculator hardware are visible to the observant user. To a
lesser extent, this is also true of calculation performed by
automatic computer using fixed-point or integer arithmetic,
especially if the user builds into his procedure appropriate
test processes [K50] such as printout of critical intermediate results.

With most modern scientific applications of high-speed
computers for numerical calculations, however, use is made
of built-in automatic normalizing floating-point arithmetic.
This feature, while providing to the user the great convenience of completely automatic scaling, also completely ob-
scures from him the internal loss of significance which may
occur because of the finite precision (i.e., limited number
of digits in each number stored and processed) of the equipment. The results can be disastrous; even for programs which
may be logically correct and which may have operated for long
periods of time without observed error, the probability is in
general never zero that new uses of the program, with even
subtly different input data, may produce erroneous results.

Some errors are sufficiently gross (e.g., a denominator
of a fraction approaching zero), to cause arithmetic fault

indication by the hardware to warn the user of trouble. More subtle difficulties (e.g., the numerator[1] of the same fraction approaching zero but with little numerical significance, or a supporting routine being used in a sequence which causes it to produce grossly incorrect results) are obscured from the user by the basic fact that arithmetic processes are invisible to him during program execution.

We mention above the class of errors due to hardware limitations, which we will call generated error. Some consideration will also be given here to input error,[2] due to inaccuracies in data and/or constants, and to analytic error, due to too-crude mathematical approximations and/or other formulation inadequacies.

The test method described in the present writing accounts explicitly for input error and displays the results of generated error. In the hands of a thoughtful user, it can be useful in leading to recognition of troubles which may be due to analytic error.

Wilkinson [K50] and Forsythe [K55] give and explain numerous examples of pitfalls in numeric calculation which can result in erroneous results from inadequate planning of calculations. Many of these pitfalls are due to machine limitations, perhaps exacerbated by use of conditionally stable calculation procedures. Wampler [K49] describes extensive tests on a class of library programs for statistical analysis, showing empirically that several widely-used program packages can yield gross inaccuracies.

With the continual growth of computer power and productivity, increasing management attention is being given to overall effectiveness of computing service to the organizations served; accordingly, less emphasis is being placed upon minor aspects of economy. Thus, modern executive systems provide improved responsiveness to many kinds of user demands, even though additional "overhead" consumption of machine resources is required to provide such responsiveness. We feel that this changing emphasis is appropriate.

[1]See the test example later in the chapter for such a case.

[2]Called "intrinsic error" by Ashenhurst and Metropolis [K56].

In scientific support programming, on the other hand, we feel that inordinate attention is still being given to speed and economy of calculation, while in many cases inadequate attention is paid to the validation of numerical results.

The test method we will describe provides a means for the user of existing programs, including those which make use of floating-point arithmetic, to trace the accuracy effects of input and generated error on intermediate and final computational results.

The method described in the chapter provides a means for automatically applying to existing programs, using actual input data, the concept of error-indicating arithmetic suggested by von Neumann and Goldstine [K57], their co-worker Metropolis, and Cheydleur [K58]. The system uses internally the notation of Gray and Harrison [K60] for keeping track of an index of significance for each quantity which is involved in or results from a calculation step. The kind of arithmetic used is significance or significant digit arithmetic, as used by Cheydleur and Ashenhurst and Metropolis, and as described by Carr [K59].

The method is also applicable to other error-indicating arithmetics, including the well-known bounds-indicating Interval Arithmetic of Moore [K61], the signed-error-indicating "n, n+1 precision" arithmetic of Moshos and Turner [K62], and (with restrictions) to nonrounding rational-fraction arithmetic [K50].

Objectives

This program test method is intended to provide means for:

1. Observing the end results on accuracy itself when input data is changed
2. Observing intermediate result accuracy effects of program parameter changes (iteration count, etc.)
3. Observing accuracy effects of precision order (single, double, multiple)
4. Localizing numeric procedures which result in excessive error growth
5. Determining the effects on result accuracy of changes in input data accuracy.

Limitations on Hand Tracing

One computation test method which is very important because of its broad applicability is that of hand tracing, in which the user performs a more or less nearly exact simulation of machine arithmetic in order to compute test results, to be compared against direct machine computational results from execution of a program in test status.

The basic limitation on this method is logistic: if used with a fixed-point desk calculator to simulate a floating-point computer, for example, the method requires that the hand-calculation execute many times the number of steps carried out by execution of the computer program. A high-speed modern computer executes perhaps a billion steps per minute, while a human at a desk calculator may execute a thousand steps per day.

Even if we ignore typical human error rates (which in practice can hardly be reduced below one error per hundred steps and which drastically reduce effective human productivity in hand computation), it is evident that hand tracing must be limited to superficial testing of programs.

The test method described here is executed entirely by the computer. Program segments being error-traced proceed only a few hundred times slower than direct machine execution, while program segments not being traced proceed at full hardware speed.

Thus, the fundamental limitation on hand tracing is not applicable to the machine method, and the latter can be applied rigorously to non-trivial computational processes.

OVERVIEW OF PROGRAM TEST METHOD   This method uses a computer software system (known as SigPac [K54]) to cause execution of a user-written program, written in a higher language (in the system described, IBM FORTRAN IV (G, H)) to be performed without human intervention or modification, other than by user insertion into his program of requests for test service from the SigPac system.

System

SigPac consists of a source-program processor (SIGSCN) which translates the user program and its service requests (known as pseudo-operations) into an artificial language version which can be compiled by a conventional compiler, together with an execution-support system (SIGLIB). The latter supports interpretive execution of arithmetic steps and intrinsic transcendental functions in single-precision and double-precision modes.

The result of execution under SigPac is conventional numerical output (unless selectively suppressed by the user), which is identical with normal execution results, plus the added output of information on the number of valid digits in each quantity on which such information is requested by the user.

The system may be stored on line, or input with user program(s) and data. It has been used in both local batch and remote batch operating modes.

The present system implementation (involving a fast compiler within SIGSCN for all of FORTRAN language plus pseudo-ops) is subject to certain parametric limitations on size of programs to be tested. Some of these limitations are due to the one-pass nature of SIGSCN's compiler, some to the existing production FORTRAN compilers used, and some to the rigid nature of FORTRAN itself.

The system has been successfully used to trace programs of which the traced segments totaled several hundred statements in size.

Usage

The primary step in SigPac usage is source program examination and planning of the testing process.

Prior to actual usage preparation, the user program is test-compiled and executed normally in order to assure that it is grammatically and otherwise acceptable to the production software.

Potentially data-sensitive aspects of the program are then identified, and desired test output is planned (with or without regular program output), by the user.

Program segments to be traced are preceded and followed by SIGENTER/SIGEXIT pseudo-op pairs.

Input data and program constants are initialized by SIGREAD, SIGSET, and SIGDATA pseudo-ops.

Special attention must then be given to particulars of the programmed process, in order to assure that service requests lead to meaningful results. For example, in iterative procedures it is often true that numerical significance may be degrading while mathematical accuracy is improving; in such processes, local significance behavior may be irrelevant to the test information desired and it may be appropriate to use the SIGSET pseudo-op to dynamically reinitialize "significance" each time the iteration loop is reentered.

This condition occurs frequently in the use of the 360 for computation of the sum of a converging series or sequence. The 360's nonrounding arithmetic causes generated error to propogate in continuously from the right-hand end (low-precision part) of the sum being developed; thus, <u>significance</u> of the result, as affected by the finite precision of the machine arithmetic, is degrading. At the same time, accumulation of successive terms is causing the result to more and more closely approximate the truth, and if the machine were executing "blackboard" (i.e., infinite-precision) arithmetic, the <u>accuracy</u> of the result would indeed be improving.

For testing purposes, we often seek to find the effective goodness of approximation to the truth, and thus must take into account both of these effects. In a typical case the system's indicated "significance" of a given result will be more realistic if the user pretends that low-order generated error is overwhelmed by accuracy improvement at each iteration. In the case of elementary function evaluation of iterative routines, this is often accomplished by dynamically resetting significance to initial-argument significance by inserting the appropriate SIGSET pseudo-operation into the iterative loop immediately following the final nonrounding arithmetic operator.

Other uses of this technique, more appropriate for more

complex situations, will become evident to the thoughtful user of the system as he gains experience in its application. We offer no rule of thumb, but merely recommend cognition in the planning of testing of programs containing iterative processes.

Examinations of SigPac test output is often found to yield surprising results. We have observed many cases in which the user was unaware that his mathematical formulation was inadequate for the results desired, until he was presented with SigPac output which was sharply at odds with known accuracy of results.

Like any other program testing tool, this kind of system is limited in effectiveness by the imagination and care with which it is applied by the user.

EXAMPLE OF USER SOURCE CODE PROCESSING We now demonstrate the mechanics of SigPac system processing of a user program, using as an example a supporting subroutine for matrix multiplication.

The subroutine MATMPY multiplies a rectangular matrix AMX1 (of dimensions IND1 by IND2) by a vector or matrix AMX2 (dimensioned IND2 by IND3) to form the product matrix AMX3 (of size IND1 by IND3). Figure 1 shows the source coding for this subroutine.

```
      SUBROUTINE MATMPY(AMX1,AMX2,IND1,IND2,IND3,AMX3)
      SUBROUTINE MULTIPLIES A MATRIX, AMX1, BY EITHER A VECTOR OR
         ANOTHER MATRIX, AMX2, TO FORM THE PRODUCT,AMX3
      IMPLICIT REAL*8(A-H,O-Z)
      DIMENSION AMX1(IND1,IND2),AMX2(IND2,IND3),AMX3(IND1,IND3)
      DO 10 I=1,IND1
      DO 10 J=1,IND3
      AMX3(I,J)=0.0D0
      DO 10 K=1,IND2
   10 AMX3(I,J)=AMX3(I,J)+AMX1(I,K)*AMX2(K,J)
      RETURN
      END
```

FIGURE 1. MATMPY FORTRAN Source Coding

In the precompiler SIGSCN phase SigPac eliminates Comments and other non-procedural source code, including all source code appearing between SIGEXIT/SIGENTER pseudo-op pairs and assigns to each variable to be traced a significance index identified by a symbol of the form $DDDDD, where "$" is a prefix designating the symbol as that of a SigPac-created index, and "D" is a decimal digit.

Arithmetic and other statements analyzed by SigPac are decomposed into precedence matrix form as in some conventional compilers, and are translated into a string of CALLs to SigPac's execution-time library, SIGLIB. Elementary arithmetic operations evoke the general-purpose arithmetic routines of SIGLIB, which are equipped with significance-prediction algorithms of general type; the intrinsic transcendentals of FORTRAN evoke modified versions of forty-four single- and double- precision routines of the FORTRAN Scientific Subroutine Library which have had added to them special-purpose algorithms for significance prediction with those particular elementary functions.

In this case, SIGSCN generates CALLs to six SIGLIB routines. Three SIGMOVE operations are required to move the matrices constituting the chosen variables and their corresponding type indicators and significance indices into temporary working storage. One SIGMUL and one SIGADD perform the desired matrix arithmetic and update the significance indices. Finally, one SIGREP "replaces" (i.e., moves from temporary to permanent storage) the computed AMX3 values and significance indices. (If mixed-mode expressions had been present, SIGREP would have performed conversions between Types of numbers according to the FORTRAN IV equivalence table, taking into account control parameters passed to SIGREP in its CALLing sequence, adjusting significance indices as required. For example, if conversion is to be made between Type INTEGER to Type REAL: Argument is left-shifted two hexadecimal places, exponent is set to 46_{16}, significance is adjusted as appropriate (set to 14_{16} if 'full-precision), and Type designator is shifted from 1 to 0 in Bit 7 of argument SIGARG4).

Figure 2 shows the actual coding generated by SIGSCN as a result of processing MATMPY. (Note that this intermediate coding rigorously follows FORTRAN language specifications, which indeed it must because it is to be compiled subsequently by the conventional FORTRAN compiler.)

```
SUBROUTINE MATMPY(AMX1   ,$00002,AMX2   ,$00003,IND1   ,$00004,IND2
1,$00005,IND3   ,$00006,AMX3   ,$00007)
 IMPLICIT REAL*8(A-H,O-Z)
 DIMENSION AMX1(IND1,IND2),AMX2(IND2,IND3),AMX3(IND1,IND3)
 DIMENSION $00002, $00003, $00004, $00005, $00006, $00007, $00008/Z01360
1000/
'INTEGER $I$(50),$$I$(50),$
 REAL $S$(99),$$S$(99),$$D$(99)
 DOUBLE PRECISION $D$(99),$$E$(8,3)
 DO 1 I=1,IND1
 DO 1 J=1,IND3
 DATA $IM/Z20187F38/
 CALL SIGREP(AMX3(I,J),$00007(I,J),0.0D0,$00008,$IM )
 DO 1 K=1,IND2
0 CONTINUE
 CALL SIGMOV($S$(2),$$S$(2),AMX3(I,J),$00007(I,J),$IM)
 CALL SIGMOV($S$(4),$$S$(4),AMX1(I,K),$00002(I,K),$IM)
 CALL SIGMOV($S$(6),$$S$(6),AMX2(K,J),$00003(K,J),$IM)
 CALL SIGMUL($S$(7),$$S$(7),$S$(4),$$S$(4),$S$(6),$$S$(6),$IM)
 CALL SIGADD($S$(8),$$S$(8),$S$(2),$$S$(2),$S$(7),$$S$(7),$IM)
 CALL SIGREP(AMX3(I,J),$00007(I,J),$S$(8),$$S$(8),$IM)
 CONTINUE
 RETURN
 END
```

FIGURE 2. CALL String Notation SigScan Output for MATMPY

EXAMPLE OF
APPLICATION
OF PROGRAM
TEST METHOD

Problem Definition

Four quantities will be of interest in our testing of the program we consider here. Pseudo-zeros and pseudo-indeterminates are so called here because they result from artifices used to gain stability, consistency, or convergence. We also consider true zeros and true indeterminates resulting from execution of the basic computational procedures.

The formulas for the integration of the equations of motion in the Goddard Trajectory Determination System (GTDS)[3] are basically of the Newtonian type, derived from standard difference operator techniques. The algorithm we use in this application of SigPac defines the Adams - Moulton predictor - corrector method for first order equations and the Störmer - Cowell predictor correction method for second order systems.

The algorithm is:

$$\dot{x}_{n+1} = h \ [\nabla^{-1}\dot{x}_n + \sum_{i=0}^{k} \beta_i \ \ddot{x}_{n+1-i}]$$

$$x_{n+1} = h^2 \ [\nabla^{-2}x_n + \sum_{i=0}^{k} \alpha_i \ \ddot{x}_{n+1-i}]$$

where β_i and α_i are the summed-ordinate Adams-Moulton and Störmer-Cowell coefficients respectively.

Our test program shows the existence of pseudo zeros in the $\sum_{i=0}^{k} \beta_i \dot{x}_{n+1-i}$ and $\sum_{1=0}^{k} \alpha_i \ddot{x}_{n+1-i}$ terms, and real zeros in both $\dot{x}$ and x.

Application Procedure

The integration algorithms are special tools used in the construction of approximations to solutions of initial value problems (In this case, orbit determination).

In order to describe the application of the test method, in this case using dummy data, let us examine the parameters used in the algorithm. We notice immediately that any solution will be dependent on the parameter k (step size).

The other variables of interest are the differences shown in the Table in Figure 3.

The summing of the first and second differences follows a stair-step pattern, with the signs apparently changing at random.

[3]GTDS Mathematical Papers preprint available from Technical Library, NASA-GSFC, Greenbelt, Maryland.

Velocities	First Differences	Second Differences
		.910 123 456 789 D + 00
	.345 678 901 234 D + 00	
.633 390 887 308 D + 00		.101 234 567 890 D + 00
	.567 890 123 456 D + 00	
.397 679 305 333 D + 00		.123 456 789 012 D + 00
	.456 789 012 345 D + 00	
—.241 798 402 347 D + 00		.123 456 789 012 D + 00
	.890 123 456 789 D + 00	
		.234 567 890 123 D + 00

FIGURE 3. Specific Difference Table

Curves of first and second differences and coefficients (for a given k) are of the shape shown in Figure 4 below.

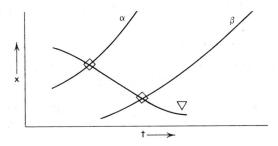

FIGURE 4. ∇, α, and β, vs. Time

It is the two intersections shown above that interest us, for it is in the approaches to these intersections that we lose significance in our computations.

The differential correction process in orbit determination is one in which the effect of machine precision limitations is of continuing and direct concern.

As an example of the requirement for control of computational accuracy, let us consider determination of a moon orbit to the not uncommon requirement of ten meters in all three dimensions, when total range is on the order of 4×10^8 meters. This brings on a requirement for a minimum of eight decimal digits of final accuracy, with a desired accuracy somewhat greater. This requirement approaches the full double-precision length of the 360's floating-point arithmetic!

Other computations may be much less demanding, and may in fact be capable of being carried out in single-length (perhaps six digits or slightly better) arithmetic.

In either case, it is necessary to have control over the resulting accuracy of calculations, as opposed to the nominal precision of the hardware.

The orbit determination calculations in general are simulated in advance of actual space flight missions; by the time it is possible to validate computational results from actual mission observational data, it is already too late to correct for errors which may have been found in the computational procedures.

Furthermore, in general, single measurements are far too inaccurate to be used for orbit validation purposes; it is only when large quantities of data can be accumulated and evaluated (e.g., doppler data over an entire mission) that observed orbits can be fully determined from measurement. Again, this is too late to be useful in mission control.

Observations on Test Program

The program chosen is extremely simple but is an actual sample problem from the Goddard Trajectory Determination System. It uses one of the linear algorithms for obtaining numerical solutions to initial value problems. The principal pitfalls we will examine are the pseudo zeros we mentioned earlier.

The numerical calculations of the summing of the ordinates were performed in both single and double precision, and with and without use of SigPac for comparison. The identical program was used in all cases, with single and double precision controlled by IMPLICIT statements, and with SigPac or normal execution selected by insertion or removal of the SigPac pseudo-ops.

This use of the testing method involved the following steps:

1. Prepare driver for subroutine to be tested.
2. Insert SigPac pseudo-ops in driver program.
3. Initialize (by assigning known or assumed accuracy/significance to) input data which are to be used for test.

4. Process driver program and test subroutine through SIGSCN precompiler.
5. Compile SIGSCN-output CALL-String-Notation program via production FORTRAN compiler.
6. Execute resulting object code with chosen and initialized data.

Figure 5 shows the driver program with the first several data elements, including the SIGWRITE and related FORMAT statements. Note that, aside from the SigPac verbs which represent a modest language extension, the program with its service requests follows FORTRAN grammar rules.

```
C           TEST DRIVER FOR XSUM
      IMPLICIT REAL*8(A-H,P-Z),INTEGER(I-N),LOGICAL(O)
      DIMENSION      SACS(11)  ,SBCS(11)  ,SUM1(3)  ,SUM2(3)  ,XZ(3)    ,
     1               XZD(3)    ,XZDD(40,3) ,II(3)
      COMMON/WORKER/ D1(3264)
      EQUIVALENCE    (D1(1)    ,XZ(1)  ),(D1(4)    ,XZD(1)   )          ,
     B               (D1(7)    ,XZDD(1,1))
     C               (D1(2647),SUM1(1)),  (D1(2650),SUM2(1)  )          ,
     A               (D1(3216)  ,H    ),(D1(3217) ,H2       )          ,
     1               (D1(3059)  ,SACS(1)),(D1(3070) ,SBCS(1)  )
      II(1)=1
      II(2)=2
      II(3)=3
      H =25.0D+00
      H2 =625.0D+00
      XZ(1)=193588.266179D+00
      XZ(2)=11737.09335772D+00
      XZ(3)=69978.5955507D+00
      XZD(1)=.0633390887308D+00
      XZD(2)=.397679305333D+00
      XZD(3)=-.241798402347D+00
      XZDD(1,1)=.063145268910D+00
      XZDD(2,1)=.631452689101D+00
      XZDD(3,1)=.314526891012D+00
      XZDD(4,1)=.145268910123D+00
      XZDD(5,1)=.452689101234D+00



            .
            .
            .



      CALL XSUM
      WRITE(6,45)
      WRITE(6,30)
      WRITE(6,50)II(1)
      SIGWRITE1(6,40)        SUM1(1),SUM2(1)
      WRITE(6,50)II(2)
      SIGWRITE1(6,40)        SUM1(2),SUM2(2)
      WRITE(6,50)II(3)
      SIGWRITE1(6,40)        SUM1(3),SUM2(3)
   50 FORMAT(4X,I1)
   30 FORMAT(76H    I                     SUM1                     INDEX
     A    SUM2            INDEX)
   40 FORMAT(4X,1X,4X,D23.16,5X,I3,5X,D23.16,5X,I3)
   45 FORMAT(1H0/1H0)
      STOP
      END
```

FIGURE 5. SigPac Test Driver Program for XSUM (with partial input data)

Figure 6 consists of an array of COMMENTS defining symbols and relationships in the subroutine being tested, together with other information for the guidance of users of the subroutine.

```
      SUBROUTINE XSUM
C     VERSION OF 1/18/71                                          00000020
C         FORTRAN SUBROUTINE FOR IBM 360                          00000030
C     PURPOSE                                                     00000040
C         TO COMPUTE STARTING VALUES FOR THE FIRST AND SECOND SUMS 00000050
C         AS REQUIRED BY THE COWELL START OR RESTART PROCESS      00000060
C     CALLING SEQUENCE                                            00000070
C         CALL XSUM
C     COMMON BLOCK VARIABLES                                      00000170
C     INPUT                                                       00000180
C         XZ   = INPUT VECTOR                             KM      00000110
C         XZD  = 1ST TIME DERIVATIVE OF INPUT VECTOR      KM/SEC  00000120
C         XZDD = 2ND TIME DERIVATIVE OF INPUT VECTOR      KM/(SEC SQ) 00000130
C         H    = INTEGRATION STEPSIZE            (SECONDS)        00000190
C         H2   = H ** 2                          (SECONDS SQUARED) 00000200
C         SACS = STARTER COEFFICIENTS FOR 1ST SUM NONDIMENSIONAL 00000210
C         SBCS = STARTER COEFFICIENTS FOR 2ND SUM NONDIMENSIONAL 00000220
C     OUTPUT                                                      00000140
C         SUM1 = COWELL 1ST SUM                           KM/(SEC SQ) 00000150
C         SUM2 = COWELL 2ND SUM                           KM/(SEC SQ) 00000160
C     REFERENCES                                                  00000230
C         GTDS TASK NAME - STARTER SUMMATION (XSUM)               00000240
C         ADAMS-COWELL ORDINATE SECOND SUM FORMULAS. EQUATIONS (6-26),
C         (6-27) CHAPTER 6
C     PROGRAMMER                                                  00000250
C         ALLEN L COHEN - COMPUTER SCIENCES CORP.                 00000260
C     MODIFICATIONS DONE BY
C               DANIELLE A. COLE FREE LANCE PROGRAMMER
```

FIGURE 6. Program COMMENTs Containing Explanation of XSUM Subroutine

Figure 7 is the tested subroutine itself, as used in the GTDS System.

```
C                                                                 00000270
C*****START PROGRAM********************************************************00000280
C                                                                 00000290
      IMPLICIT REAL*8(A-H,P-Z),INTEGER(I-N),LOGICAL(O)            00000300
      COMMON/WORKER/ D1(3264)                                     00000310
      COMMON/NONAME/       S        ,SUM1I    ,SUM2I    ,FISHER  ,00000320
     1            I        ,J        ,M        ,N        ,K       00000330
      DIMENSION   SACS(11) ,SBCS(11) ,SUM1(3)  ,SUM2(3)  ,XZ(3)  ,00000340
     1            XZD(3)   ,XZDD(40,3)                            00000350
      EQUIVALENCE (D1(1)   ,XZ(1) ),(D1(4)    ,XZD(1)   )        ,
     B            (D1(7)   ,XZDD(1,1))                           ,
     C            (D1(2647),SUM1(1)),(D1(2650),SUM2(1)  )        ,
     A            (D1(3216),H    ),(D1(3217) ,H2       )         ,
     1            (D1(3059),SACS(1)),(D1(3070),SBCS(1)  )         00000370
C                                                                 00000380
C     START VECTOR COMPONENT LOOP                                 00000390
      DO 20 I=1,3                                                 00000400
C                                                                 00000410
C     INITIALIZE SUMMANDS                                         00000420
C                                                                 00000430
      SUM1I = XZD(I) / H                                          00000440
      SUM2I = XZ(I) / H2                                          00000450
C                                                                 00000460
C     START SUMMATION                                             00000470
C     THE FORMULA IS PROGRAMMED FOR ORDER 5.
C                                                                 00000480
      M = 5
      N = 2*M+1
      DO 10 J=1,N                                                 00000490
      K = N+1
      S = XZDD(K -J,I)                                            00000500
C                                                                 00000510
C     ADD ON NEXT TERM TO SUMMANDS                                00000520
C                                                                 00000530
      SUM1I = SUM1I - SACS(J) * S                                 00000540
      SUM2I = SUM2I - SBCS(J) * S                                 00000550
   10 CONTINUE                                                    00000560
C                                                                 00000570
C     STORE RESULTS                                               00000580
C                                                                 00000590
      SUM1(I) = SUM1I                                             00000600
      FISHER = M+1
      SUM2(I) = SUM2I+FISHER *SUM1I
   20 CONTINUE                                                    00000620
  999 RETURN                                                      00000630
      END                                                         00000640
```

FIGURE 7. Subroutine XSUM (FORTRAN Source Language Form)

Figure 8 shows initialization of data in COMMON storage by use of the BLOCK COMMON Subroutine which is required by FORTRAN language usage rules. The SIGDATA pseudo-operation is used to assign initial significances. In this test, full significance is assigned to each datum, in order to show effects of machine arithmetic for a case in which it is certain that data accuracy does not limit result accuracy. The same effect could have been achieved without separate initialization by allowing SigPac to assign "default initialization" (viz., full precision) to each datum; but initialization was set up in its complete form in this case so that other assumptions could be applied by merely substituting other numerical values for initial significances of various data.

```
     BLOCK DATA
     IMPLICIT REAL*8(A-H,P-Z),INTEGER(I-N),LOGICAL(O)
C        WORKER BLOCK DATA
     COMMON/WORKER/XZ(3)      ,XZD(3)    ,XZDD(40,3),XV(3,20)  ,XVD(3,20),WORK    7
   1           XVDD(40,3,20)         ,SUM1(3)   , SUM2(3)   ,SV1(3,20),WORK    8
   3           ALPHAB(11),BETA(11) ,BETAS(11),BETAB(11),             WORK   10
   2           SV2(3,20) ,ALPHA(11),ALPHAS(11)                       WORK    9
   4           ACS(11,10),BCS(11,10)           , SACS(11) ,SBCS(11) ,WORK   11
   5           C1        ,C2        ,XOLD(3)   ,XDOLD(3)  ,           WORK   12
   6           YOLD(3,20),YDOLD(3,20)          , SPV(3)   ,SPC(3)    ,WORK   13
   7           T         ,H         ,H2        , TOL(10)  ,STPMIN    ,WORK   14
   8           RD(15)    ,HD(15)    ,POS(3)    , VEL(3)   ,           WORK   15
   9           IR        ,KK        ,N1        , N2       ,NEQ       ,WORK   16
   *           MAXIT(5)  ,NSMAX     ,NRUN      , NSTR                 WORK   17
     COMMON/NONAME/         S         , SUM1I    , SUM2I    ,FISHER   ,00000320
   1           I         ,J         , M        , N        ,K          00000330
C        ADAMS MOULTON PREDICTOR-CORRECTOR COEFFICIENTS
     DATA SACS      /                                                 WORK  254
   1           -0.100007722834328600 01,-0.99903812012319410D 00,WORK  255
   2           -0.100572851844335800 01,-0.97752126924002470D 00,WORK  256
   3           -0.107289995064734400D 01,-0.50000000000000520D 00,WORK  257
   4            0.728999506473496000D-01,-0.224787307599817000D-01,WORK  258
   5            0.572851844336216400D-02,-0.961879876810325400D-03,WORK  259
   6            0.77228343287347690D-04                         /WORK  260
C        STORMER-COWELL COEFFICIENTS
     DATA SBCS      /                                                 WORK  264
   1            0.499999739863487300+01,  0.400003991130841000+01,WORK  265
   2            0.299969211665964900+01,  0.200169170826768080D+01,WORK  266
   3            0.991263903618643900D+01,  0.979632565544433000D+01,WORK  267
   4           -0.873609648135701000D-02, 0.169170826786920800D-02,WORK  268
   5           -0.307883340349845400D-03, 0.399113084107410700D-04,WORK  269
   6           -0.260136512837748200D-05                          /WORK  270
C  INITIALISE COMMON FOR SIGPAC
     SIGDATA    XZ/  3*Z01360000/,   XZD/  3*Z01360000/,
   1           XZDD/120*Z01360000/,
   7           SACS/11 *Z01360000/,  SBCS/11 *Z01360000/,
   3           SUM1/  3*Z01360000/,  SUM2/  3*Z01360000/,
   9           SUM1I/  Z01360000/, SUM2I/   Z01360000/,
   9           FISHER/ Z01360000/, S   /    Z01360000/,
   A           H2/     Z01360000/,   H/     Z01360000/,
   A           I/      Z801F0000/,   J/     Z801F0000/,
   B           M/      Z801F0000/,   N/     Z801F0000/,
   C           K/      Z801F0000/
     END
```

FIGURE 8. Data Initialization for XSUM Test

Figure 9 gives the declarative preface generated by the SIGSCN precompiler, prior to generation of executable statements. Note that SIGSCN has generated initial values for significance indices for all variables to be traced, as well as having established control vectors for storage management.

```
SUBROUTINE XSUM
IMPLICIT REAL*8(A-H,P-Z),INTEGER(I-N),LOGICAL(O)
COMMON/WORKER/ D1(3264)
COMMON/NONAME/         S        ,SUM1I    ,SUM2I    ,FISHER   ,
1              I        ,J       ,M        ,N        ,K
DIMENSION      SACS(11) ,SBCS(11) ,SUM1(3)  ,SUM2(3)  ,XZ(3)   ,
1              XZD(3)   ,XZDD(40,3)
EQUIVALENCE    (D1(1)   ,XZ(1) ),(D1(4)    ,XZD(1)   )         ,
1              (D1(7)   ,XZDD(1,1))                            ,
1              (D1(2647),SUM1(1)), (DI(2650),SUM2(1)   )       ,
1              (D1(3216) ,H     ),(D1(3217) ,H2        )       ,
1              (D1(3059) ,SACS(1)),(D1(3070) ,SBCS(1)  )
COMMON /$WORKE/$00002(3264)
COMMON /$NONAM/$00003,$00004,$00005,$00006,$00007,$00008,$00009,$0
10010,$00011
DIMENSION $00012(11),$00013(11),$00014(3),$00015(3),$00016(3),$000
117(3),$00018(40,3)
EQUIVALENCE ($00002(1),$00016(1)),($00002(4),$00017(1)),($00002(7)
1,$00018(1,1)),($00002(2647),$00014(1)),($00002(2650),$00015(1)),($
100002(3216),$000 19),($00002(3217),$00020),($00002(3059),$00012(1))
1,($00002(3070),$00013(1))
REAL $00002, $00003, $00004, $00005, $00006, $00007, $00008, $0000
19, $00010, $00011, $00012, $00013, $00014, $00015, $00016, $00017,
1 $00018, $00019, $00020, $00021/Z801F0000/, $00022/Z801F0000/, $00
1023/Z801F0000/
INTEGER $I$(50),$$I$(50),$
REAL $S$(99),$$S$(99),$$D$(99)
DOUBLE PRECISION $D$(99),$$E$(8,3)
```

FIGURE 9 SIGSCN Output (Preface to XSUM)

Figure 10 is the procedural portion of the result of the SIGSCN precompilation process applied to driver and subroutine. (Remark: The 17-statement source language representation of the subroutine has caused generation of 23 CALLs and 8 other statements in this case of a procedure with very simple control; a more complicated control structure would have resulted in a substantially higher ratio of precompiler output to input FORTRAN statements.)

```
      DO 1      I=1,3
      DATA $IM/Z20187F38/
      CALL SIGMOV($D$(1),$$D$(1),XZD(I),$00017(I),$IM)
      CALL SIGDIV($D$(2),$$D$(2),$D$(1),$$D$(1),H,$00019,$IM)
      CALL SIGREP(SUM1I,$00004,$D$(2),$$D$(2),$IM)
      CALL SIGMOV($D$(1),$$D$(1),XZ(I),$00016(I),$IM)
      CALL SIGDIV($D$(2),H2$(2),$D$(1),$$D$(1),H2,$00020,$IM)
      CALL SIGREP(SUM2I,$00005,$D$(2),$$D$(2),$IM)
      CALL SIGREP(M,$00009,5,$00021,$IM)
      CALL SIGMUL($I$(1),$$I$(1),2,$00022,M,$00009,$IM)
      CALL SIGADD($I$(2),$$I$(2),$I$(1),$$I$(1),1,$00023,$IM)
      CALL SIGREP(N,$00010,$I$(2),$$I$(2),$IM)
      DO 2      J=1,N
      CALL SIGADD($I$(1),$$I$(1),N,$00010,1,$00023,$IM)
      CALL SIGREP(K,$00011,$I$(1),$$I$(1),$IM)
      CALL SIGSUB($I$(1),$$I$(1),K,$00011,J,$0000R,$IM)
      CALL SIGMOV($D$(3),$$D$(3),XZDD($I$(1),I),$00018($I$(1),I),$IM)
      CALL SIGREP(S,$00003,$D$(3),$$D$(3),$IM)
      CALL SIGMOV($D$(1),$$D$(1),SACS(J),$00012(J),$IM)
      CALL SIGMUL($D$(2),$$D$(2),$D$(1),$$D$(1),S,$00003,$IM)
      CALL SIGSUB($D$(3),$$D$(3),SUM1I,$00004,$D$(2),$$D$(2),$IM)
      CALL SIGREP(SUM1I,$00004,$D$(3),$$D$(3),$IM)
      CALL SIGMOV($D$(1),$$D$(1),SBCS(J),$00013(J),$IM)
      CALL SIGMUL($D$(2),$$D$(2),$D$(1),$$D$(1),S,$00003,$IM)
      CALL SIGSUB($D$(3),$$D$(3),SUM2I,$00005,$D$(2),$$D$(2),$IM)
      CALL SIGREP(SUM2I,$00005,$D$(3),$$D$(3),$IM)
10    CONTINUE
2     CONTINUE
      CALL SIGREP(SUM1(I),$00014(I),SUM1I,$00004,$IM)
      CALL SIGADD($I$(1),$$I$(1),M,$00009,1,$00023,$IM)
      CALL SIGREP(FISHER,$00006,$I$(1),$$I$(1),$IM)
      CALL SIGMUL($D$(1),$$D$(1),FISHER,$00006,SUM1I,$00004,$IM)
      CALL SIGADD($D$(2),$$D$(2),SUM2I,$00005,$D$(1),$$D$(1),$IM)
      CALL SIGREP(SUM2(I),$00015(I),$D$(2),$$D$(2),$IM)
20    CONTINUE
1     CONTINUE
999   RETURN
      END
```

FIGURE 10. SIGSCN Output of XSUM (Call String Notation)

Figure 11 shows the final result of execution, using the run-time interpretive processing library SIGLIB, with the given input data, of the machine-language program created by compilation of SIGSCN output by means of the regular FORTRAN compiler. (In this case, FORTRAN IV G Level 20.1 was used for final compilation. The system is also used with the OS/360 FORTRAN IV H compiler, usually with optimization level OPT = 2.)

SUM1 is a result of simple operations performed, in this test, on full-significance numbers which are well scaled. SigPac shows, as it should, that the results have not degraded in significance.

SUM2, on the other hand, shows serious degradation of significance, corresponding to accuracy loss of about seven decimal places.

Following localization of the trouble source to the three expressions in lines 600 of Figure 7, by means of SigPac usage, it was possible to apply independent tests on the troublesome procedure. These tests confirm the accuracy loss predicted by SigPac tracing of the entire program.

As a result of use of this testing process, it is possible to experimentally modify the SUM2 calculation in the offending area in order to develop a procedure which will preserve essentially full accuracy in limiting cases such as the one tested here.

The testing process will then have concluded with uncovery and correction of a small but serious weakness in a large and complex numerical procedure.

SUM1	INDEX	SUM2	INDEX
0.3012657813159927D 01	54	0.3146495183620493D 03	35
0.2339658870467145D 01	54	0.2365153327508063D 02	32
-0.3082954999652428D 01	54	0.1060490067977732D 03	33

FIGURE 11. XSUM Test Execution Output

DISCUSSION OF ECONOMICS OF USAGE
We consider the present version of SigPac to be a validation and diagnostic tool rather than an alternative (accuracy - monitored) means for running production computation. This is because of the high cost of executing the error-indicating arithmetic interpretively. In any machine with normalized floating-point hardware, and especially in a hexadecimal machine (because of the complexity of the arithmetic itself and because of the need to test for pathological cases in individual program steps), such execution must be expected to be costly. In large 360/370 machines, for instance, the SIGLIB routines execute 212 to 248 instructions per floating-point arithmetic step.

In practice, we have found it possible to gain useful information by using SigPac selectively, tracing only those parts of programs which may be expected to be data-sensitive. In important test cases, this selectivity has resulted at the low end of the cost range in CPU execution-time increases as low as 10% to 15%, as contrasted with the hundredfold-increased execution times which would have been expected from indiscriminate application of the test system.

In addition to the execution time increase which should be expected under SigPac, the user must plan on the precompilation SIGSCN phase (which is comparable to FORTRAN compilation time), as well as regular FORTRAN compilation of the SIGSCN output (essentially the same as compilation time for the program used without SigPac) and for LINKEDIT or loader time for housekeeping on related supporting routines.

Space requirements in main memory will be larger than for conventional compilation and execution, but in many cases will be less than twice "normal" space needs. Several fairly large test cases have SIGSCN'ned in about $400K_{10}$ bytes, which is well below twice "normal" space for these cases, and also executed in less than twice non-SigPac space.

Actual determination of time, space, and communication requirements is a complex process. The above discussion is intended merely to point out that logistics requirements for use of the system, carefully applied, may not be prohibitive.

As a final remark we believe that the real potential for production application of error-indicating arithmetic will be realized in the future not thorough development of special-

purpose computing hardware but through use of microprogramma-
ble "firmware" in which error-indicating arithmetic algorithms
can be implemented (and changed) as required in the light of
non-trivial experiences in using all-software systems such
as SigPac.

APPLICABILITY   As in the case of usage logistics planning,
OF TEST METHOD   we will present no simple rules of thumb
                 for deciding when the method and the SigPac
System may be applicable to program testing.

As preliminary guidelines, however, we have recommended
to users of one large 360 system that they consider application of SigPac to the testing of apparently-correct programs
when one or more of the following conditions exist:

1. Numerical results cannot be positively validated (e.g.,
   extrapolation);
2. Large amounts of double-precision computation;
3. Ordinary Differential Equation system integrations
   and other kinds of calculations which are recognized
   as being subject to rapid and/or unpredictable error
   growth; and
4. Programs which have been in satisfactory operation
   on a continuing basis but which may be data sensitive:
   i.e., which occasionally give, for particular values
   of input data, results which are surprising and which
   have not been justified to the complete satisfaction
   of responsible investigators as being numerically
   correct.

One basic guideline cannot be overemphasized: A fully
mechanistic testing process such as use of the SigPac System
can test only what is presented to it. Thus, if logic errors
may exist in a program for some conditions, or if the computational procedure expressed in the program to be tested is
mathematically inadequate to solve the given problem (e.g.,
inadequate approximation), this test method will tell the
user only how well the given program, with the data being
used for test, is executed in the specified hardware environment.

For this reason, any experimental use of this test should
be preceded, as a precaution, by "normal" execution of the pro-

gram and data which are to be test-executed under control of the system. (We have found, to our dismay, that "correct" programs, delivered for testing, in surprisingly many cases contain errors of obvious and trivial nature.)

TESTING
LARGE SOFTWARE SYSTEMS

VI

It is a combination of the imperfection of written specifications and the fallibility of those who program from them which contributes to the need for extensive testing to achieve a workable system.

– Robert V. Head

The stress has always been on larger and more powerful systems in spite of the fact that the available programmer competence is unable to cope with the complexities.

– Peter Naur

DEVELOPING AND TESTING A LARGE PROGRAMMING SYSTEM, OS/360 TIME SHARING OPTION

14

Allan L. Scherr

IBM, Poughkeepsie, N. Y.

INTRODUCTION   This chapter presents an overview of the
process used to design, develop, and test
the Time Sharing Option (TSO) of Operating System/360. This
project was one of the largest programming releases ever produced by IBM and during its development involved over 1000
people in several geographic locations. Described are the
overall processes used for the coordination of the system design, the building of the various versions of the system required for its development, and the testing done at each
phase. TSO represented a significant modification and extension to OS/360, a widely used control program that had been
in existence for some years prior to the advent of TSO. The
problems associated with integrating the two and the techniques used to overcome these problems are discussed. Finally, a number of conclusions are drawn which are felt to be
generally applicable to the implementation and testing of any
large programming effort.

The chapter first gives a general discussion of the design, size, and complexity of TSO with some facts regarding
the environments in which TSO is used. Next is an overview
of the type of development process used for the design, implementation, and testing of TSO. Then, the various types of
testing used throughout the cycle are described with emphasis
on their relationship to the various stages of the development process. The last section summarizes conclusions regarding the techniques used on TSO and their effectiveness as
well as some recommendations regarding improvements and the
importance of emphasizing early testing.

TSO   TSO adds general-purpose time sharing capa-
DESCRIPTION bility to OS/360. The broad objectives for
             TSO were to provide comprehensive interact-
ive facilities for terminal users while maintaining compatibil-

ity of this support with existing OS/360 programming and data.
TSO users can run almost all existing OS programs interactively. Programs developed under TSO can be run in a batch environment, and the same data can be accessed from either environment. Interactive use of ALGOL, BASIC, COBOL, FORTRAN,
PL/I, and assembler language is supported.

TSO is built upon the MVT configuration of OS/360 and is
based upon the technique of swapping the programs that are
conversing with users at remote terminals. Swapping is simply a technique for sharing an area of the system's main storage among the programs associated with various users. In TSO,
each user is associated with a program, and only one program
may be in a predefined area of main storage or a "region" at
a time. Thus, when a user's program is given a time slice,
it is first brought into main storage from a disk or drum
storage device, allowed to execute, and then copied back out
to the auxiliary storage device. Since this operation typically causes the replacement of one program in main storage
by another, the technique is called "swapping". Up to fourteen regions of main storage may be used simultaneously for
swapping. In this case, the total number of users would be
divided into fourteen groups, each group permanently associated with a region. Regions may be of various sizes to accom-
modate the requirements of the system's users. Users entering the system or "logging on" are assigned to whichever region is large enough to satisfy their size requirements, and,
where there is a choice, the region with the lightest load is
selected.

Before discussing the techniques used to build and test
TSO, the complexity and size of the problem will first be
discussed. As stated, TSO was a substantial increase to OS/
360, itself a large program. Prior to TSO the OS/360 system
(at the Release 19 level), including compilers, totaled over
1.6 million instructions, represented by almost 2.3 million
lines of code (including comments) in 4637 modules. (A module is normally a unit of programming able to be separately
assembled or a macro definition. The average size of a module is approximately 500 lines of code.) The inclusion of
TSO into OS/360 resulted in the addition of 547,000 instruc-

[1]Further details on TSO facilities and the internal structure
of TSO can be found in Time Sharing for OS, A.L. Scherr and
D.C. Larkin, Proceedings of FJCC, 1970 and IBM System/360
Operating System Time Sharing Option: Planning for TSO, IBM
Corporation, Form GC28-6698, White Plains, 1971.

tions to OS/360 for a new total of nearly 2.1 million instructions and three million lines of code. Figure 1 summarizes
this data:

	Release 19	Release 20 (TSO)	% Change
Modules	4637	5352	+13
Lines of code	2.29M	2.97M	+30
Instructions	1.65M	2.07M	+25

FIGURE 1

The above statistics do not represent the total magnitude of
the TSO effort since substantial modifications were made to
the OS/360 base. Of the 5352 modules comprising Release 20,
over 40% of them were either new or modified.

OPERATIONAL   The complexity of TSO as a program could
ENVIRONMENTS   well be illustrated by enumerating its
                     functional content. However, another as-
pect of the system's complexity is the broad variety of environments that TSO and OS/360 are designed to run in and
the large number of installations that actually use it.

TSO is designed to run on any of ten different System/
360 or System/370 Central Processing Units with main storage
in the range of 384K bytes through 4 million bytes inclusive.
A broad variety of I/O devices are supported as well. For example, TSO supports seven different direct-access storage devices (disks and drums) for swapping. Any of the seven types
can be used singly or in combinations. Overall, there are
literally thousands of possible hardware configurations.

The usage of TSO is also varied. TSO is used not only
in areas where time sharing has traditionally played an important role: academic, scientific, and engineering establish-
ments; but also in many commerical environments: banks, insurance companies, etc. Limiting the scope of a program is
an obvious way to insure that it can be tested and debugged
efficiently. In the case of TSO, it was a clear objective
to design a system with a potential usage that was as unlimited as possible. Usage of OS/360 for applications not
directly considered by its designers is not only

desirable but very common.

The design and development cycle for TSO spanned approximately 3 1/2 years. During this time, the OS/360 base upon which TSO was being built underwent two major functional enhancements, releases 18 and 19. While the system changed somewhat less for these than for TSO, they also represented substantial modifications to the system. Moreover, another set of functional enhancements, for release 9 months after TSO, were also undergoing design and development. Thus, TSO was designed, implemented and tested during a period when other substantial development projects, both preceding and following it, were underway. Another complication in developing TSO was that implementation was done in a number of geographically dispersed locations. Roughly twelve different groups in seven distinct locations were involved. Because of this and the large size of the system, there were relatively few people who understood the total system in a detailed way. Using these critical resources effectively was an important aspect of the development process.

THE DEVELOPMENT PROCESS   Developing a program the size of TSO in the environment described above requires significantly more formalization and structuring of the development process than would be the case for a small program. Figure 2 shows an overview of the various types of documentation produced during the design phases.

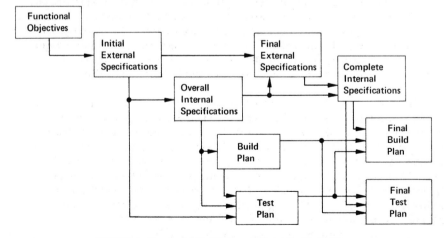

FIGURE 2. Documentation Produced During the Design Phases

DEVELOPING AND TESTING A LARGE PROGRAMMING SYSTEM

The initial technical efforts for TSO involved only a handful of people engaged in determining the technical feasibility of the program. However, during this period, a number of marketing studies were done to determine the functions which had to be provided, the necessary performance levels, and the environments within which the system would have to operate. The primary output of this phase was a relatively small document (50 pages) which defined the functional requirements of the system, the expected types of usage, the hardware configurations to be supported, and the desired performance and size characteristics. This objectives document did not specifically describe implementation or design techniques, but rather attempted to characterize the usage that TSO would have and to prioritize the various functions requested. The primary purpose of the objectives document was to concisely communicate to the designers the overall goals of the system and to provide a yardstick against which the design could be measured. The functional objectives were created with a high degree of interaction between the marketing-oriented groups and the designers to insure that the objectives were achievable.

The initial overall design of the system was done with a relatively small number of people working together as a single group. Their goal was to bring the design of the system to the point where its components could be developed more independently. The result of this initial design effort was a description of the external characteristics of the system and the interfaces between the major components. The external description included material defining the terminal user command language, central operator commands, assembly language macros for new system services, main storage estimates, performance specifications, etc. (For a discussion of the specification and testing of performance for TSO see [J11]). The inter-component interface descriptions consisted primarily of definitions of control tables, calling sequences, parameter values, subroutine return codes, error conditions, and implementation guidelines. The latter included coding standards, error recovery practices and other material oriented toward insuring consistency across the system. The initial version of the external specifications was completed approximately one year after the start of the project and was about 600 pages in size. In parallel with this external design, a central team, including representatives from the outlying groups, began the overall internal design.

During the last few months of this activity, a prototype version of TSO was implemented on the then latest version of OS/360, Release 16. It incorporated the major control flow but had relatively little function compared to the final system. The purpose of this prototype was to help determine the technical feasibility of the fundamental TSO design and to provide a vehicle for establishing performance projections.

The next phase of the project can best be described as an iterative one. The initial specifications were extended with added detail, modifications made to reflect problems and improvements found during the internal design work, and certain additional functions identified by later marketing studies as being required. Internal specifications were developed to finer levels of detail, in some cases to flow charts at the 5-10 instructions per box level.

Internal specifications are derived from external specifications. In the same way the build plan is derived from the internal specifications. The build plan describes the sequence in which the various components of the system will be combined to achieve the final version. Generally two types of code enter into the build process: code implementing the new function, in this case TSO, and code representing fixes to errors found in the previous releases. Because of the volume and complexity of the code, this process is incremental and can extend over a period of six months or more. Generally, the process is aimed at getting the core of the system running on a single configuration, performing a simple workload and then gradually adding more function and capability. The test plan, describing the various stages of program testing, is dependent upon the external and internal specifications for the obvious reasons and upon the build plan because testing is the primary way to determine that a particular phase of the build process has been successfully completed. The development of the above documentation is iterative because, in many cases, extensions and increased detail in a higher level document, e.g., external specifications, are possible only after working at a lower level, e.g., internal specifications. The build and test plans are related in this way. The build plan may also effect the specifications in that sometimes it is necessary to redesign or drop function to shorten a critical path in the schedule or to make it easier to build and test the system in an orderly way.

Figure 3 shows a typical segment of the build test plan.

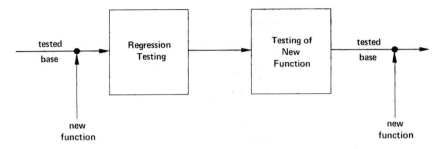

FIGURE 3. Typical Step in the Build/Test Plan

After successfully testing a level of the system, new function
in the form of additional and/or modified modules is added.
Next, tests are performed to insure that the new function
did not cause problems with previously added function. After
these "regression tests" have been successfully completed,
the new function is tested and the next step is taken. Another aspect of the build/test is that the code representing
new function is not integrated into the system without first
undergoing preliminarly testing. This is accomplished by
scheduling into earlier steps of the build process functions
which are dependencies for code to be added in a later cycle.
Thus, this early level of the system can be used for preliminary, pre-integration testing of function to be added in
a later level. Figure 4 shows this relationship in a simplified form.

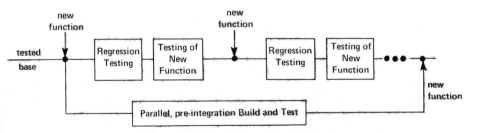

FIGURE 4. Example of Use of Earlier Level of the Base for Preliminary
Testing of Function Scheduled for a Later Base

From the standpoint of a given module, the development process can be characterized as shown in figure 5.

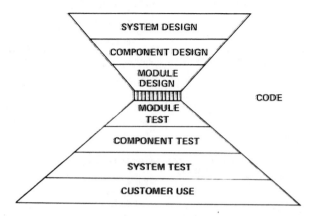

FIGURE 5. Outside-in Design: Inside-out Testing

The design generally proceeds from the global to the specific. That is, the design begins at the system level and gradually becomes more and more detailed until it is sufficient to allow a module to be coded. Once coded, the module is tested by itself, typically in an artificial environment. Next the module may be tested in combination with other modules. Larger and larger numbers of modules may be used, each combination providing a bigger function. At some point, the module as part of a larger collection of modules performing a particular set of functions is integrated into the system and finally tested in a complete environment. Thus, while the design goes from the system to the module, the testing goes in the opposite direction.

TESTING   Introduction

The most obvious problem with testing in the manner described in the previous paragraph is the danger of postponing the discovery of system-wide problems until late in the cycle. There has been work on approaching the testing problem from the opposite direction via structured programming techniques (see [B10] for example), but there is very little evidence to indicate that the process will work in the desired way for a large system developed under the constraints of TSO.

DEVELOPING AND TESTING A LARGE PROGRAMMING SYSTEM

Another problem is that the cost of finding and fixing
an error in the system increases as the process comes nearer
to completion. A bug found during the design phase costs a
negligible amount to correct. During coding and module-level
testing, errors are detected and fixed for a relatively nominal cost. During the component and system level testing, errors are dramatically more expensive. More people are involved and communication is necessary between at least two
groups. In the unfortunate case that a bug is found by a
user after the system is shipped, the costs are higher still:
the same bug is often found by more than one installation,
the field support organization is involved, temporary fixes
or bypasses are required in serious cases, and the user's
operation is disrupted. The last point is a cost to the organization producing the program whether or not it is part
of the same company as the end user.

It should be noted that the closer the project is to
completion, the more important it is to minimize the time
taken to correct an error. Often for a difficult error, it
may take many days for diagnosis and correction. During this
time the source of the error may manifest itself in a variety
of ways, causing the effort per error to mushroom. This is
particularly important at the end of the cycle because of the
larger number of components, and therefore programmers, involved.

Importance of Early Testing

These two problems have essentially the same solution:
early testing. While this statement is admittedly glib, it
represented a key ingredient to successful completion of the
TSO project. As stated previously, the creation of a complete and correct written specification for the system is
necessary to ensure that the parallel, dispersed development
can be feasibly done. The development of this specification,
actually a series of specifications, proceeds from the system
level to the module level, as shown in Figure 5. What must
be recognized is that the specifications can be tested. In
particular, the creation of each successive level of detail
of the specifications is a form of test of the previous level.
Typical questions that occur when designing a module are:
Is there a message in the external specifications appropriate
to a particular error condition which occurs in the module
being designed? or Is there a control field in the interface
between two modules that are being designed which will allow
for necessary synchronization, etc.

The fact that a module can be completely designed from a higher level specification is, in a sense, proof that the specifications are correct and complete. In general, many of the advantages cited for structured or "top-down" programming can occur for structured or "top-down" design. In the former, both the order of design activity and the structure of the resulting design are "top-down", in the latter, only the design activity is necessarily sequenced this way.

Specification and Paper Testing

In addition to the valuable but incidental kind of testing mentioned above, formal testing of specifications can occur even in the case, as in TSO, where the specifications are written in English and not a formal language designed for the specification of programs. These tests can take several forms, all of which are relatively simple. First, the answers to several very general questions can be tabularized. Thus, a form of test can be the generation of a table of functions, derived from the external specifications, and modules or components, derived from the internals. The resulting matrix would then be filled in to represent where each function is implemented. This process, and several stages of elaboration, can be used to cross-check the external and internal specifications. Another approach is to list the inputs and outputs of a process in the external specifications and derive cause-effect relationships. This type of exercise is useful in ensuring that the specifications are complete, it can be used to test externals as well as component interface definitions, and it may also provide the raw material for the definition of test cases (i.e., programs designed to run on the new system to test whether it was properly implemented).

Another type of paper analysis is the "walk-through" where the logic of the design is simulated by a group of people working their way through the internal specifications. Typically, a test case is chosen (e.g., "What happens when a user enters a 'LOGON' command?"), and the flow of the program is worked through on paper by a group of people. The value of this type of exercise is highly dependent upon the value of the test cases used and the thoroughness and skill of the participants.

Experience has shown that such paper tests are extremely valuable and that they find problems earlier in the development cycle, where they can more easily be corrected. In TSO, most of the design testing emphasis was placed at the detailed module logic level. In retrospect, this emphasis was misplaced. The reason for this is that immediately following the generation (and testing) of module logic specifications, these specifications are coded, and the resulting code tested at the module level. Because of the time proximity and the relative ease with which errors at this level can be detected and corrected during module test, the payoff in running through a rigorous paper test of the detailed logic specifications is relatively small. Another aspect of this argument is that with the use of higher level languages, detailed flow charts for modules are essentially redundant. Testing this level of specification by testing the program using a computer, (as opposed to a paper "walk-through") is usually, but not always, more effective. The qualification in the last sentence is there because several times during the development of TSO, skilled programmers found a significant number of errors that had escaped detection in actual execution simply by carefully reading the listing of the program. This fact is one of the principle reasons why it is believed that analysis of design prior to implementation can be extremely valuable.

It has been stated that tests of the specifications are valuable but that testing the detailed module logic specifications has a relatively low payoff. Where should the emphasis be? Since component and system level testing of the code occurs late in the cycle when error detection and correction is most costly, the early testing of the design should be oriented toward finding and fixing problems of the type that are not found in module-level testing. Thus, the emphasis of design testing should be at the system and component levels. The highest priority should be placed on ensuring that the interfaces between modules and between components are correct and that the overall flow of the system is correct. The objective should be to have a design that is good enough so that all errors found during the system test can be corrected by changing a single module, rather than a set of modules scattered all over the sytem.

Module Testing

Testing techniques used for module, component and some of the TSO system testing are widely known and therefore will be only briefly discussed. The selection of test cases was done using a number of methods, depending largely on whether the component to be tested was new for TSO or merely a

modification. Reference [J1] discusses one that was used
widely for new TSO code. The coverage of test cases was
measured by a program which interpretively executed the code
being tested and produced a report showing which instructions
had been executed by the test case and which way conditional
branches were taken. Typically, criteria were established
for an acceptable set of test cases for a program in terms
of the percentage of the instructions executed and the percentage of branch instructions taken both ways.

Module-level testing and some component testing was done
using interactive, dynamic debugging packages, such as TSO
TEST. This tool allows the user to suspend program execution
at prespecified locations, to examine the contents of main
storage and the registers, to make modifications to the program, and then to continue from the point of interruption,
etc. TEST was implemented on the TSO prototype and was used
in this way to debug a large portion of the code for the final
TSO system. System-level testing of TSO was done in three
ways.

Functional Testing

Test cases originally designed for component-level testing, augmented by several system-level test cases comprised
one form of testing. These test cases were run in the form
of a stream of batch jobs or from a TSO terminal as appropriate. In the latter case, the entry of input from the terminal was accomplished either manually or by one of two programs which simulated traffic from terminals. One form of
this type of terminal traffic simulator ran in a second system connected to the TSO system via a communications control
unit.

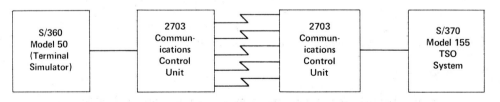

FIGURE 6. Typical Configuration for Testing TSO under Simulated Terminal Load

DEVELOPING AND TESTING A LARGE PROGRAMMING SYSTEM

To the TSO system it looked as if it were connected to low-speed terminals when, in fact, the terminals were being simulated by the second system. Another program could simulate message traffic by replacing the terminal I/O component of TSO with a package that would read input from a set of tapes. In both cases, reading the output produced by the TSO system and comparing this with the expected output was a fundamental part of the operation. Where deviations occurred between the expected and the actual output, error messages were printed for later analysis by a programmer.

Toward the end of the development cycle, TSO was subjected to heavier and heavier loads in an effort to cause a system failure. These loads were placed upon the system using a second system to simulate terminals. Interaction rates were increased and more complex test cases were introduced to push the system to its limits.

Performance Testing

The second form of testing was for performance. Throughout the development of TSO, projections were made of the final performance of the system. Configurations of the type shown in Figure 6 were used with the appropriate instrumentation. The techniques used are discussed in more detail in [J11] but it is worth pointing out that a large number of program errors were detected by trying to solve performance problems. In any complex system designed to recover from its own or its users' errors, there is enough redundancy so that many errors successfully pass through the functional test cases and can be detected only because the performance of the system is not what it was expected to be. Such errors frequently show up as gross performance anomalies which can be detected because they are simply unreasonable. Therefore what constitutes reasonable performance for various functions must be carefully predicted so that errors of this type can be found.

Environment Testing

The third type of testing was an attempt to use the system in a more realistic environment. Live users were recruited and invited to try to "crash" the system. A group was formed to try to use TSO for a new application program. TSO was used prior to its formal availability date in a number of installations. Generally, this type of testing did not yield a high number of errors detected for the time and effort

spent. The problem is that workload levels found in realistic environments do not generally test a large system efficiently. The most useful feedback from this type of testing was on the suitability of the design of TSO, its ease
of use, etc.

Before TSO was formally made available for general usage,
certain pre-established reliability, performance, and error
criteria were met. One criterion specified the performance
of TSO on a given set of hardward configurations with a given
terminal workload. The error criterion stated than no known
errors above a certain severity and only a limited number below this severity would be allowed in the final system. The
reliability criterion was expressed as a minimum mean time
between failures caused by the software. This was measured
over a period of several weeks, essentially non-stop, running
a predetermined "realistic" workload. If an identified error was the cause of more than one failure, it was only count-
ed once. Such errors were fixed prior to release of the final
system.

CONCLUSIONS   The description of the TSO development cycle
                   in this paper is, by necessity, somewhat
idealized and sketchy. It does, however, describe the overall
process used by TSO in enough detail to be meaningful. Several
additional complications were omitted because they add little
to the understanding of the basic process. One of them is
worth noting because of its importance to the individual programmer. In many cases, a module for TSO or MVT is used almost without change in several other systems as well. Therefore, for such modules parallel development activity is extremely heavy and the cost of an error late in the cycle is
all the more costly.

The importance of early testing cannot be emphasized
enough. Code should be exercised with as many test cases as
possible as early as possible. Test cases should not be
"saved" until an appropriate point in the cycle. The argument that a programmer's code is not ready for being subjected to test cases is valid only up to a point. Given that a
certain function in the system is being tested; all test cases
pertaining to that function should be attempted. If an aval-
anche of errors are detected, it is better to know sooner
than later that the associated code is poor. Furthermore,

errors can frequently be corrected more efficiently in a batch than one at a time. Taken to the extreme, it is more efficient to re-write a program all at once than a little at a time.

Because of the iterative nature of the design phase, changes will occur to all of the documents at almost any point in time. As a result of testing the design and ultimately the code, errors will be found whose correction will require design changes. Accurate documentation is essential in a large project like TSO, especially if later follow-on development is planned. Moreover, it is important to control all forms of change to the design because of the need to inform the large numbers of people involved. For all of these reasons, a design change procedure is extremely valuable. It allows all changes to be formally accepted by all effected parties and can ensure that documentation changes are synchronized. Another positive benefit is that by keeping track of the number of design changes, the reasons why they occur and the areas they affect, it is possible to evaluate the quality of the design and to spot potential trouble spots.

The introduction of the TSO function into MVT had a rather interesting effect on the reliability of the functions existing in MVT prior to TSO. TSO makes extremely heavy use of the facilities of MVT, sometimes in new ways and combinations. In shaking TSO down, a number of MVT errors were found which, in some cases, had existed for several prior releases. The result was that the MVT capability in the TSO release came through with substantially better reliability. The conclusion drawn from this fact is that TSO placed a significantly heavier load on the MVT base than it had ever been subjected to in the past. This load allowed these latent errors to be detected and corrected. Once a system achieves a mean time to failure on the order of days, the efficiency of detecting errors drops off quickly. The only way to effectively test such a system is to subject it to loads that are orders of magnitude heavier than any it will have in its intended environments. TSO provided such a load for MVT. A similar stress test was created for TSO by greatly increasing the number and complexity of the transactions that it was made to process.

The most important ingredient in the quality of any program is the quality of the people who implement it. While some might be dissatisfied with the design specification

-179-

analysis techniques described earlier because of their relative informality and dependency on human ingenuity, these traits are precisely the strengths of the technique. Given the opportunity, a relatively small number of dedicated, skilled programmers can conduct the type of reviews described and achieve truly worthwhile results.

Acknowledgements

Most of the ideas presented in this chapter are not those of the author. They were developed over a period of years by the people who implemented OS/360, MVT, and TSO. Their contributions are gratefully acknowledged. The author would like to thank Mr. Richard T. Pierce of IBM, who managed a good portion of the TSO Build and Test Activity, for his helpful suggestions regarding this chapter.

AUTOMATED SOFTWARE QUALITY ASSURANCE

J. R. Brown, A. J. DeSalvio, D. E. Heine,
and J. G. Purdy

TRW Systems, Redondo Beach, California

> " . . . *the Air Force can expect to spend
> almost half of its software budget . . .
> on the checkout and test phases of compu-
> ter-program implementation. . .*"
>
> Barry Boehm [A2]

INTRODUCTION   TRW Systems has been involved with the de-
                 velopment of a number of large-scale com-
puter programs. Many different efforts have been made to
automate the checkout and testing of these systems. In this
paper, three example testing modules are described which
have been implemented or are in the process of implementation.
The authors (and TRW) believe automatic testing and analysis
of computer software will generate significant rewards during
the 1970's. The three case studies presented here demonstrate some of our recent achievements.

We shall use the phrase *software quality assurance* to denote any activity that can be employed to verify the correctness of a computer software system, whether it be a small
sub-program or a large system. The purpose of having software quality assurance is, of course, to produce a more reliable end-product: the deliverable software system.

A quality software system may be defined as one which
performs satisfactorily according to the system's specifications. The ability to determine if a computer program does
indeed satisfy its specifications has largely been accomplished to date through "experience" in using the software.
In general, the quality of computer software increases as
the software is used and failures are discovered and corrected. A measure of the variety of ways in which a computer
program is tested (or not tested) and an accumulation of

program performance can combine to form a software "*experience index*".

A formal *automated* software quality assurance system can provide three capabilities that are not as easily attained with standard manual testing and checkout procedures. These capabilities are:

1. Quantification of Test Effectiveness. Various methods are employed to measure how well a software system has been tested. It provides a set of measures or experience indexes; a simple example would be the percentage of statements executed for a given test case.

2. Automation of the Testing Process. It is common experience during the checkout of large software systems that many processes performed manually could be performed automatically. An example would be a test case librarian program to control execution of test cases.

3. Increased Reliability. By providing measures of test effectiveness and automating the testing process, more reliable software will obviously result. When the values of the testing quantifiers are not acceptable, the testing is modified, e.g., to test more paths in the program. The quantifiers provide a common denominator for measuring the reliability of software.

Through these three capabilities, software quality assurance controls the development of computer programs and guarantees to the procurer a quality product.

For the sake of discussion in this paper, let us define a software system as represented by the three modules shown in Figure 1. The system is composed of: a Data Base module, which includes both data and program inputs, a Program module, which includes all machine instructions, and a Results module, which includes all forms of output, irrespective of the storage medium.

The first case study is concerned with the first module of Figure 1 on the next page. It is an automatic method to compare data bases. The second study describes an automated system which provides a first-order measurement of the ef-

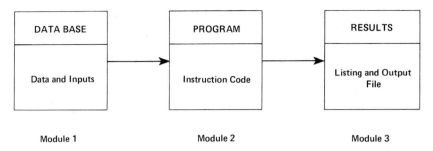

DATA BASE	PROGRAM	RESULTS
Data and Inputs	Instruction Code	Listing and Output File

Module 1	Module 2	Module 3

FIGURE 1. Schematic Representation of a Software System

fectiveness of program testing and explicit results which lead to increased effectiveness. The third study concerns the automation of comparing computer program output test results.

CASE STUDY ONE: A development group at TRW is responsible
A PROGRAM TO for the development and maintenance of a
COMPARE large command and control software system.
DATA BASES This system operates on a CDC 3800 with two
banks of memory each of which is 32K. The
software was developed in the JOVIAL language and uses its
associated COMPOOL[1] facility.

System testing required the generation of many different data bases for the associated test cases. It was necessary to maintain strict control of the data bases which included the identification of their similarities and differences. This task was virtually impossible without an automated processor, so the TRW Data Base Compare ('TDBCOMP) program was designed to automate the comparison function.

Basic Description.

'TDBCOMP is designed to compare and summarize the differences between two data bases in one of three modes. In all modes, comparison is between a data base tape and an active data base on disc. The *normal mode* is a complete validation in which each data base on a tape is compared item-by-item with the active disc data base.

[1]The COMPOOL facility in JOVIAL provides automatic linkage between items, arrays, and tables to the data base.

-183-

BROWN, DESALVIO, HEINE & PURDY

A *suppress* mode permits user specification of those blocks, files, and records to be ignored when making a complete tape validation. The *select mode* allows comparison of only a user specified set of blocks, files, and records. In each mode a comparison of each block is made on a word-by-word basis until a miscompare is encountered, and then an item-by-item comparison is made using the related COMPOOL description of the block. Each miscompare is converted according to its JOVIAL description in the COMPOOL along with appropriate units conversions. Table entry numbers or array dimensions are also output where applicable.

Input Definition.

The operation of 'TDBCOMP is controlled by a single input card. The definition of the inputs is given in Figure 2.

---

*'TDBCOMP *in'unit* [*mode*] [*out'unit*] [*block'name* [F *file* [R *record*]] (s)] $

---

where:

Field Parameter	Field Identifier	Field Parameter Size (Type)	Field Description
in'unit	I	IXX(I)	Logical input unit for data base tape (e.g., I3)
mode	-	XXXX(H)	Mode in which 'TDBCOMP will compare blocks
			SUPP - suppress comparison of those blocks input on this request
			ALL - complete tape validation
			blank -selective comparison of those blocks input on this request
out'unit	-	XX(H)	Output unit SO = System Output Tape PR = On-line Printer and System Output Tape blank = System Output Tape
block'name	-	XXXXXXX(H)	Block name to be compared or to be suppressed. Must begin with prime.
file	F	XXXXXXX(I) or XXXXXXX(H)	File number or name. If blank, all files of block will be compared or suppressed
record	R	XXXXX(I)	Record number. If blank, all records of specified file will be compared or suppressed.

Note -- Brackets mean the input field is optional.

FIGURE 2. Input Definition for 'TDBCOMP Data Base Comparator

Some example input requests are the following:

-184-

1. *'TDBCOMP I5 ALL $
   Compare complete tape on unit 5.
2. *'TDBCOMP I5 'CAM 'CND 'DREEK F O R 2 $
   Compare only 'CAM, 'CND, and 'DREEK (file 0, record
   2) data blocks from tape on unit 5.
3. *'TDBCOMP I5 SUPP 'VEBKI F 1 PR $
   Compare complete tape on unit 5 except 'VEBKI, file
   1, and output on-line as well as off-line.

These examples demonstrate the flexibility of 'TDBCOMP.
With a small amount of input specification, a large number
of comparisons can be performed automatically.

Output Description.

'TDBCOMP produces three types of output – one for each
of its three processing modes:

1. Complete tape validation mode – the output consists
   of data block identification including a block name,
   file, and record, compool ID, tape and disc data
   base ID's. For each miscompare the COMPOOL tag,
   JOVIAL description, tape and disc values, relative
   location in block, type of item, table name and entry (if applicable), array dimension (if applicable),
   and overlay flag (if applicable) are displayed. If
   there are no miscompares in a block nothing is displayed. If no miscompares are encountered in the total data base comparison, the message
   "**NO MISCOMPARES FOUND**" will be output.

2. The suppress mode – The output is the same as 1. a-
   bove except at the top of the first page the following will appear:

** COMPARE ALL BLOCKS EXCEPT THE FOLLOWING **

BLOCK	FILE	RECORD
'XXXXXX	XXXXXXX	XXXXXX
.	.	.
.	.	.
.	.	.

3. The select mode – The output is the same as 1. above
   except that if a requested block contains no mis-

compares the message "NO MISCOMPARES IN BLOCK 'XXXXXX FILE XXXXXX RECORD XXXXXX" will be output. In addition the top of the first page will summarize those blocks that are to be compared:
** SELECTIVE DATA BASE COMPARISON OF THE FOLLOWING DATA BLOCKS ONLY **

BLOCK	FILE	RECORD
'XXXXXXX	XXXXXXX	XXXXXXXX
.	.	.
.	.	.
.	.	.
.		

'TDBCOMP has been employed in an operational environment and has provided a cost-effective contribution towards assuring software quality.

CASE STUDY TWO: A SYSTEM TO MEASURE TEST EFFECTIVENESS   The Product Assurance Confidence Evaluator (PACE) System is a development effort of TRW's Software Product Assurance office. This effort has been directed toward development of some general purpose automated software "tools" which would provide significant aid in performance of a software quality assurance activity.

The PACE System's automated techniques assist in attainment of a high " *experience index*" initially through minimum (but comprehensive) testing and quantification of the index for meaningful software evaluation. Thus, PACE is an automated quality assurance system designed to provide programmers with debugging tools and managers support in determining and controlling computer program quality.

Basic Description

PACE is a collection of automated tools which assist in the planning, production, execution, and evaluation of computer program testing. PACE usage consists of four phases as follows:

1. Test Planning (Preparation of test materials)
   . Analysis of computer program anatomy to determine what must be tested

- Instrumentation of the program to render it measurable as a test item
- Development of test data to exercise the desired portions of program anatomy

2. Test Production (Synthesis of test materials into a test package)
   - Synthesis of test stimulus data for a test
   - Selection of test driver and data environment structure for a test
   - Selection of test measurement and recording software
   - Configuration of a test job containing the above materials ready for execution

3. Test Execution (Operation of the computer program with test data)
   - Computer execution of the instrumented test item
   - Measurement and recording of test output

4. Test Evaluation (Analysis of test results and program performance)
   - Analysis of execution frequency of program elements
   - Analysis of comprehensiveness of test execution
   - Assessment of validation confidence

The objective of PACE is not to find errors, per se, but to quantitatively assess how thoroughly and rigorously a program has been tested and to use this information in the improvement of test design in order to prescribe and carry out the conditions for validation.

PACE has been used to assess the test effectiveness of several large FORTRAN programs and is currently being used in the validation of large operational assembly language programs for crucial defense applications.

The prototype PACE capability was developed in FORTRAN IV for the CDC 6500 and IBM 360 and in FORTRAN V for the Univac 1108 to process FORTRAN computer programs. A highly modular design approach was taken to reduce and isolate machine/language dependent PACE System characteristics to assure easy implementation on a variety of computers.

The initial implementation or instance of PACE was the FLOW module. FLOW analyzes a FORTRAN program and instruments

it in a way which allows subsequent compilation and execution
of the program. FLOW provides for an accumulation of frequencies with which selected elements (e.g. statements, small
segments of code, subprograms, etc.) are exercised as the
program is being tested. A modification of, and extension to,
FLOW was recently completed for NASA/MSC on a Univac 1108.
This system is called AVS (for Automated Verification System),
and it includes a subsystem called TDEM (for Test Data Effectiveness Measurement).

The TDEM subsystem is comprised of three distinct elements. The first is QAMOD, the code analysis and instrumentation program. The second, QAPROC, monitors execution of
the program and provides summary statistics on the frequency
of use of program elements as well as detailed trace information and an indication of the effectiveness of the test
data. The third, QATRAK, uses these results and finally displays internal program transfer variables which can be changed
to effect execution of the unexercised code. QATRAK also
displays the statements which compute or input the transfer
variables. Figures 3 and 4 illustrate the program and data
file interfaces of the TDEM subsystem.

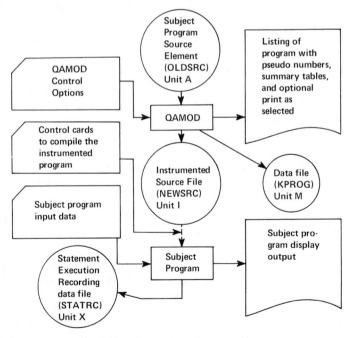

FIGURE 3. TDEM/QAMOD Interfaces

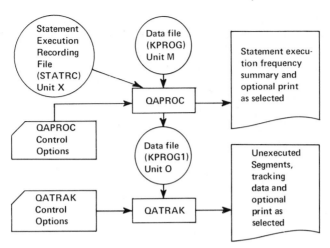

FIGURE 4. TDEM/QAPROC-QATRAK Interfaces

Code Analysis and Instrumentation Program

The QAMOD program sequentially analyzes each statement of a FORTRAN source program, which may be input via cards or Univac 1108 Program Complex File (PCF) tape. As each statement is read, the following analysis is accomplished:

1. The first executable statement of each element (i.e., subroutine or main program) is assigned a pseudo statement number of one. Each subsequent statement is assigned a sequential pseudo number and the statements are displayed with their pseudo numbers. Statements are later referenced from QAPROC and QATRAK by element name and pseudo number.
2. The code is instrumented by the insertion of traps to an execution monitor subroutine. The function of these traps is the generation of a recording file during execution of the instrumented program. The recording file registers the execution of each statement and the order of execution.

After completion of the analysis of all statements, the instrumented source program is output to a file, NEWSRC, for compilation and execution. Except for the generation of the recording file, this program executes exactly as the original subject program.

As the program is being processed by QAMOD, a data file

(KPROG) is also generated. The KPROG file consists of information describing each statement and information relative to program size and structure. A sample output of QAMOD is given in Figure 5.

```
                    ***** QAMOD INPUT DESCRIPTION *****
          NAME   VALUE   DEFINITION

          KRE      5    SYSTEM CARD READ FILE
          KPR      6    SYSTEM PRINT FILE
          KPN     -3    SYSTEM PUNCH FILE
          OLDSRC   1    INPUT SUBJECT PROGRAM SOURCE TAPE
          NEWSRC  11    OUTPUT INSTRUMENTED SOURCE TAPE
          NFILES   1    NUMBER OF FILES ON OLDSRC TAPE
          KPROG   15    PROGRAM STRUCTURE DATA OUTPUT FILE
          NOPRNT   0    DISPLAY NOMINAL PRINT
          KLIST    0    DO NOT DISPLAY KPROG DATA
          ISEG     0    NO SEGMENTATION IS BEING PERFORMED
          TRPEND   0    DO NOT INSTRUMENT FORTRAN 'END' STATEMENTS
          IFA      1    INSTRUMENT ARITHMETIC 'IF' AS 4 STATEMENTS
          NINOPT   1    INPUT SOURCE ELEMENTS FROM TAPE
          NOTOPT   1    OUTPUT SOURCE ELEMENTS TO TAPE
          LEVEL    1    INSTRUMENT SUBJECT PROGRAM AT LEVEL 1
          LIMSEG   0    NO INTERMEDIATE INSTRUMENTATION LEVEL SELECTED
          SPECIFIED ELEMENTS ARE -
          *ALL
                    ************************************

     ELEMENT MAIN                                                  0
          DIMENSION  STATE(8) , ITITLE(14) , X(3),Y(3),Z(3)        0
          COMMON /MODS/ MOD2,MOD3,MOD5,MOD7                        0
          DATA  STATE / 8*0. / , I1 / 8 / , I2 / 9 /               0
          INPUT = 0                                                1
          REWIND I1                                                2
          READ (5,100)  ITITLE                                     3
     100  FORMAT ( 14A6 )                                          0
     110  READ(6,500) MODEL, (STATE(I),I=1,8)                      4
                 .                                                 .
                 .                                                 .
                 .                                                 .
          CALL  XYZ(X,Y,Z,MODEL)                                  27
          IF ( INPUT.LT.6 )   GO TO 110                           28,  29
          STOP                                                   30
          END                                                     0

     ELEMENT XYZ                                                   0
          SUBROUTINE XYZ(X,Y,Z,MODEL)                              0
          DIMENSION  STATE(8),X(3),Y(3) , Z(3), XDOT(3),YDOT(3),ZDOT(3)   0
          COMMON /MODS/ MOD2,MOD3,MOD5,MOD7                        0
          DATA  IFLAG/0/                                           0
     C    IFLAG = 0 AT FIRST CALL                                  0
          IF (IFLAG.NE.0)  GO TO 200                               1,   2
          IFLAG = 1                                                3
          DO 100 I=1,3                                             4
          XDOT(I) = 0.0                                            5
                 .                                                 .
                 .                                                 .
                 .                                                 .
          GO TO 2050                                             238
     1000 CONTINUE                                                239
     1100 CONTINUE                                                240
          RETURN                                                  241
          END                                                       0

                    ***** QAMOD SUMMARY PRINT *****
          THE   25 ELEMENTS ANALYZED CONTAINED THE FOLLOWING -
          2210 STATEMENTS, 1637 WHICH WERE TRAPPED AT LEVEL 1
             31 ENTRY POINTS
              3 STOP STATEMENTS
              0 END STATEMENTS
          1810 KPROG RECORDS
                    ********************************
```

FIGURE 5

Execution Monitor Program

The QAPROC program accesses the statement execution recording file generated by execution of the instrumented subject program and produces an evaluation and summary of the test case executed. The recording file is sequentially accessed and the data are assimilated into an internal table, MAPTAB. At times designated by the input control options, a display is printed which includes the following:

1. A map, delineated by subroutine, indicating the number of executions which have been recorded for each statement.
2. Statistics indicating the percentage of the total executable statements which were executed.
3. Statistics indicating the percentage of the total number of subroutines which were executed.
4. A list of the names of subroutines which were not executed.

After processing the entire recording file, statement usage frequency information is added to the data from the input KPROG file and this revised information is output on a data file KPROG1.

Statistics from several recording files (i.e., several executions of the subject program) may be summed and a cumulative summary compiled. The nominal display from QAPROC is shown in Figure 6.

```
                  ***** QAPROC INPUT DESCRIPTION *****
        NAME   VALUE      DEFINITION

        STATRC  27    STATEMENT EXECUTION RECORDING FILE
        MAPSAV   0    OUTPUT MAP SUMMARY FILE
        MAPIN    0    INPUT MAP SUMMARY FILE
        BEGNTR   0    NUMBER PAIR AT WHICH TRACE BEGINS(0=NO TRACE)
        ENDTR    0    NUMBER PAIR AT WHICH TRACE ENDS  (0=NO TRACE)
        IMAP     0    MAP DISPLAY WILL BE OUTPUT
        MAXPAR 100000 NUMBER PAIR AT WHICH TO DISPLAY FIRST MAP
        INCPAR 200000 NUMBER OF PAIRS TO PROCESS BETWEEN MAPS
        MAPMAX  10    MAXIMUM NUMBER OF MAP DISPLAYS REQUESTED
        NOTAB    0    MAP SUMMARIES WILL BE CUMULATIVE
        KLIST    0    DO NOT LIST KPROG1 FILE
        NCASES   1    NUMBER OF CASES BEING PROCESSED
        KTRACK   0    SUBTRK FILE WILL NOT BE OUTPUT
                  *****************************************

        **QAPROC MAP PRINT**

        --------------------
          ELEMENT MAIN
        PSEUDO NO. FREQ. PSEUDO NOS. FREQ  PSEUDO NOS. FREQ  PSEUDO NOS. FREQ
          1 TO  3=  1     4 TO 29=  6     30 TO 31=  1

        --------------------
          ELEMENT XYZ
        PSEUDO NOS. FREQ  PSEUDO NOS. FREQ  PSEUDO NOS. FREQ  PSEUDO NOS. FREQ
          1 TO  1=  6     2 TO  2=  5     3 TO  7=  1     8 TO  8=  6
          .
          .
          .

        --------------------
        **QAPROC USAGE SUMMARY AFTER    122462 NUMBER PAIRS(ENTRY/EXIT SEGMENTS)

          THE TEST DATA EXERCISED  1514 OF  1637 EXECUTABLE STATEMENTS.
          THE TEST EFFECTIVENESS RATIO AT THE STATEMENT LEVEL IS   .92

          THE PROGRAM CONTAINS  3 TERMINATION POINTS, ONLY ONE OF WHICH WAS
          EXECUTED.  THE CORRECTED TEST EFFECTIVENESS RATIO IS  .93

          THE TEST DATA EXERCISED  26 OF THE   31 ENTRY POINTS.
          THE TEST EFFECTIVENESS RATIO AT THE ENTRY POINT LEVEL IS   .84

        THE FOLLOWING ELEMENTS WERE NOT CALLED -
        ADBARV MDBARV RNIT   SINGLE SUVW
```

FIGURE 6

BROWN, DESALVIO, HEINE & PURDY

Test Analysis Program.

The QATRAK program accesses the KPROG1 data file generated by QAPROC and displays information indicating the variables whose values could be changed to provide more comprehensive verification of the subject program. For each unex-
ecuted block, or segment of code, the following information
is displayed:

1. A listing of the statements in the segment.
2. An explanation of why the segment was not executed.
3. All statements from which a transfer could be made
   to the segment.
4. All computations of the branch control variables involved in the decision to transfer to the segment.

Through the optional track-back feature, the user may
also select to track the computation and input of the branch
control variables within all subroutines executed prior to
the segment being analyzed.

The QATRAK displays provide aid to the user in the selection of new input data to effect execution of the unexercised segments, thereby generating a more comprehensive test
data base. An example of QATRAK output is given in Figure 7.

FIGURE 7

-192-

The TDEM Subsystem provides a meaningful measure of the effectiveness of test data and aids modification of the data to achieve more comprehensive verification of software. After applying TDEM to assure that 100 percent of the executable statements and transfers in the subject program have been exercised, the user will have generated a basic test data base. Although TDEM focuses upon comprehensive usage of a program's logical properties (i.e., statements and transfers), valuable information is provided to support manual assurance that all functional requirements have been satisfied.

CASE STUDY THREE: The ACTRAC program developed by TRW is a
A SYSTEM TO   large scale (>300 subroutines) multiple-pur-
COMPARE TEST   pose orbit determination program. It was
RESULTS   developed using the FORTRAN IV language and
                 operates on an IBM 360/65 under OS. ACTRAC
is typical of a large class of scientific application programs which operate in a batch mode, utilizing the line printer as a principal means of output communication with the analyst/user.

A comprehensive library of test cases for ACTRAC is stored on magnetic tape and can be readily processed by ACTRAC when operating in its TEST mode. Each test case deck is numbered according to the module or function to which the case pertains and the category of test: *engineering valida-tion* or *logic check.* The user selects test cases for execution by entering TEST cards in the input stream containing the four digit numbers of the cases to be executed. This semi-automatic system proved very useful during program development and verification testing.

As the program grew in size and complexity, the library of test data also grew. At the current state of program development, ACTRAC requires (for a complete retest) approximately 18 hours of 360/65 CPU time, yielding from .85 to 1.1 million lines of printed output. Before this retest can be accepted, its output must be compared against previous test case output and discrepancies justified. Three man weeks are required to do this task manually.

While great strides were taken to improve the efficiency of actually executing the test cases (the ACTRAC TEST mode) little concern was originally given to the problem of evaluating the "mountain" of output produced during a complete retest operation. This study discusses the elements of a new approach proposed to aid in automating this procedure.

The goal of the approach to improve retesting efficiency is a reduction of computer and personnel time and, concurrently, maintenance of program reliability. To achieve this goal, the following steps had to be taken.

1. Substantially reduce the volume of test output for comparison, thus reducing computer time.
2. Automatically compare the results of the test to those of previously verified cases.
3. Incorporate data management features to allow for expansion and flexibility of the retesting procedure.

A fully automatic method, that is, one which generates a file of complete ACTRAC retest results to be compared byte for byte to a master file, is unacceptable. Computer time would be increased as well as storage requirements for the resulting output files. It was felt that a complex comparison program to recognize intentionally added and deleted output characters would have to be developed. The comparison could, of course, be done by a clerical staff using documents indicating which data are to be compared, but maintaining such documents and controlling the inherent human error could seriously downgrade ACTRAC's reliability.

The decided upon approach, called the RETEST mode of operation, is automatic and is currently being implemented.

Basic Description.

For each test case, the analyst must identify from the printed output those data which best reflect the correctness of the tested capability. These data will form a critical subset of the total output and will be used as the criteria for determining whether the program capability has been disturbed following modifications. If these "key numbers" agree from version to version, the program will be accepted as validated.

Once identified, the key numbers must automatically be extracted by ACTRAC from the printed output and saved in a file for later processing. The file produced will become an "answer" file containing the essential output for each test case in the library. Later, following modifications, a new file can be generated containing the new "answers". Automatic comparison of these files (the old and new "answer" files) will provide the necessary validation information.

The key to the RETEST method is the identification of the key comparator data. What is needed is a system of identifying uniquely every piece of data that is produced by ACTRAC on the line printer. In addition, the identifiers must be relatively insensitive to most program modifications. In other words, once a piece of data has been located in the output stream, its identifier must be valid from program version to program version.

The scheme adopted requires that an additional piece of information be produced on every line of ACTRAC output. This data is a line identifier, and it is printed at the extreme right edge of the form (beyond the eleven inch perforation). The line identifier is a nine digit alphanumeric character string composed as follows:

MRREEELLL

The M field identifies the module of ACTRAC currently executing and varies from A through Z. RR is an identifier for the routine currently executing. Every subroutine of ACTRAC is given a unique two letter code from AA to ZZ. EEE is a three digit numeric field identifying the entrance number of the routine (RR) producing the current line of print (varies from 001 to 999). LLL is a sequence number for each line of print produced on the EEE entrance. These line identifiers are generated automatically by the FORTRAN I/O package (IBCOM) using data available in ACTRAC regarding module and routine execution.

As an example, if subroutine CD appears in both modules A and F, and each entrance to CD produced two lines of output, the lines would be identified in the printed output as follows:

ACD002001 ACD002002	First two lines produced on entrance two of routine CD in module A.
ACD003001 ACD003002	First two lines produced on entrance three of routine CD in module A.
FCD002001 FCD002002	First two lines produced on entrance two of routine CD in module F.

Once a line has been identified, the analyst may select comparator data by indicating the relative position of the printed data within the line (in accordance with the list appearing in the FORTRAN WRITE statement). These identifiers are punched on cards and input to the FILGEN program along with tolerances to be assigned with each data value. The input to FILGEN is described in Figure 8. The output from FILGEN is two disc files, COMPID and TOLERANCE, structured according to Figure 9 and 10.

COLUMNS	ENTRY DESCRIPTION
1-9	Line identification $(MREL)^+$ from ACTRAC of line containing comparator.
11-26	Location of comparator within line. 16 column flag field. i^{th} column non-zero means comparator is i^{th} element in line ($i \leq 16$).
27-28	RE-repeat the identifier in columns 1-9 RE times while incrementing E, i.e., MREL, MR(E+1)L, MR(E+2)L ... RE allows lines from successive subroutine entries to be identified. (RE < 128)
29-30	RL-repeat the identifiers in columns 1-9 RL times while incrementing L, i.e., MREL, MRE(L+1), MRE(L+2), ... RL allows successive lines printed from a single subroutine entry to be identified (RL < 128)
31-39	Tolerance lower limit
40	Tolerance lower limit type. Enter P if Tolerance lower limit is percent deviation
41-49	Tolerance upper limit
50	Tolerance upper limit type (as shown)
60	Blank-ignore this and next field; A - add data to an existing file and case; C - change corresponding data in existing file and case. D - delete data in corresponding file and case
61-69	The line identifier (MREL) at which the option A or C is to be activated. Not needed for D

+ M = module, R = routine, E = entrance number, L = line sequence number

FIGURE 8

DIRECTORY		DATA RECORDS	
Words	Description	Words	Description
1-2	Reserved for FORTRAN control	1-2	Reserved for FORTRAN control
3	Number of entries in directory	3	Number of entries in record
4	Reserved	4	Reserved
5	Case ID/version number (binary half-words)	5	String of comparator identifiers in the following format:
6	Creation date-year/day (binary half-words)	:	$MRRFEEELLLLNNR_ER_L$ (1 byte/character)
7	Time created-hours/min/sec (1 byte each)	:	M - module identifier
8	Location of first comparator identifier for case/number of comparator identifiers for case (binary half-words)		RR - routine
:			F - Repeat values (R_E, R_L) present
			EEE - routine entrance number
			LLLL - line number
			NN - comparator's position in line

One set for each case (brace spanning words 5-8)

FIGURE 9. Format of Comparator Identifier File (COMPID)

AUTOMATED SOFTWARE QUALITY ASSURANCE

DIRECTORY

Words	Description
1-2	Reserved for FORTRAN Control
3	Number of three-word entries in Directory
4	Case ID
5	Date created year/day number (half word binary)
6	Location of first tolerance for case/number of tolerances for case (half word binary)

DATA RECORDS

Bytes	Description
1-8	Reserved for FORTRAN Control
9-12	Number of two-items entries in record ($\leq$ 69)
13	Item 1 - Tolerance type (0-value; 1-percent)
14-17	Item 2 - Tolerance

For each comparator { 13, 14-17 }

FIGURE 10. Format of Tolerance File (TOLERANCE)

The COMPID file is input to ACTRAC when operating in the RETEST mode. Test cases are called for execution using TEST cards as described above, and the COMPID file is processed by the modified IBCOM routine during execution. Each line of output is checked by IBCOM to determine whether the current line identifier matches one in the COMPID file. If no match, the line is suppressed (no printout) and execution continues. If the identifiers match, the appropriate item in the line is saved in a buffer (the data item is extracted from core memory using the FORMAT statement and WRITE list) and eventually routed to disc into the MASTER answer file.

Following modifications, this process is repeated with the new answers routed to the NEW answer file. The structure of the NEW and MASTER files is given in Figure 11.

DIRECTORY

Words	Description
1-2	Reserved for FORTRAN Control
3	Number of five-word entries in directory
4-5	Reserved
6	Case ID/Version ID (binary half-words)
7	Date case run - year/day (binary half-words)
8	Time run - hrs/min/sec (1 byte each)
9	Location of first comparator for case/number of comparator records for case (binary half-words)
10	Logical checksum of comparator records for this case

Repeat for each case in file { (words 6 through 10)

DATA RECORD

Bytes	Description
1-8	Reserved for FORTRAN control
9-12	Number of words in record
13-16	Logical checksum of this record
17-24	Reserved
25-28	Information supplied by IBCOM for converting comparator data
29	Comparator data for case (variable length)

FIGURE 11. Format of MASTER and NEW Files

A compare program processes entries in the NEW file and compares the results with those stored in the MASTER file. The deviations permitted between comparator data is prescribed by the TOLERANCE file. Messages are output indicating the success or failure of each test case comparison. In the case of failure, the entries will be printed and identified for further analysis. In this way, the analyst devotes his time to analyzing only those cases which do not match from version to version rather than laboriously comparing all data. A sample output from the compare program is given in Figure 12.

AUTOMATED SOFTWARE QUALITY ASSURANCE

********************************* TEST CASE 1052 DISCREPANCIES *********************************

OLD ANSWERS DERIVED FROM PROGRAM VERSION 9.2 GENERATED ON 71/10/ 9 10:15:26.842
NEW ANSWERS DERIVED FROM PROGRAM VERSION 9.3 GENERATED ON 72/ 2/14 3: 5:15.022

COMPID	ITEM	OLD ANSWER	NEW ANSWER	DIFFERENCE	ACCEPTABLE TOLERANCE	TOLERANCE TYPE
CQB001025	1	8.92516382D-01	8.82516382D-01	1.00000000D-02	1.00000000D-03	VALUE (LOWER)
CQB001025	2	NOT ECLIPSED	ECLIPSED	**************	0.	VALUE (UPPER)
CQB001025	3	364580	465660	101080	1000	VALUE (UPPER)
CFA020001	10	2.09257382D 07	2.09257383D 07	1.00032000D-01	0.	VALUE (UPPER)
CCC102001	4	6.00000000D 03	6.60000000D 03	1.00000000D 01	5.00000000D 00	% (UPPER)
DQB003050	6	6.00000000D 03	5.40000000D 03	1.00000000D 01	5.00000000D 00	% (LOWER)

****

THE FOLLOWING TEST CASES MATCH

```
                                    1020
                                    1021
                                    1030
                                    1040
                                    1050
                                    1051
                                    1053
                                    9021
                                    9872
                                    9875
                                    9876
                                    9880
                                    9881
```

FIGURE 12

The entries in the COMPID file form a unique set of line identifiers insensitive to many types of program modifications. Changes to routines which do not disturb the order and amount of printed output have no effect on the COMPID file. Changes in one module will have no effect on line identifiers in another module. Changes which cause lines to be added or deleted within routines that do not produce "key numbers" (they do not appear in the COMPID RR field) are similarly accepted without change. System messages do not disturb this process since they are not handled by ACTRAC and, thus, do not alter the numbering scheme.

Of course, modifications will be made which invalidate certain COMPID entries so that the item identified in the MASTER file does not correspond to that in NEW. These cases will be caught by the compare program and properly identified. The analyst will then have to compare the full printout from the master version with that of the new version.

While these techniques are specifically directed toward ACTRAC operating in a batch mode, they are applicable to any program for which:

1. Periodic modification is anticipated
2. A high level of reliability is to be maintained.
3. Test cases have been developed demonstrating current capability.
4. Program validation of modified versions requires re-running the test cases and comparing current results to past results, i.e., by retest evaluation.

SUMMARY   We have examined three instances of auto-
REMARKS   mated software quality assurance. Each of
              these studies provides, to some degree, all
three of the capabilities mentioned earlier, i.e., they each
provide some form of testing quantification, they all are
automatic, and they all serve to increase confidence in the
reliability of the software being tested.

Cost Benefits.

The cost of testing is one of the major elements of the
cost of developing operational software (software which is
to be used in a production mode). On the Apollo program according to estimates by NASA/MSC, testing accounted for a-
bout 80% of the cost of developing on board software. Although this probably represents a high figure because of the
thoroughness required in Apollo testing, similar estimates
for the development of operational software for other applications have produced figures of 30% to 60% of the total development cost as the amount assignable to testing.

In spite of the large amounts of time and money that
are spent on software testing by manual methods, it is generally agreed that the results are less than satisfactory.
Software delivered from the developer to the user is usually
far from error-free. The user generally finds a number of
errors. These errors may show themselves in the program
failing to run for certain inputs or they may become evident
because the computed results are clearly in error. More
troublesome are the cases where the error is more subtle and
the error in the results is not found until they have been
used with some consequent bad effects. The cost to the user

can be rather substantial.

The high error content of developed and tested software is only partly due to poor workmanship on the part of the developers and testers. It is also due to the complexity of large computer programs and to the lack of techniques for dealing adequately with the complexity. The amount of testing required to thoroughly test a program has generally been regarded as too costly or time consuming to be fully accomplished. The major reason that errors remain in software released to operational use is that the developer has been unable to determine whether the testing he has performed is sufficient.

Considering this, one has to ask if automated testing methods are cost-effective. Can the additional cost for the development of automated software quality assurance systems be accounted for? The answer is a strong "Yes".

Let us assume an automated software quality assurance system costs $200,000 for each particular implementation. For a program development activity in which 50% of the cost is in software testing, the use of an automated software quality assurance system should reduce the testing cost by 10 to 20 percent. This means that in an activity that operates at a level of $1,000,000 per year, the payoff should occur in less than two years; i.e., the total cost of program development and testing for two years using the software quality assurance system should be less than if it were not used and the thoroughness of manual testing was substantially increased. If the programming activity is at the level of $5,000,000 per year, payoff should be achieved in less than one year.

As an example of this cost benefit, consider the case of the application of PACE/FLOW to the testing of the HOPE (Houston Operations Predictor/Estimator) program, a trajectory program used on a production basis by TRW's Houston Operations. HOPE is a large program: it has over 400 subprograms and is extensively overlaid for operation on the Univac 1108. Before the use of FLOW, testing – after major updates – involved the use of 33 test cases requiring 4-1/2 hours of computer time and 35 to 50 man hours for examination and analysis of test results. Use of FLOW showed that this amount of testing exercised only 85% of the sub-programs. From data obtained from the use of FLOW, 6 test cases were designed, which could

be selectively used, and which would exercise 93% of the subprograms. Minor modifications to this basic test case set can
be easily made to effect execution of all subroutines as required. Testing with these test cases requires less than
three hours of computer time and less than 24 man hours for
examination and analysis of test results. Thus, in this case
an increase in thoroughness of testing was obtained with a
decrease in the cost of testing and a reduction in the e-
lapsed time of testing. The decrease in cost of the test
runs more than offset the cost of making the initial FLOW
analysis of HOPE; and continued use of FLOW has resulted in
savings which are greater than the initial development costs
of FLOW.

The increase in running time of test cases, when the program has been instrumented to collect data on the testing,
increases the cost of each run. Although this increase may
range from 20% to several hundred percent, in most cases, the
increase will be offset by savings in the number of cases
that need to be run to achieve an acceptable degree of thoroughness. Because of the aids to designing improved test
cases, the degree of thoroughness in the testing will, in
most cases, be increased.

The cost benefits of the use of automated software quality assurance methods can be summarized as follows:

1. Reduced cost of testing to achieve a given degree of
   thoroughness; usually, both the cost of testing can
   be reduced and the degree of thoroughness increased.
2. Increased thoroughness of testing significantly reducing the number of errors encountered in operational
   use with consequent reduction of the cost of maintenance and the cost of servicing customer complaints;
   to the customer, the reduction in errors reduces the
   cost to him of having errors occur in production use.
3. The visibility of execution logic provided by automated software quality assurance will, in many cases,
   simplify the diagnosis of problems and significantly
   reduce the time and effort to find and correct errors.

The net effect of these benefits - when compared to the
cost of obtaining and using automated software quality assurance technology is very substantial.

Expectations.

There is definitely a good future for the capability
of automated software quality assurance. Large funding agencies like NASA and DOD are beginning to include requirements
for software quality assurance in their software procurement
procedures. Automated software verification systems will be
merged with automated methods to aid in the development phase,
e.g., greatly extended automatic debug facilities and their
associated compilers.

The PACE system is under current development at TRW, and
in the near future (< 5 years), such a system as PACE or one
of its descendents will become an integral part of every
software development project at TRW. With the complexity of
software systems increasing, automated verification is, indeed, becoming a requirement instead of a desire.

Acknowledgement

The work presented in this paper involved many people
besides the authors. Recognition should be given to A.C.
Arterbery, R.H. Hoffman, C.P. Lucas, E.R. Mangold, E.C. Nelson, L.J. Carey and W.W. Royce.

A SOFTWARE TESTING CONTROL SYSTEM

16

E. P. Youngberg
Univac, Blue Bell, Pennsylvania

INTRODUCTION   Recently, the concept of a specialized
monitor or *test control system* to test
software has been considered. The idea seeks to use the
software system to fullest advantage to reduce the time required for testing as well as simplify the task of test sequencing, result analysis, data generation and other related
procedures.

This chapter discusses the design of a particular test
control system called the Validation Control System (VCS).
VCS is made up of a number of basic parts or *tasks*. These
include:

1. A control routine that interfaces with the test at a subroutine level; this is defined as the "control nucleus".
2. Modular test "kernels" that contain the necessary service
   request calls to the control nucleus. These test kernels
   are "self-checking" so that valid pass/fail decisions can
   be made at execution time.
3. An active job interrogator that communicates with the
   control nucleus (via file communication entries) which
   is linked with the test kernel. This is defined as the
   "interrogator".
4. A parameter driven routine that selectively structures
   executable programs from a base of test kernels. This
   routine will also update the kernel identifier entries in
   a test requirements file and is defined as the "structurer".
5. A parameter driven routine that randomly selects test executions and feeds them to the host systems scheduling
   facilities. In addition, this routine will create the

job control streams that are associated with the test executions. This is defined as the "JCL generator".
6. A facility to generate data records as a pre-process or dynamically during the test execution. This will be defined as the "data generator".
7. A result analysis mechanism that interprets codes previously stored in the result file by the interrogator, and produces a testing report for the selected test mix. This will be defined as the "result reporting routine".

The next three sections of the chapter give an overview of the part VCS plays in testing at the unit, component and systems level. The rest of the sections cover a more detailed description of each of the various tasks in VCS. The last two sections discuss advantages and conclusions.

THE SOFTWARE UNIT LEVEL   This is the level at which unit test kernel development occurs and code is implemented for future interface in the control system. Test kernels for early unit testing would be designed with the following characteristics:

1. Interface coding for later link-up with a control nucleus subroutine.
2. Self-checking code to allow pass/fail result data to be passed to the control nucleus.
3. Modular test design for ease in later structuring of load modules.

Unit test kernels, designed for later inclusion in VCS, cover the finite areas of the software. This would include parts of the supervisor (e.g., SVC calls, transients, etc.) and other early implementation items. Ideally, many of the available software options are checked out prior to full component integration. Figure 1 is a block diagram of a simple unit kernel which tests the decimal feature of the assembler. Interface coding, with a control nucleus driver, is bypassed at this level.

THE SOFTWARE COMPONENT LEVEL   When the software component is first implemented, unit test kernels are normally debugged and running. At this level,

SOFTWARE TESTING CONTROL SYSTEM

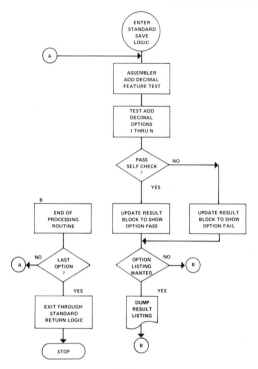

FIGURE 1

there exists a software component (assembler or job control) that coexists with a complete set of unit test kernels for that component. Unit kernels test all the features and options of the described component.

The new objective, at the component level, is to allow variability by interaction of units within the component. Two factors now enter into the VCS test kernel building plan. They are:

1. Develop a "driver" type program to handle execution scheduling and parameter passing within the load module (i.e., several kernels linked with the driver). The driver would ultimately be joined with the control nucleus, either by another level of subroutine, or by building the control nucleus logic into the driver.
2. Build a data generator interface to the test kernels that use data records. Variable patterns can now be substituted for previously fixed data. Formats and

E.P. YOUNGBERG

block/record sizes would be passed by parameters to the driver which would then make an internal data request and return
the variable record to the test kernel.

Figure 2 is a block diagram of a sample component driver.
Coding for the control nucleus is bypassed at this level.
Instead of result blocks being passed to the VCS by way of
the nucleus they are optionally listed by the driver.

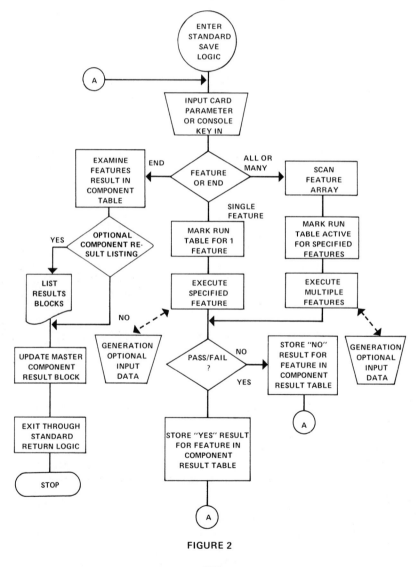

FIGURE 2

-208-

SOFTWARE TESTING CONTROL SYSTEM

THE SOFTWARE   VCS is a complete control system at the
SYSTEMS LEVEL   software systems level. Functional mechan-
                      isms are built in which enable a test pro-
grammer to make complete use of the operating system. Services are provided to permit the running of test kernels in
a highly controlled environment. These services not only
control execution, but offer ways to accomplish the tasks of:

1. Job control stream generation.
2. External data file generation.
3. Internal data generation for purposes of self-checking.
4. Structuring of load modules from a base of test kernels.
5. Result reporting using coded blocks that are passed
   from the kernels to the interrogator's result file.
6. Snap shot services for kernel usage.
7. Execution sequencing.

Figure 3 graphically represents the VCS at the software
systems level.

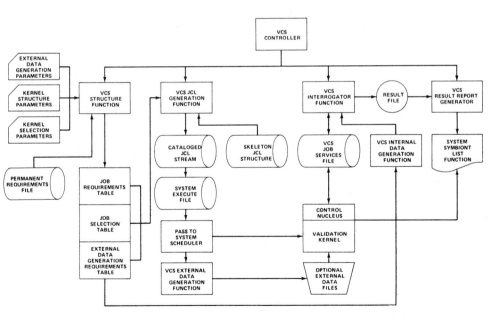

FIGURE 3

Generally, parameter cards are input to the "structurer" function of VCS to define job requirements, selection, and external data files (if used) for the test kernel. This information, along with prestored data in the permanent requirements file (a file maintained by the structurer that stores kernel definition data) is stored as separate job entries in the job requirements, selection, and external data tables. In this way, the beginning of a validation job is defined for control stream preparation. Control is passed to the JCL generation function (JCLGEN) which accesses the tables built by the structurer. Using this information, the JCLGEN creates the control stream for the host machine. The JCLGEN uses a skeleton control stream (created by a pre-process) when possible. The stream may be generated with an optional external data generation step supplying the test kernel with data files for input functions. Later, the kernel would make an internal data request (using the same type parameters), via the interrogator, for purposes of self-checking record processing.

Once a job control stream for the selected validation jobs is generated it is passed to the scheduling facilities of the host machine. The order and priority of execution is predetermined and is reflected in the order of the run streams. When possible multitasking is used.

Control is now passed to the VCS interrogator function. If the running load module (control nucleus kernels) is to invoke job services, the interrogator will be notified through continued examination of the Job Services File (JSF). JSF will contain entries for interrogation words that both the control nucleus and interrogator utilize. Result blocks, requests for data, or snaps of kernel areas will be handled by the interrogator.

After an accumulation of result data, and all other VCS activities are complete, the result report function is initiated. The accumulated data is sorted and a result report, by kernel, is printed. In the following sections the various elements in the VCS system are discussed in detail.

CONTROLLER ROUTINE   This element of VCS is initially loaded and represents the resident core of the system. The controller's main function is to schedule the particular VCS overlay that is needed to service the

validation jobs. This includes structuring, selection, and
inter-job services.

When one VCS element has successfully performed a task,
control is released to the controller routine. Then the
next overlay function is scheduled and gains control when
called for by the controller. The controller is resident
for the duration of the VCS run.

Another function that is served by the controller is to
house the VCS system tables. Table definitions will be discussed as they are used in other VCS elements.

STRUCTURER   The structurer routine accepts control cards
ROUTINE   that define the desired synthetic mix of
                test kernels to be linked with a control
nucleus. This information is combined with previously stored
kernel information in the permanent requirements file (PRF).
Collectively, information is placed in the three VCS tables
shown in Figure 3 (job requirements, selection, and external
data tables). This data is later used in creating the run
streams to link and execute the jobs.

Job Table

The job table is resident in the controller part of VCS.
In the example used (Figure 4), the job table has a maximum
of 99 job entries with up to 20 kernels (tests) per job.

6	Job Name	8	Kernel Name and Entry Point
2	Job Number	1	Kernel Order Number
1	Job Mode	1	External Files
1	Job Mix	8	Kernel Name
1	Job Order	1	Kernel Order Number
1	Job Type	1	External Files
1	Job Priority	8	Kernel Name and Entry Point
1	External Files	1	Kernel Order Number
2	Number of Kernels in Job	1	External Files

FIGURE 4. Field Names and Lengths in Job Table

The job portion of the table is taken from VCS parameter
cards. For example, the first item, job name, is made up
from a job number supplied by the user and a constant furn-
ished by the structurer. Important to the VCS job is the
kernel entry point. The control nucleus uses this entry to
transfer control to a given kernel within the load module.
Since the control nucleus can not determine what kernels
might be linked with it, there has to be a structure list
that defines the entry point.

The technique used preconstructs a branch table in the
run stream. This branch table element is actually source
code that is assembled and linked into the control nucleus.
Information, for the entry point, is obtained from the kernel name in the job table.

Permanent Requirements File

The Permanent Requirements File (PRF) is an indexed sequential file that supplies the VCS job requirements. Items
that are not described in the VCS parameter cards are permanently stored, and maintained on the PRF. Data from the
PRF is placed in the VCS tables by the structurer routine.

An example of PRF type information is the kernel name
and number of external files per kernel (Figure 5).

8	Kernel Identification	3	Record Count for Start of Sequencing
30	Component, Feature, and Option Codes	1	Field Number
1	Kernel Mode	1	Field Sequencing
1	Number of Files. Packed Left 4 bits = Total No. of files. Right 4 bits = No. of Internal Files.	1	Character Mode
		1	Start Character
		4	Number of Characters
		4	Field Starting Address
2	Kernel Size (Packed)	1	Field Number
30	File Identification	1	Field Sequence
1	File Number = VCS file ID	1	Character Mode
1	File Mode = Internal or External	1	Start Character
		4	Number of Characters
2	File Type	4	Field Starting Address
4	Record Size	1	Field Number
4	Block Size	1	Field Sequence
4	Number of Records	1	Character Mode
2	Blocking Factor	1	Start Character
1	Blocked or Unblocked File	4	Number of Characters
1	Variable of Fixed Lengthed Records	4	Field Starting Address
1	Sequencing, Ascending, Descending or None	1	Field Number
		1	Field Sequence

FIGURE 5. Field Names and Lengths in Permanent Requirements File

JCL GENERATION
ROUTINE

The JCL generation routine (JCLGEN) has the task of creating job control streams for:

1. Assembling the branch table
2. Linking the control nucleus and kernels
3. Generating external data
4. Execution of the load module (control nucleus and kernels) that was linked previously.

To accomplish control stream generation, JCLGEN must access information in the VCS tables and a file of JCL skeletons that was created by a preprocess. The JCL skeletons are associated with each kernel that is run under VCS control.

Additional JCLGEN functions which are complete when the generated run stream is passed to the host computers scheduling mechanism are:

1. Supply the branch table source code so that the control nucleus can enter the kernels when they become part of the load module.
2. In addition to the external data generation control stream, supply the parameters that are required to generate proper data files.
3. Establish the execution sequence and priority of the VCS load module.

After the run streams for several jobs have been generated, JCLGEN places the output on a direct access device. Run streams are now filed, to the systems file, and control is released to the scheduler. Figure 6 represents graphically the entire JCLGEN process.

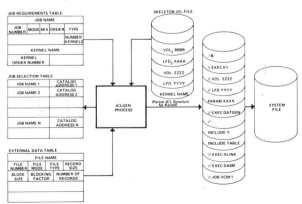

FIGURE 6

E.P. YOUNGBERG

It should also be pointed out that JCLGEN maintains the skeleton library. Updates can be made according to changes in the kernel requirements.

Inter-Job Communications.

The interrogator's primary function is to service the running validation load modules. This is accomplished through interjob communications (IJC). The IJC function is handled through an intermediate index sequential file called the Job Services File (JSF).

To communicate, the control nucleus places a job service request in the JSF. The control nucleus action is initiated by a subroutine call from one of the linked kernels. Once the request has been placed, the interrogator, which is continually scanning the JSF, services the request.

Job Services File (JSF).

As previously mentioned, the JSF is shared by the interrogator and all the active control nucleus/kernel load modules. The number of entries in the file are equal to the number of multiprogramming levels supported by the operating system. Accordingly, if there are ten levels of multiprogramming, then ten file entries would exist.

Figure 7 represents a sample JSF control entry.

	BYTE 1							BYTE 2							
FIELD	A	D	DR	R	TR	T	S		AKN				DFN		
BITS	0	1	2	3	4	5	6	7	8	9	10	11	12	13	14	15

LEGEND:

```
A    — Active Bit
D    — Data Requested
DR   — Data Ready
R    — Results Ready
TR   — Termination Requested
T    — Terminated
S    — Snap Requested
AKN  — Active Kernel Number (Binary)
DFN  — Data File Number
```

FIGURE 7

The bit entries will be described along with the interrogator and control nucleus actions.

-214-

SOFTWARE TESTING CONTROL SYSTEM

Services Provided.

The 'A Bit' is initially set to one by the control nucleus requesting service. Upon finding the active bit set, for this JSF entry, the interrogator then picks up the active kernel number 'AKN'.

Now that the interrogator has detected an active service request, and the requesting kernel number, a service scan takes place. The 'D' bit is next examined for an internal data request from the kernel. If the 'D' bit is on, the interrogator picks up the 'DFN' data file number entry. This 'DFN' value is passed to the internal data generator, along with the kernel number 'AKN'. The internal data generator then goes to the external data table and gathers information on the format of data to be generated. The record is placed in a JSF buffer common to the interrogator and control nucleus. At this point, the 'DR' bit is set on.

If the control nucleus does not need data, it may pass a result block to the interrogator. Accordingly, the control nucleus will place the result data in a common JSF buffer and set the 'R' (results ready) bit. The interrogator sees this and picks up the result and writes it to the result file. When that is finished, the 'R' bit is reset by the interrogator. Continuous results may be passed by the control nucleus.

A test kernel may request a snap dump. The control nucleus will load a common JSF buffer with the beginning and ending addresses of the desired snap area. It then sets the 'S' (snap requested) bit. The interrogator sees this and calls the snap transient, and passes the addresses. When the snap completes the 'S' bit is reset.

The last bits to be analyzed concern termination of the interrogator/control nucleus inter-job communication link-up. When the control nucleus has received termination requests from all active kernels, it sets the term request (TR) for the active load module. The interrogator is notified and services any outstanding requests. Then the termination bit (T) is set by the interrogator which tells the control nucleus to terminate the load module.

E.P. YOUNGBERG

CONTROL NUCLEUS In the previous section we showed how the
KERNEL INTERFACES different bit settings triggered interrogator action. Now we will consider how
the kernel causes the control nucleus to set all of the job
service bits.

Initialization.

Figure 8 shows the sequence of actions necessary to request service (ie., set the 'A' bit).

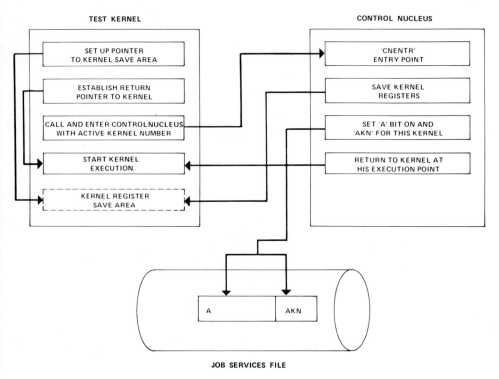

INITIALIZATION OF TEST KERNEL

JOB SERVICES FILE

FIGURE 8

Internal Data Request.

The kernel may request an internal data record generated previously. In making this request the conventions
shown in Figure 9 cause the D, DR, and DFN entries in ISF to
be initialized.

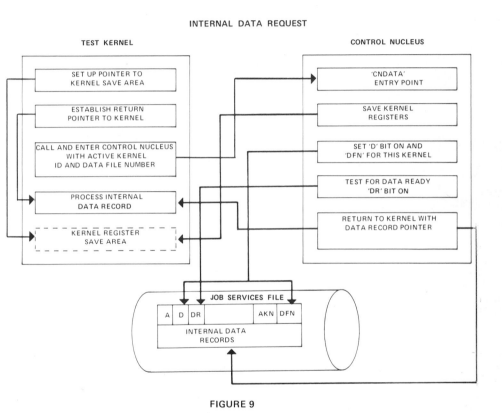

FIGURE 9

Kernel Snap Dump Requests.

The kernel may have internal areas snapped. This is
accomplished by a subroutine call to the control nucleus at
the entry point 'CNSNAP'. The action of calling CNSNAP will
cause the beginning and ending addresses of the desired snap

area to be picked up and the 'S' bit set on.

Figure 10 shows the necessary conventions to be followed.

KERNEL SNAP REQUEST

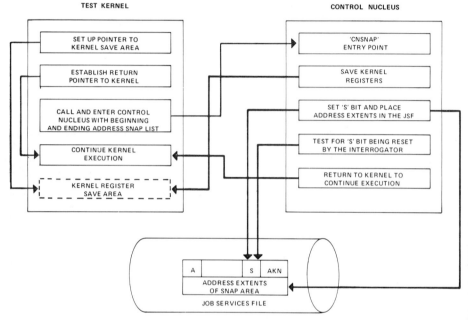

FIGURE 10

Control Nucleus Request for Result Reporting.

In order for the test programmer to pass results of
self-checking options in his program to the control nucleus,
certain report code standards must be followed.

The following is a list of information that must be supplied upon any kernel entering the control nucleus.

1. Result Flag. This is used to indicate the results
   of a given option. The value of a character 0 (F0)
   indicates pass; a character 1 (F1) indicates fail.
2. Component Code. This is an alpha code for the type
   component being tested.
3. Feature Code. This value indicates the feature being tested.

4. <u>Option Code</u>. This byte is used to describe up to six options for any given feature. The test programmer has the choice of Codes 1 through 9, A through Z, to be used as an Option Code.

5. <u>Kernel Name</u>. Supplied by the kernel to identify the reporting initiator.

Figure 11 represents the interface convention.

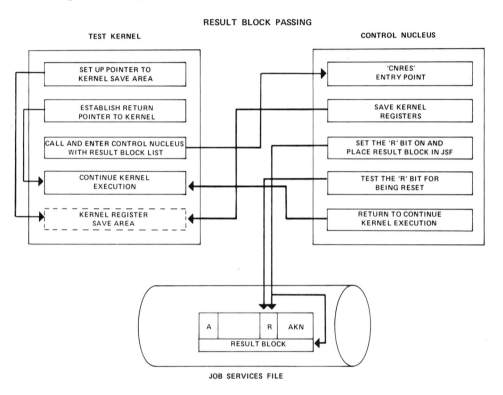

RESULT BLOCK PASSING

TEST KERNEL   CONTROL NUCLEUS

TEST KERNEL	CONTROL NUCLEUS
SET UP POINTER TO KERNEL SAVE AREA	'CNRES' ENTRY POINT
ESTABLISH RETURN POINTER TO KERNEL	SAVE KERNEL REGISTERS
CALL AND ENTER CONTROL NUCLEUS WITH RESULT BLOCK LIST	SET THE 'R' BIT ON AND PLACE RESULT BLOCK IN JSF
CONTINUE KERNEL EXECUTION	TEST THE 'R' BIT FOR BEING RESET
KERNEL REGISTER SAVE AREA	RETURN TO CONTINUE KERNEL EXECUTION

A		R	AKN
RESULT BLOCK			

JOB SERVICES FILE

FIGURE 11

E.P. YOUNGBERG

Control Nucleus Termination Request.

When kernels are linked with the control nucleus, for service requests, the interrogator must be notified of impending load modules termination. This is accomplished by the kernels first notifying the control nucleus, which in turn notifies the interrogator that the load module is about to terminate. The effect is scheduled termination, for the load module, and the interrogator deallocates the job service link. Control is eventually returned to the control nucleus which issues and end-of-job routine.

The control nucleus accumulates a list of kernels in a load module and marks them deactive. The 'TR' bit in JSF is set when all kernels are complete. The control nucleus then waits for the 'T' bit to be set on before issuing an EOJ. Figure 12 shows the kernel interface conventions.

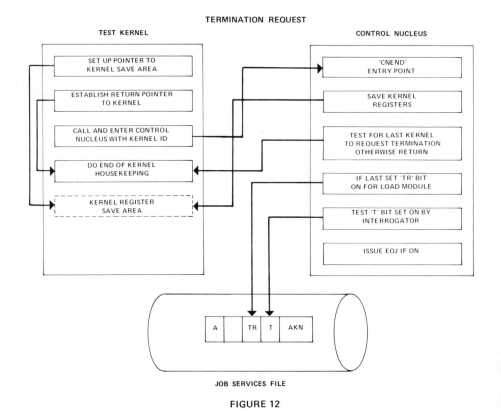

FIGURE 12

EXTERNAL
AND INTERNAL
DATA GENERATOR

External Generation.

The external data generator will be executed as a job
step prior to the kernel executions. In this way files may
be generated for those kernels that are testing a data management type component. Information for the generator is
obtained from the external data table. The use of an external data generator relieves the test programmer of creating
and maintaining data files.

Internal Generator.

The internal data generator is a subroutine that operates under the control of the interrogator and passes a record formatted to specifications in the external data table.
The maximum length of an internally generated record is 256
bytes and the maximum number of files to be generated at one
VCS execution will be four times the number of multiprogramming levels. The interrogator will pass the element name to
DATGEN to be looked up on the external data table, which
will contain the information necessary to generate the file.
The problem program will be responsible for any blocking or
IOCS.

The advantage of an internal data generator is to compare records read using data management, against an internally generated record. If the specifications are the same,
the records should be equal. This is a major requirement of
the testing process.

RESULT   This final element of VCS is written as a
REPORTING   separate program and executed as a job step.
ROUTINE   The result reporting routine takes data that
                  has been collected on the result file, and
sorts it by kernel name, component and feature. The data is
then printed in a report for later analysis.

E.P. YOUNGBERG

ADVANTAGES OF   The advantages of a testing control system
A TESTING   are:
CONTROL SYSTEM

    1. Efficient use of the host computer.
    2. Interaction of software functions at the component
       level.
    3. Interaction of software functions at the systems
       level.
    4. A powerful tool to ease the tasks of data generating
       and result analyzing in the test process.
    5. A rigorous control of the test application to easily
       pinpoint failure areas.
    6. A vehicle to help evaluate system degradation.
    7. Most of all, a way to ensure a systematic approach
       to the testing process.

CONCLUSION   A testing control system is the next step
                in the evolution of software validation.
Many groups are now attempting to provide still further sophistication of testing philosophies. The concepts and tools
discussed here have been implemented, thus proving their
feasibility. It must be seen if what remains to be developed
and what remains for experimentation will prove just as feasible. Whatever the outcome, the need for a control mechanism
that fully validates the system software is necessary for today's complex operating systems. Finally, the sophisticated
user community demands, and deserves, software packages that
perform optimally, as specified.

MODELS
OF PROGRAM BEHAVIOR

I cannot refrain from feeling that many testing aids that are en vogue now are invented as compensation for the shortcomings of a programming technique that will be denounced as obsolete within a short time.

— Edward Dijkstra

In the study of ideas, it is necessary to remember that insistence on hard headed clarity issues from sentimental feeling, as it were a must, cloaking the perplexities of fact.

— Alfred North Whitehead

THE COMPLEXITY OF PROGRAMS

Harlan Mills

International Business Machines Corporation
Gaithersburg, Maryland

17

INTRODUCTION   We consider the complexity of programs to be
the "third dimension" in data processing, in
addition to the dimensions of storage and processing requirements. This third dimension is more difficult to quantify
but no less important. We have seen great strides in the
past twenty years in both the amount and speed with which data can be stored, retrieved, and processed. But we have seen
little corresponding improvement in our ability to handle
complexity in programming.

Fifteen years ago it was confidently predicted that in
ten years the chess champion of the world would be a computer, but that hasn't happened. Ten years ago there were
much more serious hopes in command and control, management
information systems, and many other areas of computer applications. And these hopes have been largely unrealized as
well. At the same time, a close examination of what computers do today could prove embarrassing in many instances.
They carry out numerical and clerical activities at great
rates, but often with very little intelligence and very much
inefficiency. It is not that intelligent and dedicated people have not tried hard. It is simply that the computers,
with their vast, but elemental, capabilities, are difficult
to harness and apply to problems requiring even a modicum of
intelligence.

The principal barrier to the application of computers to
intelligent problem solving, or even intelligent assistance
for human problem solving, is the barrier of complexity.
Computers go fast enough and store enough data to do much
more than they do now, but they are not programmed to do so.
And the barrier of complexity which limits the development
of applications programs is largely generated by the programmers themselves. The first layers of software we create to
deal with programming problems become so complex that we have

little remaining intellectual capacity to deal with problems by programming. As Pogo once said, "We have met the enemy, and he is us."

THE
COMPLEXITY
BARRIER
It is difficult to recognize a barrier without knowing that it exists. Five hundred years ago the world did not know that air had weight. Air is hard to measure, hard to put on a scale, and seemingly, of no weight at all as we move within it. Yet, in retrospect, we now know that air has weight -- at set level the weight of a column of water some 34 feet high.

Imagine the frustrations of a well pump manufacturer 500 years ago, whose hypothesis is that "nature abhors a vacuum." By constructing a pipe with a plunger containing a one-way valve, one can draw water up from a well 15 feet deep on the premise that nature abhors a vacuum. By tightening the seals on the plunger one can draw water from a 25 foot well. By continuing to tighten seals and to machine the inside of the pipe to closer and closer tolerances, water can be drawn higher and higher. But in attempting to raise water 35 feet, no amount of care will avail.

In hindsight, it is all too easy to see the well pump manufacturer's difficulty. He is up against a barrier of which he has no inkling. When that barrier is discovered, his whole approach to making well pumps changes accordingly and he becomes less frustrated and more effective in his manufacturing operations.

In computer programming, we have not yet discovered that complexity has weight. We know that programs require both storage and processing time. We can measure and control these effects. But we do not measure complexity -- the effect of adding one more branch or one more shared data reference to a program. As a result, we run into the same difficulties as our imaginary pump manufacturer, in hitting an unknown barrier with no inkling that it exists.

SYSTEM
DEVELOPMENT REALITIES

In human terms, not being able to measure and control complexity means that it is practically impossible to conduct an intensive development of a set of integrated programs over more than a three to four year time period. By that time we have a set of programs that are so complex and so unwieldly that we can do little more than try to keep them running, as we often uncover more and more obscure errors that plague the operation under changing data conditions. In a real sense, such a set of programs has become a victim of its own complexity. As time and personnel pass, such programs become harder to maintain and modify. Up to now, we have had the ultimate excuse of "conversion" to a new hardware base, in which the program is redone, but usually with little better results than before, in controlling complexity.

The first 25 years of hardware development has been so effective and explosive that programs have needed to be redone in new, more efficient, architectures. The development in hardware is maturing, however, so that breakthroughs in the storage and processing will be stretched out in time. The present generation of hardware will be viable from an economic and engineering standpoint over much longer time frames than before. These longer, viable hardware possibilities provide a new potential in programming which is presently frustrated by the complexity problem. It is the potential of evolving systems over as long as 25 years of continuous and intensive programming. As noted, we cannot now program more than three to four years intensively, without a system becoming a victim of its own complexity. But the potential is there in hardware to produce almost unlimited capabilities in clerical, numerical, and eventually semi-intelligent activities, if, in fact, the complexity barrier can be understood and removed.

THE ROLE OF
STRUCTURED
PROGRAMMING

The development of structured programming, as initiated by Dijkstra [B20], is motivated by the problem of complexity. It is a first broad attempt to deal with the complexity of control logic in programs, although not much has been developed for the control of data reference complexity as yet. The main feature in structured programming is the connection between static text and dynamic execution of programs. Programmers can inspect static text and more easily visualize its dynamic execution than is otherwise possible.

The rigorous use of structured programming principles can change the programming process in a radical way and bring it under effective manufacturing control for programs of a few tens, or even hundreds, of thousands of instructions, in which a relatively small team of programmers can cooperate on a prescribed problem, as reported by Baker [B1]. One characteristic of the intelligent use of structured programming techniques is high precision coding, in which a significant fraction of program modules are correct from their inception with practically no debugging, and in which the global structure of a program is highly visible for maintenance and modification.

However, as programs grow in size and in unexpected ways because of new functional requirements or opportunities, additional advantages of structured programming emerge. The initial advantages of structured programming accrue from an intelligent, goal-directed form of programming, in which the goals are known a priori. With unexpected evolution, it often occurs that incidentals and accidentals of previously written programs become important, either for their use or in their limitations. And the structured evolution of such programs permits the control of complexity which would grow dangerously otherwise.

Structured programming entails inefficiencies in storage and processing, but in practice, these inefficiencies appear to be outweighed by the better mental control programmers have over the development and maintenance of programs. In retrospect, it appears that programmers are "penny-wise and dollar-foolish" in trying to program without sufficient structure. In contrast, structured programming is obviously "penny-foolish" and possibly "dollar-wise." It is not a foregone conclusion that programmers will be "dollar-wise" with structured programming, but the possibilities are there, if the programmers are so capable.

THE COMPLEXITY OF UNDERSTANDING PROGRAMS These problems and possibilities motivate a deeper investigation into the measurement and control of complexity. We recognize that we are dealing with a human problem, rather than a logical one. The computer never gets "mixed up". We do not need to control complexity because of any difficulty in the computer following its instructions. The control is necessary because people get confused, in developing and interpreting instructions for the computer. In illustration, we point out that the computer never knows that it is engaged in multiprogramming -- it simply executes instructions one after another. One instruction may load a program, but the computer cannot tell that from data. Another instruction may jump to a new program for execution, but the computer cannot tell that from an internal jump to another part of some presently executing program. In short, the whole fabric of programming theory in terms of subroutines, multiprogramming, etc., represents attempts to factor problems of complexity into smaller units to be treated by human intelligence.

A PRINCIPLE OF
EQUIVALENCE
We postulate that the complexity of a program is equivalent to the difficulty of proving the program correct. This equivalence may seem impractical at first glance, but we will see that it is capable of theoretical quantification and heuristic evaluation on a pragmatic basis. Proving a program correct is, ultimately, a subjective activity, even though more or less formal logic can be used to articulate and bound the limits of that subjectivity. The difficulty of proving any theorem depends on the logical theory within which the proof process is carried out. That is, the complexity of a program turns out (by this principle of equivalence) to be relative to the subjective basis for deciding on its correctness. While this may seem paradoxical, we believe further reflection will demonstrate the necessity for such a human-oriented consequence.

We also take the proof of correctness of a program to be synomonous with its documentation. Thus, we are also saying that complexity is equivalent to the difficulty of providing adequate documentation for a program. More precisely, we define documentation to be a correct abstraction of program execution into some context - as coined by Floyd [E4], assigning a "meaning" to a program.

A proof of correctness of a program can be carried out at many levels. At the lowest level is a direct appeal to intuition - the mathematician's "it is obvious that...".

H. MILLS

For example, in the sum program,

```
sum:   s = 0

       do i = 1 to 10

             s = s + x(i)

       end,
```

it is "obvious" that s receives the sum of the first 10 elements of array x. But even this simple sum program can be
proved correct more formally, through an induction argument
on i and on the relationships of various intermediate values
of i and s. Floyd [E4], Naur [E23], and Mills [G4] have
given formal procedures for proving the correctness of programs. In particular, Mills has given a set theoretic procedure for proving the correctness of structured programs,
which reduces to verifying equality among pairs of finite
sets. Eventually, it is expected that the number of steps
required to make these verifications will be related to a
quantitative measure of the complexity of a proof of program
correctness.

RATIONAL   Every program begins its existence, at
PROGRAMS AND   least in conception, as a realization of
NATURAL PROGRAMS some idea or purpose. But when the program
                 comes into being, it exists independently
of whether that purpose was well served or not. A large program, or programming system, will go through a typical history, from its conception to implementation, and on to usage,
maintenance, and further modification, often by programmers
not fully familiar with the program in its entirety. In this
lifetime, such a program becomes more and more mysterious in
its internal mechanisms, and knowable primarily through its
external behavior.

We will use the terms *rational* and *natural* to refer to the
knowledge available about the internal mechanism of a program. A rational program is one whose internal mechanism is
transparent to some set of people; a natural program is one
whose internal mechanism is known to no one. Clearly these
terms rational and natural are subjective, and describe the
ends of an entire spectrum of partially understood programs.

But the distinction is an old one -- a cow is a natural mechanism, while a clock is a rational one. We can study cows to make better use of them, and even evolve better strains, even though the biological and genetic processes are mostly mysterious to us. But we can fix a clock by replacing critical parts of its mechanism in a way we cannot fix a cow -- in the latter case veterinary medicine primarily provides an environment for a mysterious, but somewhat predictable, process of healing.

It may seem curious, but there are useful natural programs now in existence -- programs in frequent use, which are known entirely by their activity -- like a cow -- while the internal mechanism is no longer known to anyone. As long as such a program is useful as it is, it will continue to serve its users. But it cannot evolve, if it becomes obsolete; it cannot heal itself if it is faced with new changes of data it cannot handle correctly. As a matter of fact, the mechanism of such a program exists for possible deciphering in its code -- much as hieroglyphics. If important enough, human energy could be put to the task. But ordinarily, there will be a better way to address the user's problem (likely in a later generation machine or programming language).

The past twenty years have seen the creation of a great many programs which have passed into the natural domain, become obsolete, and died "natural deaths." These programs represent, collectively, a considerable waste of mental effort that went into their conception and implementation. As noted, up to now the pace of hardware improvements, with the escape of "conversion" has masked this waste. But we continue this waste at our peril, in limiting the growth of programming applications.

In our terms, a natural program is one whose complexity has become extremely large. The difficulty of understanding it, and proving it correct, has become so great that it is no longer worth doing. Conversely, our objective in measuring and controlling complexity is to keep a program rational -- to maintain its structure and documentation in such a form that its internal mechanism remains transparent for repairs and evolution as usage dictates. It is evident that the "aging" of a program from a rational state to a natural state is inevitable under enough stress and evolution. But our objective is to increase the "rationality phase" from a typical three years or so to thirty.

MEASURING   It does not take very much thinking to dis-
COMPLEXITY   cover that measuring the complexity of programs
is no simple task. It is easy to form sim-
ple hypotheses about such measures, but it is just as easy
to demolish them with counter-examples of common experience.
The idea of equating complexity with the difficulty of understanding a program has been generated out of the frustrations of concocting and demolishing more simple-minded direct ideas, such as counts of branches, data references, etc.

Our expectation is that the idea of proof provides an
especially concise and precise model of understanding, and
will be amenable to counting processes, which we can interpret
as measurements. As in the construction of any theory, of
course, we do not seek ultimate truth -- rather we seek a
set of ideas rooted on a small enough base of agreeable axioms that we have some confidence for a reasonable life ex-
pectancy before the inevitable inconsistencies and inadequacies begin to appear.

FUNCTIONS AND   We emphasize the common mathematical notion
PROGRAMS   that a <u>relation</u> is a set of ordered pairs,
c.f. Halmos[1], say f. If, in addition, the
first members of such pairs are all distinct, we say f is a
<u>function</u>, as well. The fact of membership $(x,y) \in f$ is often
written as $y = f(x)$ from custom; x is called an <u>argument</u>, y
the <u>value</u> of the relation or function f. The sets of first,
second members of the ordered pairs of a relation or function,
are called the <u>domain</u>, <u>range</u> of the relation or function, respectively.

Since relations or functions are sets, it makes sense to
use the terms "empty relation," "empty function," etc., and
to consider set theoretic operations, such as union, intersection, difference, etc., on them. Relations are closed

[1]Halmos, Paul R., <u>Naive Set Theory</u>, D. Van Nostrand Col, Inc.
(Eds. J. L. Kelley, P.R. Halmos), Princeton, New Jersey,
(1960).

under union, intersection and difference.

We abstract the commonly known idea of a (computer) program as a finite set of finite functions, called instructions, each with finite domain contained in a common set, called the data space of the program, and range contained in the cartesian product of the data space and the program, called the state space of the program. A member of the data space, state space, is called a data value, state value, respectively.

A program execution is a sequence of state values, say

$$s_i = (d_i, f_i), \quad i = 0, 1, \ldots$$

such that

$$(d_i, s_{i+1}) \in f_i, \quad i = 0, 1, \ldots$$

which terminates, if ever, when $d_i \notin \text{domain}(f_i)$. Since the state space is finite, it is decidable, for every initial state value $s = s_0$, whether that execution terminates, and, if so, what the final state value is, say t. Therefore, a program automatically specifies a set of terminating executions $\{(s=s_0, s_1, \ldots, s_n=t)\}$ and a set of ordered pairs $\{(s,t)\}$ defined by the terminating executions, called the program function. The program function of program f is denoted by $[f]$.

We note the well known distinction between a function and rule, and recognize, in retrospect, that a program is, indeed, a rule for calculating the values of its program function. In fact, the foregoing provides a set theoretic basis for the concept of rule, which is often introduced as a primitive notion in a function theoretic discourse.

We also abstract the idea of an indeterminate program as a finite set of finite relations, called indeterminate instructions, with data space and state space defined as above. The idea of execution follows precisely as given above, and an indeterminate program thereby specifies a relation between initial states and final states, called the (indeterminate) program relation.

-233-

THE CONTROL
PARTITION OF
A PROGRAM

As Dijkstra [B2] has pointed out, a program exists in two forms, as *static text* and *dynamic process*. The static text describes the set of instructions, usually in some typographical format with the control logic partially shown in the text sequence. The dynamic process is given by the executions of a program. Note the terms "static" and "dynamic" are human-oriented terms, rather than logical terms -- the executions exist as logical objects just as much as the instructions.

If the text of a program is limited enough in extent, and simple enough in control logic, and if the functions are simple enough as well, a programmer can inspect the static text and visualize the dynamic process directly. That is, in Floyd's [E4] terms, the programmer can understand the meaning of a program, see what the program does with data. The mental process involved with understanding the meaning of a program -- or, involved with constructing a program with an intended meaning -- is an extremely complicated inductive/deductive human activity. But we can outline some of its features for common agreement and analysis. One major step in connecting text and process is the mental expansion of text into branch free text sequences, corresponding to classes of executions using identical instruction sequences. A second major step is the mental execution of instructions along those branch free sequences. These two steps are often intermingled in a mental visualization of the process invoked by the text.

The first step can be identified with a partition of a program function, or more readily with a partition of the set of all terminating executions of a program. Every terminating execution defines a unique composition of functions each of whose domain and range is included in the data space of the program -- the data space projections of the instructions. But many executions may define the same composition. In this way, we define the *control partition* of a program to be the partition of its program function which identifies members defined by identical compositions.

We believe that the control partition of a program identifies a major part of the mental difficulty in connecting static text with dynamic process.

The control partition of a program is related to its branches -- but it is deeper than that. A program with no branches has a one element partition, namely the entire program function. But a program with branches may also have a one-element partition. In particular, the sum program:

```
sum:    s = 0

        do  i = 1 to 10

               s = s+x(i)

        end
```

has a one element partition. The control logic contains branches, but the branching depends solely on the "bound variable" i, and is independent of the data in array x. On the other hand, the program

```
        s = 0

        do i = 1 to 10 while x(i) ≥ 0

               s = s+x(i)
        end
```

which adds the elements of the array x up to the first negative element, if any, has an eleven element partition.

PROGRAM   Given a function (or relation) g and a pro-
CORRECTNESS   gram (or indeterminate program) f, we say f
                is correct with respect to g if [f] = g. In
theory, the determination of correctness reduces to the e-
quality of sets [f] and g. But ordinarily, it is not practical, even though logically decidable, to carry out this comparison in complete detail. Therefore, we introduce measures of program correctness to describe human credibility
about the possible outcome of such a comparison, even though
it may never be made. In this connection, we observe the
remark of Dijkstra [B5], "Program testing can be used to show
the presence of bugs but never to show their absence." That
is, we need find only one element in one, but not both, of
[f] and g,. to show [f] ≠ g; but to show [f] = g we must examine every element of both [f] and g.

In seeking human credibility about the correctness of programs, we identify three general levels of consideration-- logical, statistical and pragmatic -- and two areas of examination -- program text and execution, as diagrammed briefly below.

	Logical	Statistical	Pragmatic
Text	Correctness Proofs	Inspection Statistics	Desk Checking
Execution	Exhaustive Testing	Usage / Test Statistics	Selective Testing

Origins of Credibility in Program Correctness

FIGURE 1

Each of these levels contains a spectrum of possibilities -- for example, correctness proofs are possible all the way from first order predicate calculus to purely verbal arguments, and desk checking may be very superficial or very thorough. It is also clear that text examination carries with it the imaginary execution of the program in order to form conclusions about correctness.

The actual measures of human credibility vary with their origins. Correctness proofs exist or not (and by authors inspiring various credibilities themselves). Usage statistics usually suggest error rates, or mean times to next errors. Selective testing provides a subjective confidence, usually inversely proportional to the number of errors turned up and corrected. In fact, selective testing often reflects an intuitive form of stratified statistical test design, based on the internal mechanisms of a program.

There is little in the literature to date on the possibility of inspection statistics, particularly those based on the intentional, but random, seeding of errors in a program, in order to calibrate the error finding process itself. A brief development of such an idea is contained in Mills [G4].

Our main emphasis here is on correctness proofs, of various levels of formality. But the other origins are noted because any treatment of complexity should include any means of credibility. Our present understandings do not address those other means, but we flag their absence and our ignorance thereby.

Proving the Correctness of Table Lookup Programs.

Consider a program which accepts a function or relation, say f, and a possible argument x , and carries out a table lookup for a value y, if any as follows:

```
y = undefined
while f ≠ ∅ do
      s ε f
      if p1(s) = x then
              y = p2(s)
              f = ∅
      else
              f = f - {s}
      end if
end do
```

Here, sεf means s is any element of the (nonempty) set f, p1 and p2 are projection operators which pick out the 1st, 2nd members of an ordered set s. This program, it is claimed, does a table lookup in f for argument x, producing a value y, if such an argument x exists in the table.

Note the program also destroys f (assigns ∅ to f) in execution. We can imagine a proof of the correctness of this table lookup program. Once such a proof and program is accepted as correct, that program can be used for various sets of ordered pairs f to realize various functions or relations. How do we prove such a program (with a specific table) realizes a function or relation correctly? We can prove it by "proofreading" the table, comparing element by element, the ordered pairs of the table with the ordered pairs of the function or relation. There are many ways this can be done. For example, let f be a set of ordered pairs (table) and g be a program function to be realized by the table lookup program. We need to verify that f = g. It is claimed that the following program will compare two sets for equality.

```
match = undefined
while f ∩ g ≠ ∅ and match = undefined do
        if f∩g = ∅ then
            match = false
        else
            s∈f∩g
            f = f - {s}
            g = g - {s}
        end if
end do
if match ≠ false then
        match = true
end if
```

Let us suppose we have also convinced ourselves of the correctness of this matching process. This process represents a certain amount of effort, in extracting elements of sets and comparing them, in deleting elements from sets, and deciding if sets are empty. We.believe the effort represented here is a reasonable upper bound for the difficulty of proving the table lookup program correct for a given table.

It clearly depends on the number of elements of a table. If bit matching procedures are used in comparison, then it depends on the number of bits required to represent the elements of the table.

ANALYZING SEQUENCES OF OPERATIONS
PERFORMED BY PROGRAMS

18

J. H. Howard and W. P. Alexander
University of Texas, Austin

INTRODUCTION   Many interesting properties of programs can
be stated in terms of the sequences of operations they perform. The uninitialized variable problem for
example can be described as a violation of the rule: "In
any computation of a program using a variable X, some operation which assigns a value to X must precede all operations
which use the value of X." A second example is found in
communication between processes in a multiprogramming system.
Correct communication requires that each process obey a protocol such as that of the "critical section"[1] in which the
process must set an interlock before accessing a shared data
structure and subsequently must release the interlock. The
objective of the research described here is the development
and automation of a procedure for verifying that programs
obey given ordering rules on the sequences of operations
they perform.

Traditional debugging by enumeration of cases breaks
down for large and complex programs such as operating systems. The procedure described here uses verification rather
than simulation techniques, which is to say that programs
are checked out by direct inspection of their source code
and are not actually run. It consists of comparing a given
source program with a prototype for correct sequences of operations and reporting those parts of the program which cannot be matched with the prototype.

The structure of this paper is as follows. The second
section describes the basic ideas of the approach, including
the description of programs and their computations by state
graphs, algorithms for manipulating state graphs, and the

[1]Dijkstra, E.W. Cooperating Sequential Processes, In Program-
ing Languages (F. Genuys, Ed.) Academic Press (1968) 43-112.

overall structure of the verification procedure. The third
section describes the realization of the procedure in an experimental analysis program and gives more detail about the
algorithms used. A point of special interest about the analysis program is that it has been applied to real programs
taken from a real operating system. The final section summarizes the applications to which the analysis program has
been put.

BASIC   This section summarizes the theoretical as-
CONCEPTS   pects of analyzing sequences of operations.
                 Although a certain amount of formalism is
used, proofs and detailed definitions are omitted for the
sake of brevity. State graphs and their correspondence to
programs are defined first, followed by a general technique
called folding for manipulating state graphs. The class of
program characteristics analyzable by the state graph technique is defined in terms of folding into a prototype graph.
Finally, the overall structure of the analysis procedure is
stated and some general considerations are discussed.

State Graphs

    A state graph is a directed graph with labeled edges.
Several edges with different labels may connect the same pair
of nodes, and a node may have several edges with the same
label entering or emerging from it. The nodes of the graph
correspond to program states, that is, to the distinct combinations of values of all memory cells used by the program.
The contents of registers, such as the instruction location
or program counter, are also included. The edges of the
graph correspond to the sequential transitions of the program
from state to state as it runs, and are labeled with the symbolic operations performed.

    Formally, a state graph is an ordered triple $G = (S, A, \rightarrow)$
where S is a set (the states), A is a finite set (the operations), and $\rightarrow$ is a subset of the Cartesian product $S \times A \times S$.
We write $x \underset{\rightarrow}{a} y$ if (x, a, y) is an element of $\rightarrow$.

    The state graph of a program explicitly describes the
set of computations of the program in terms of paths through
the graph. Sequences of operations, or traces, are simply
the sequences of edge labels along such paths. Unfortunately,

the state graphs of actual programs are quite large if not infinite, so it is impossible to deal directly with them. A general technique called folding is used to compress and modify state graphs in finite space and time.

Folding

Folding is the merging together of states while preserving the edges involving them. This is formalized as follows. A homomorphism of graph $G = (S, A, \rightarrow)$ into a graph $H = (T, A, \rightarrow)$ is a mapping $f: S \rightarrow T$ such that

$$x \xrightarrow{a} y \text{ in } G \text{ implies } f(x) \xrightarrow{a} f(y) \text{ in } H.$$

If such a homorphism exists then H is a folding of G. A thorough discussion of graph homomorphisms is given by Hedetniemi.[2]

It is easily shown that since a folding preserves individual state transitions, it preserves paths and thus sequences of operations. Said another way: If ab...c is a sequence of operations in G, and H is a folding of G, then ab...c is also a sequence of operations in H. Note however that the converse is not true. A folding can introduce spurious traces unless its inverse is also a folding. Whether or not the spurious traces do any harm in the analysis depends on the context in which the folding occurs. The general strategy is to keep the state graph as folded as possible without introducing undesirable spurious traces.

The foregoing definition gives no hint as to what an appropriate homomorphism is like. In analysis of programs, foldings almost always can be defined by ignoring selected program variables. If the variables of a program are divided into two sets, one to be preserved and one to be ignored, then the program's state set can be considered to be a Cartesian product $S = A \times B$, where A represents the values of the interesting variables and B those of the uninteresting ones. Assuming this has been done, an appropriate folding is the projection mapping $f(a,b) = a$, which simply discards the uninteresting variables. Actual foldings can be much

[2] Hedetniemi, S.T. Homomorphisms of Graphs and Automata. Technical report, Communication Sciences Program, The University of Michigan, 1966.

more selective than this, ignoring variables only in parts
of the state graph for example.

Assembly language programs themselves are extreme examples of folding of their state graphs, in which every variable except the program counter is ignored. The states correspond directly to the addresses of instructions (program counter values) and the symbolic instructions label the transitions from state to state. Throughout we label the edges
corresponding to conditional branches with the outcome of the
branch. The folded state graph directly defined by a program
is a simple modification of the program's flowchart, with the
operations labeling the edges rather than the nodes.

Uses of Folding

Folding has several uses in the analysis of programs using state graphs. It allows finite representations of infinite state graphs. It may be used to manipulate a state graph
by unfolding it in some ways and refolding it in others to
get a more explicit or compact representation of interesting
sequences of operations. Last but not least, it provides a
characterization of the kinds of properties that can be ana--
lyzed using state graphs. The last will be described next,
using an example and then a definition.

Dijkstra's "critical sections" are a tool for coordina-
ting asynchronous parallel processes. They are defined in
terms of four primitive operations:

P - set an interlock which prevents any other process
    from performing the P operation until this process
    has performed a V operation.
V - Release the interlock.
A - Access the shared data structure protected by the P
    and V operations.
ϵ - Any other (irrelevant) operation.

A process is defined to be correct in its usage of these
operations if and only if its state graph can be folded into
the prototype of Figure 1 which follows on the next page.

The node at the left represents the noncritical part of
the program, and the node at the right is the critical section. The correctness criterion defined by the prototype is
that a program may not access the shared data or do a V operation if it is not in its critical section, that it may not

-242-

halt or do a P operation when it is in its critical section, and that the P and V operations switch the program between the noncritical and the critical sections.

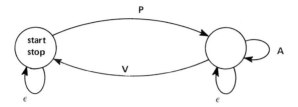

FIGURE 1. Origins of Credibility in Program Correctness

As suggested by this example, the properties which can be verified using state graphs are those which can be stated by defining a prototype into which any correct program should be foldable. All program verification techniques must eventually appeal to intuitively acceptable standards of what makes a program correct. The prototypes play this role here. The objective is not to verify the prototype in any way, but rather to decide if a given program can in fact be folded into the prototype.

Comments on the General Technique Used

The technique for verifying that a program can be folded into a given prototype is divided into three steps:

1. Convert the program's symbolic source deck into the flowchart-like folding which ignores all variables but the program counter.
2. Transform the initial folded graph to represent distinctions in the values of "critical" variables and to eliminate superfluous detail.
3. Attempt to fold the transformed graph into the prototype and report success or failure. If failure is reported, identify the portions of the program which could not be folded into the prototype.

The details of automating these three steps are discussed in the next section. There are, however, several points which deserve further discussion.

Referring back to the critical section prototype, note

that all "uninteresting" operations were lumped together in a single operation labeled ϵ . Note also that the prototype allows such operations in any legal sequence. This is a common phenomenon in prototypes and deserves some special treatment as it can be used to fold considerable uninteresting detail out of the state graph.

An operation is "unitary" if it appears in the prototype only on unit loops. (A unit loop is a transition $x \xrightarrow{a} x$ which does not change the state.) It is "uninteresting" if it is unitary and every state of the prototype has such a unit loop. In the critical section prototype, A is a unitary operation and ϵ is uninteresting. An edge of the program state graph is unitary or uninteresting if it is labeled with a unitary or uninteresting operation. Uninteresting edges are also called null edges. Such edges provide a special opportunity for folding the program state graph as follows:
1. Any two nodes connected by a unitary edge may be folded together. The resulting graph will be foldable into the prototype wherever the original was, because the two states in question must fold into the same state of the prototype due to the unitary edge connecting them.
2. Once the above folding has been accomplished, all unitary operations in the program state graph appear as unit loops. For uninteresting operations these loops may be eliminated entirely since it is known that they will be allowed in the prototype.

It should be noted that the general folding technique described above can introduce spurious illegal sequences if an illegal sequence already exists. For example, consider the effect of adding a null edge in parallel with the V edge in the prototype graph of Figure 1. This corresponds to a program's illegally jumping out of its critical section without releasing the interlock. The illegal sequences generated contain an excess of P operations. If the two states are folded together then spurious illegal sequences containing an excess of V operations are also generated.

The algorithms described in the next section avoid the generation of spurious sequences by constraining the application of folding. For example, the "only successor" rule allows folding of nodes x and y with the null edge $x \xrightarrow{\epsilon} y$ whenever y is the only successor of x. Such restrictions make it considerably easier to reconstruct the illegal path in the source program given an illegal sequence in its folded version.

The need for the second step of the technique which unfolds and refolds the state graph is best illustrated by an example. The following fragment of an Algol program contains a disguised critical section.

.
.
.

for I:= 1 step 1 until 3 do

begin

if I = 3 then V;

if I = 2 then A;

if I = 1 then P;

end;

.
.
.

Figure 2

Here P, V, and A are the primitive operations to be matched against the critical section prototype defined earlier. The initial state graph generated from this program fragment has the form:

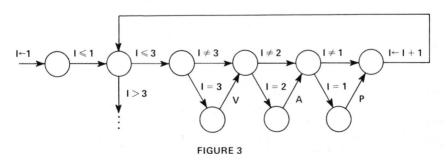

FIGURE 3

In this example the variable I is critical in the definition of the actual as opposed to apparent flow of control.
If the graph were simply folded to eliminate all operations
except for P, A, and V the result would be:

FIGURE 4

This graph cannot be folded into the prototype. Thus the
graph must be unfolded to reflect the distinct values of I,
giving the intermediate result:

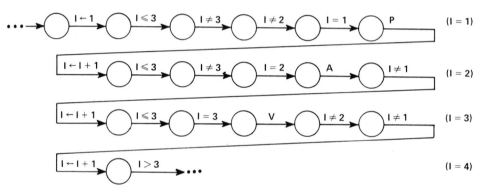

FIGURE 5

If this second graph is folded by deleting insignificant
operations, the result is

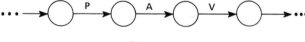

FIGURE 6

which obviously does fit the prototype.

The point of this example is that the initial folded
graph may need to be unfolded for certain variables which
play a critical role in determining the sequences of significant operations. The unfolding is done by splitting selected
nodes of the graph into separate copies for each different
value of the critical variable. This implies that a finite
set of such values must be known. This is a restriction on

the method, but fortunately critical variables usually satisfy the restriction.

The splitting procedure has been automated with one major omission: the identification of critical variables.
This is accomplished manually by input to the analysis program. Overlooked critical variables are quickly found since
they result in spurious paths which cannot be folded into the
prototype.

One major class of critical variables is identified automatically. This is the class of subroutine returns. State
graphs represent subroutine structure as follows. With each
subroutine is associated a variable the values of which
identify the points at which the subroutine is called.
This return variable is set before the subroutine is called,
and the subroutine returns to the proper point by branching
on the value of the return variable. The return variables
are automatically considered to be critical by the analysis
procedure, with the result that a separate copy of the subroutine is inserted at each point of call by the splitting
procedure. The finitude restriction on critical variables
implies that recursive subroutine calls cannot be handled.

The final step, folding the transformed state graph into the prototype, is accomplished by a straightforward matching process which defines the desired homomorphism. The process starts by matching the starting state of the program to
the starting state of the prototype, and extends the matching
to the rest of the graph by propagating matches based on the
homomorphism rule that $x \xrightarrow{a} y$ implies $f(x) \xrightarrow{a} f(y)$. It is simplified by requiring that the prototype be deterministic.
This is easily accomplished manually, either by inspection
or by the use of the power set technique borrowed from the
theory of finite automata.

TECHNIQUES   The ideas and methods of the previous sec-
              tion have been implemented in a program
called TRACE. TRACE is divided into three independent sections which sequentially perform the major steps in producing a compact state graph for a given object program. BUILD
reads the source code and generates an initial state graph.
SPLIT resolves questions which arise when the program branches
on the values of critical variables. CLEANUP performs final

folding and outputs the graph in various forms suitable for external analysis, and may also immediately verify that the object program does or does not conform to the order-of-operation rules specified by the user-supplied prototype graph.

Building the State Graph.

The only major inputs to TRACE are the source code of the object program and a list specifying which instructions or operations in the source code are to be considered interesting. This list must always contain all instructions which affect the flow of control within the object program such as jumps, branches, subroutine calls and returns, and program stops and ends. Additional items on the list will depend on the application. In the table interlock example, the operations which reserve, access, and release the table will be included.

In the present version of BUILD if these operations of interest are not explicitly coded in one or two lines or with a macro, the source code must be "doctored" by the user; a unique instruction must be invented to represent the interesting operation, and must be inserted at the appropriate points in the code and included in the list of interesting instructions. Occasionally unobvious code may have to be re-written; for example, table jumps must be replaced with explicit branches.

BUILD reads the source code one line at a time selecting those lines which have location labels or whose op-code is on the interesting instruction list, and ignores all other lines. For these interesting lines, appropriate additions are made to the state graph. Labels cause the creation of a new node corresponding to the state of the machine just before the labeled instruction is executed. This new node then becomes the "current" node. These program location labels are attached to the nodes so that later the user may easily see which nodes correspond to which sections of the source code. Jumps cause the creation of a null edge between the current node and the node corresponding to the location jumped to, and the creation of a new current node. Application-dependent interesting actions such as semaphore operations cause the creation of an appropriately labeled edge from the current node to a new node corresponding to the new state of the machine after the interesting action has taken place.

BUILD may be told by the user to keep up with the value
of certain critical variables which affect the flow of control within the object program. When these variables are set
to a value in the object program, this information is attached to the current node. When the program branches on the
value of these variables, BUILD creates two null edges from
the current node, and tags the edges with the condition under
which each path is taken. For example, if the variable
SWITCH has been designated critical, the segment of source
code in figure 7 will result in the graph segment of figure
8.

```
           JPOS    LOC1      branch to LOC1 if (acc) ⩾ 0
           P       J         reserve table J
           LOAD    1
           STORE   SWITCH    SWITCH ← 1
           JUMP    LOC2      unconditional jump to LOC2
                   .
                   .         (uninteresting code)
                   .
   LOC1    LOAD    0
           STORE   SWITCH    SWITCH ← 0
                   .
                   .
   LOC2            .
                   .
                   .
           LOAD    SWITCH
           JZERO   LOC3      branch to LOC3 if SWITCH = 0
           V       J         release table J
   LOC3            .
                   .
                   .
```

FIGURE 7

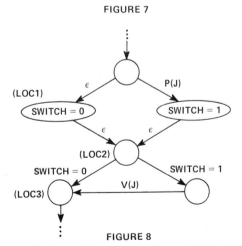

FIGURE 8

When a branch is made on a value which BUILD has not
been told is critical, two untagged edges result, and the
state graph contains a nondeterministic branch such as the

-249-

one from the top node of figure 8. BUILD automatically handles subroutine calls and returns as setting and branching on, respectively, the value of a generated critical variable.

Splitting.

The directed graph produced by BUILD contains complete information about the sequence of operations which the object program does, or may, perform, but it will generally be too large and too complex to be useful. The folding techniques for reducing the size of the graph are described in the next paragraph. The complexity arises because of the conditional edges which result from subroutine returns and from branches on other critical variables. SPLIT resolves such conditional paths by creating two or more copies of the graph segment corresponding to the (possibly) different sequences of actions performed as the critical variable takes on its range of values. This splitting process begins at the node from which there are conditional edges and propagates backward along the directed graph to the nodes at which the critical variable acquired known values. For example, from the graph segment of figure 8, SPLIT will produce the graph segment of figure 9.

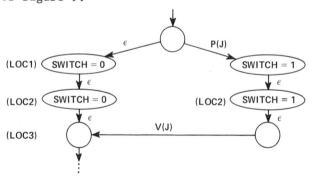

FIGURE 9

SPLIT keeps a pushdown stack of "question nodes", nodes from which there are conditional edges. This stack is initialized to contain all the question nodes in the graph originally produced by BUILD. SPLIT begins each execution of the splitting algorithm by considering the top node of the stack. If it does not have associated with it answers to all of the questions on its outgoing edges, this node is split, the questions propagated back onto its incoming edges, and all of its predecessor nodes are pushed onto the stack. Loops are handled by marking each copy of the split node with the corresponding value of the critical variable. When the stack is empty, SPLIT terminates.

Folding.

The initial state graphs produced by BUILD can be quite large; for example the graphs representing operating system programs written in CDC6600 peripheral processor assembly language average about one node for every three lines of executable source code, and about 1.5 edges per node. (These ratios will probably vary depending on the source language and nature of the program.) The splitting algorithm greatly increases the number of nodes. Thus both to conserve memory and in order to reduce the amount of work to be done by subsequent portions of TRACE, it is imperative to reduce the size of the graph as much as possible at each stage of the process. This reduction is accomplished by folding. Folding may introduce new traces into a graph, and although the general folding rule given in the second section will never introduce spurious illegal traces into a graph which did not already contain at least one, the folding rule can be modified so as never to introduce them. It can be easily shown that applying the following two rules will never introduce spurious illegal traces:

1. If node I is directly connected to node J only by a null (ϵ) edge from I to J, and either a) I has no other successors, or b) J has no other predecessors, then I and J may be combined.
2. If there is a null edge from node I to J and a null edge from J to I, then I and J may be combined.

In addition, null edges from a node to itself, and one of a pair of identical edges between the same two nodes, may be eliminated. When two nodes are combined, location labels and information regarding the value of variables attached to either of them are attached to the combined node, with duplications eliminated. Nodes connected by a conditional edge are never combined.

The above rules are incorporated into a routine called FOLD which applies them in turn to each node in the graph. If any combinations were made in a pass through the whole graph, then FOLD again applies the rules to every node, and the process is repeated until a pass has been made in which

no new combinations occurred. Applying FOLD to the graph
segment of figure 9 produces the graph segment of figure 10.

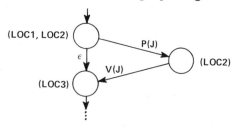

FIGURE 10

FOLD is applied to the graph as soon as BUILD has finished and is usually able to cut its size in half. During
the execution of SPLIT, FOLD may be called whenever memory
gets crowded, and is always called when SPLIT has finished.
It has been found that at this point even very large object
programs will be represented by graphs having no more than
40 nodes, and usually less. It therefore becomes practical
in CLEANUP to apply folding rules with more sophisticated
criteria for combining states:

3. Any two nodes whose sets of outgoing edges are identical, with respect to both labels and successor
   nodes, may be combined.
4. If there is a closed path, no matter how long, consisting entirely of null edges from a node back to
   itself, then all the nodes along this path may be
   combined into one node. (Notice that this is a gen-
   eralization of rule 2; in rule 2 the length of the
   path is just two).

When all of the folding rules have been applied to every
node in the graph without any new combinations occurring,
the graph is completely folded. CLEANUP will then output the
final graph and may also try to match the graph against a
prototype graph.

APPLICATIONS   The program called TRACE, described in the
AND CONCLUSIONS previous section, is an experimental version
                 of what we hope will become a useful tool
for program verification and system debugging. Its primary
purpose so far has been to verify that the techniques described in this paper are in fact practical. In its present

form TRACE is written in FORTRAN and requires 42000_8 words of memory on a CDC 6600. From the runs that have been made, it appears that TRACE requires less than 2 seconds of central processor time per 100 lines of source code to produce the final state graph for a program.

Despite its experimental nature, TRACE has been used to verify one aspect of the UT2 operating system used at the University of Texas Computation Center. TRACE has been run on 6 of the system programs which access the Job Status Table to verify that they all adhere to the semaphore protocol. It can be used in its present form to verify that all programs adhere to the correct protocols for reserving channels, disk and ECS space, etc.

The state graphs produced by TRACE are of use in connection with a major performance measurement and evaluation project currently in progress on the UT2 operating system. This project includes an event driven trace which eventually produces directed graphs representing sequences of actions actually taken by programs including system programs.[3] All these events can be detected by TRACE in the source code of the same system programs. Thus the graphs produced by TRACE can be used to preset the event trace. In addition, comparison of the two graphs produced by these two different methods helps to verify each method and may indicate sections of source code seldom or never executed, sections which are heavily used, etc.

Most of the problems encountered so far in implementing the techniques described in this paper arise in the input and recognition phase in which the initial state graph is produced from the source code. Not all interesting actions are automatically recognized. The value of critical variables may be set by an input statement. At present such problems must be handled by modifying the source code. An average of about one modification per 75 lines of source code have had to be made by hand to enable TRACE to correctly recognize all interesting operations.

[3] Sherman, S.,Howard, J.H., and Browne, J.C. A Comparison of Deadlock Prevention Schemes using a Trace-Driven Model. Sixth Annual Princeton Conference on Information Sciences and Systems, Princeton, N.Y., March 1972.

Another area for future research is language independence. The fact that the source code operations which are to be considered interesting are input at run time indicates that TRACE could be run on programs written in different source languages with little or no modification, but this hypothesis has yet to be tested.

A great deal of research needs to be done to determine just how many interesting properties of programs can be stated purely in terms of the sequences of operations they perform, and for those properties which cannot be so described, whether or not any state graph techniques can be applied to them.

EXTENSION OF HARDWARE FAULT DETECTION MODELS TO THE VERIFICATION OF SOFTWARE

19

Jean-Claude Rault

Central Research Laboratory, Orsay, France

INTRODUCTION   Until now, the general problem of testing digital systems has been tackled mainly from the hardware side for which numerous proven methods have been devised and are presently used in industrial environments.

On the other hand, as a survey of the technical literature immediately reveals [E13], the software side has been comparatively less developed.

This state of affairs has an historical reason. Until some time ago hardware cost was far greater than software cost in complex systems; today the situation is reversed and software takes the main share. Consequently there is a stringent need to develop aids for fast and economical software design.

CHARACTERISTICS   Until a few years ago, software design was
OF SOFTWARE   considered more of an art rather than a
PRODUCTS   science [A12]. As a consequence software
                    products have the following characteristics:

1. the probability of being faulty is great.
2. a low transferability.
3. a high disparity between the costs, the delays for production and the performance of several products having the same function but different origins.
4. reduced capabilities for changes: experience shows that it is generally more economical to construct a totally new product rather than to modify an existing one.

These findings have induced the software developers to

look for rational methods for designing software. Such methods are generally referred to as "Software Engineering."

IMPROVING
SOFTWARE

Three methods have been used, so far, for improving the quality of software products and for easing the programmer's task.

Improvements in Program Writing Methods:

This approach mainly concerns improvements at the programming language level. It is supported by the fact, generally admitted, that nearly half of the errors have to be imparted to the language alone: either it lacks generality or versatility, or it includes too many inconsistencies, or it may even burden the programmer with too many constraints which are not relevant to the problem he is dealing with.

A programming language can be improved either through its definition itself, or by combining software and hardware [M7]. This latter technique is well exemplified by hardware protection devices which check that array bounds are not exceeded during computation. This is not the case in FORTRAN.

Use of Elaborate Debugging Aids:

This is certainly the technique most in use nowadays. It consists simply in writing a program and then running it. In case of improper results, the programmer resorts to the debugging aids he may have at hand; among them one generally finds [M4, M6]:

1. syntax checking
2. selective trace
3. programmed stops
4. monitoring of certain significative variables
5. semantic analysis at the compilation level [D11]

The efficient use of these tools is highly dependent on the programmer's skill.

Formal Proof of Program Correction:

Many valuable research studies have been undertaken in this field. In spite of interesting results in particular cases one cannot expect, within the near future, a dramatic solution to the verification of complex programs.

EXTENSION OF HARDWARE METHODS TO SOFTWARE DIAGNOSIS   The techniques described above allow one to assure software quality only to a certain extent. One may wonder whether they are the only ones and whether it would not be possible to take advantage of methods intended for hardware in order to devise new methods for software verification and fault detection.

One will first be inclined to apply hardware reliability theory to the assessing of software quality. This does not seem to be possible since software products differ too much from hardware ones. In particular, no parallel between the ways that software and hardware age can be drawn. A software product is never frozen and is undergoing continual modifications.

Nevertheless there is another direction where promising extensions could be found: methods for fault detection and location in digital circuits.

As a matter of fact, the analogy between digital circuits and programs is quite natural. It is usual to derive for both programs and circuits a graph whose nodes correspond respectively to primary logical functions and to instructions. The generation of input test combinations corresponds to the generation of test cases for programs.

Methods of generating test sequences for digital circuits proceed from two main principles: one is deterministic, the other probabilistic.

Deterministic principle

Under this heading are gathered methods by which input sequences for detecting and/or locating faults from a given list are derived either through analysis or synthesis.

This principle has been applied to software fault diagnosis by means of the D-cube algebra, which is a formalization of the concept of path sensitizing for faults in digital

J. C. RAULT

circuits[1].

For the time being this extension is limited to certain programs written in a simplified language for algorithm specification [A20].

Probabilistic principle

Two general schemes proceed from this principle.

The first one, pertaining to analysis, consists mainly in deriving though simulation the possible faults detected by random input combinations. Such a method allows one to determine quickly detection tests for a fairly high percentage of the total number of possible faults. However, this method is no longer economical for 100% detection.

This scheme has been used in the generation of test programs for checking compiler front ends [H3]. A program produces randomly built tests, syntactically correct but without any semantic meaning, written in the language of the compiler to be checked.

In the second testing scheme both the circuit being tested and a fault-free reference circuit are fed in parallel with random input signals. The output signals are monitored and compared. Should a discrepancy be detected by the comparator, the testing is stopped and the tested circuit is declared faulty.

The question is to know how to run the test for a given probability of error, or in other words, what is the number of random input combinations to be imposed before a circuit is considered "good."

We intend, in what follows, to extend this testing scheme, devised for LSI circuits, to program verification.

---

[1] J.P. Roth = Diagnosis of Automata Failutes - A Calculus and A Method, IBM Journal of Research and Development, Vol.10, No.4, P.278-291, July 1966. and - Programmed Algorithms to Compute Tests To Detect and Distinguish Between Failures in Logic Circuits, IEEE Transactions on Electronic Computers, Vol. EC-16, No.5, P.567-580, October 1967.

In fact this statistical and comparative scheme corresponds to a new programming technique which has been in an experimental stage for a year and a half since the introduction of an APL system in our Research Laboratory.

CHECKING PROGRAMS THROUGH COMPARISON   In order to apply this statistical and comparative testing scheme to program checking, a reference program, the counterpart of the reference circuit mentioned above, has to be determined first.

Reference Program Determination:

In the case of digital circuits, the reference is either a simulation program or a real circuit built in a technology more favorable for total testing.

In a similar way in the case of programs, the reference may be taken as another program written in a language different from the one used for the final product but allowing fast and economical debugging.

In other words the reference program is written in a very high level language intended for specifying algorithms accurately and quickly rather than for executing them efficiently. Several languages possessing such characteristics already exist, but only a few of them have been implemented [F10, F15, F14, F16, F17].

Among the possible languages is APL, which, in spite of certain limitations well known to its detractors, allows one to produce quickly executable first versions of complex programs.

This possibility led us to a new programming technique, which, in spite of being highly empirical, seems to be rewarding after real life experiments.

This programming technique consists of two phases:

During the first phase, the algorithms entering in a complex program are defined and checked with an APL system.

In the second phase, the APL functions obtained in the

J. C. RAULT

first one are then translated into another more classical
language (usually FORTRAN) and allowing efficient executions
on present computers.

The APL program version allows one to determine random
test cases and to get the corresponding results the tested
program is supposed to provide. Two types of results are
monitored: those after execution is performed and the intermediate results obtained at the different test points placed
at certain strategical places. The choice of these points
is still empirical and calls for skill on the programmer's
part. However this choice could be made automatic if the
program graph is analyzed by means of one of several segmentation techniques presently available. [C1, C8, C12, C17,
C21].

DETERMINATION   In order to assess such a checking method
OF THE   quantitatively it is important to connect
TEST LENGTH   the number of test cases to be randomly
                 drawn (or the test length) to the allowed
probability to declare a faulty program "good."

The number of test cases may be determined through the
following reasoning:

Let P be the allowed probability and Pe the probability
for proper functioning of a faulty program.

The test length L should be such that:

$$(Pe)^L < P$$

$$\text{or} \quad L > \frac{Log\ P}{Log\ Pe}$$

The minimal value of this length is given for the maxi-
mal value of Pe, the probability for the tested program to
behave correctly in spite of errors.

The worst case value for Pe, depending on both the program function and the program structure, can be computed in
theory. However, its rigorous computation may not be feasible due to the combinatorics involved in it.

Nevertheless some computation may be contemplated. Consider Pe_i the probability associated with each node i in the graph, i.e., with each instruction in the program. This probability can be considered as a product of two coefficients: the first one corresponds to the probability of reaching instruction i in the program, the second one corresponds to the probability of the effect of a fault being detected at one of the program exit points.

Computations of this type are similar to those necessary for propagating random signals in graphs derived from digital circuits [C18] or from programs [D9, C11].

For programs written in classical programming languages these computations may not be feasible practically. The use of a high level language such as APL, tending as a rule to reduce the complexity of the program graph, should result in great simplifications for computing the two coefficients in Pe_i.

In fact, having an accurate value for Pe_i is of no real concern, an approximation is sufficient. An heuristic method, based mainly on graph theory, is presently under investigation.

CONCLUSION   The testing strategy described above is not intended to provide a radical solution to the question of program checking and proof of correction. However, we contend, in spite of its present empirical features, that it should lead, as preliminary experiments have demonstrated, to rewarding practical results.

This technique assumes the availability of a high level language, such as APL, being simultaneously well suited to the specifying of algorithms and run on present computers. Several other languages meeting these requirements are under development; among the most typical is the SET language [F15].

The use of such languages is not restricted to the field of program verification.

When used concurrently with a second language of lower level but potentially more efficient, they are a good aid for introducing the notions of quality and reliability in the

J. C. RAULT

early stages of program design.

As a matter of fact the two-phase programming technique has many advantages over conventional techniques:

As a first phase provides a concise program, the designer is thus able to get a general overview of complex programs. This is not the case with conventional programming techniques in which the programmer is forced to have in mind simultaneously both the abstract concept of algorithms and the problem of their practical implementation on a computer.

The ease with which the programmer obtains an executable version without having to tackle the inner and intricate details of a definitive implementation is a high incentive for him to experiment with different possibilities in order to reach the best arrangement for the program under development.

With conventional techniques the designer must wait until the whole program is completed before he can really experiment. And generally, after a long and costly development, he is either not prone to or does not even have the opportunity to undertake the necessary iterations. In short, as the programmer himself is well aware, the final product is not optimal.

This program writing and verification technique should find full scope with the advent of programming systems which allow, in the same program the simultaneous presence of modules written in the two languages mentioned earlier and the automatic translation from one to the other.

Such a scheme would allow translating naturally and directly the definition of algorithms into their practical computer implementations while assuring a full agreement between the end product and its specifications.

In conclusion, these systems would be an intermediate step toward filling the chasm between the conciseness in algorithm definition and their present materialization as computer programs.

Acknowledgement

The author wishes to express his gratitude to Dr. J.P. Vasseur of Thomson-CSF and to Pr. J.J. Arsac of the University of Paris for their advice and many stimulating discussions.

ACCEPTANCE TESTING FOR APPLICATIONS PROGRAMS

J. Grant Holland

Naval Systems Support Activity, Washington, D. C.

INTRODUCTION   Applications program acceptance testing affects anyone who designs, develops, moni-
tors or uses functional systems. But it is a subject which
has received little serious consideration--either procedural
or theoretical.

Two types of persons are interested in testing applications programs: the developer and the acceptance tester
(user). The essential distinction between the two is that
the developer must be assured that every detail of his program functions properly, whereas the acceptance tester is interested in the validity of the final product. An immediate
consequence of making this distinction is that the developer
is operating from a position of knowledge about the program,
and is therefore able to approach testing deductively and
analytically. On the other hand, the acceptance tester,
operating under the constraints imposed upon him by his assumed ignorance of the program and, in general, his lack of
interest in its detailed structure, must approach the program
as a "black box" into which he places inputs and from which
he receives outputs. That is, his approach to testing will
be empirical. Consequently, theory and methodology for two
types of testing must be developed.

Previous work on computer program testing has concentrated in areas that are of more interest to the developer than
to the acceptance tester. London has reported several methods for proving programs correct (all deductive in nature),
and Good has developed a mathematical model for computer programs which he uses to prove that certain methods for proving
programs correct are, indeed, valid. On the other hand, a
thorough search has found no literature on acceptance testing.

In this chapter, pertinent literature is reviewed, the
acceptance tester and the developer in a common environment

are compared, and the implications of that comparison to developer and acceptance tester are discussed. Some considerations toward development of a theoretical model which treats
an acceptance test as an empirical rather than an analytical
process are suggested. In so doing, Good's mathematical model of computer programs, which he calls an *a-process*, is relied on heavily.

REVIEW OF   Substantial work has been done in the area
PERTINENT   of proving programs correct. This approach
LITERATURE   is characterized by Good [14]; *It has been
             argued...that correctness of programs
should be "proved" in the same sense as one might prove a
mathematical theorem.* London [E16] discusses six techniques
for proving program correctness and gives examples for each.
Among these techniques are case analysis, assertions, mathematical induction, and prose proof. Good [14] defines a
mathematical model of which a computer program is a special
case. From this model he generates the technique of proving
programs correct called the inductive assertion method. He
then presents some considerations toward a man-machine system
of proving programs correct which can be applied to nontrivial,
real-life programs.

London [E13] presents a bibliography on proving the correctness of computer programs, while Prokop in Chapter four of
this book presents a synopsis of the development of proving
program correctness. Prokop concludes that *we are not very
much advanced in the art or science in proving programs correct* and that ... *the emphasis really should be placed on
the applicability of techniques in a production environment
to computer programs which are somewhere in the middle of
this continuum which goes from trivial to impossible.*

Rubey, et al [G6] defines seven groups of attributes,
or properties, which one thinks a computer program should
possess. These include program correctness, time and memory
utilization optimization, program intelligibility, easiness
to modify, easiness to learn and use, program design and accuracy. The report points out how metrics may be defined to
measure the degree to which a program possesses each of the
attributes.

Vander Noot [A7] expresses the lack of articles that can

be found on the subject of "systems testing", and, from a
practical viewpoint, considers the complexities of testing
a system of application programs for a production environment.

Gruenberger [A7] expresses his belief that ...*testing is
more of an art than a science. There are no rules for testing...*, and that *the program must be run with known test data
that leads to known answers*. But, his comment that *The goal
is to increase our confidence level in the ability of the program to perform its task* is found more interesting.

ACCEPTANCE TESTER   "Acceptance Tester" rather than "user" is
VS. DEVELOPER IN   used because the two are not necessarily
A COMMON   equivalent. Frequently, the acceptance
ENVIRONMENT   tester is a middle man between the develop-
                    er and the user. This situation arises
when the user is not ADP oriented and secures the services of
someone who is to test a program that is being developed for
his use. Another case is that of the facility which operates
the program in a production status. Its concerns are (1) that
the program does not impact or abuse the facilities, and (2)
that the user is satisfied with the program as it operates
in the production environment.

In any event, the acceptance tester exhibits the following properties: first, due to reasons of time, inclination,
or funding, he cannot assimilate as much knowledge about the
information flow internal to the system as the developer
possesses and second, he is interested in maximizing the
probability that the program is all that he wants it to be.
That is, he wants to increase his confidence in the program.
And what does he want his program to be? Rubey, et al, elaborate on attributes a program may or may not possess and the
degree to which it possesses these attributes. These attributes can be summarized as follows:

1. The program is valid. A computer program is designed to
   represent some information process, P. The acceptance
   tester asks the questions, Does the program represent P
   rather than some other information process?, and Does
   the program represent P accurately? This is validity.
   The tester is interested in maximizing the probability
   that the program is valid.

2. The program makes efficient use of the hardware/software environment in which it operates. The tester is interested in minimizing the probability that the program will impact the production environment, or malfunction due to some incompatibility with the environment. The program design should reflect awareness and familiarity with support software and hardware configuration and consideration of possible future changes in such. Also, backup procedures should be developed and tested in order to decrease the likelihood that the program will not be operational at any time.

3. The program is easy to learn, use, and modify. Has the program automated as much data manipulation as is feasible? Does the program inform the user when he has input nonsensical data, and does it pinpoint his input error? Does the documentation assume that the user knows more about the program than he needs to? And, from a pedagogical standpoint, is the documentation well designed?

The developer is likewise interested that his program is valid, that it makes efficient use of available hardware/software, and that it is easy to learn, use, and modify. However, he exhibits two properties that make his approach to testing different from that of the acceptance tester. (1) Because he designed and coded the program, he can determine by deduction precisely what the sequence of executions and data generations should be for any set of parameters that one inputs to the program, and, (2) consequently, he is in a position to prove his program correct, and also to prove that his hardware/software utilization has been optimal[1].

Example

As an example of an environment in which both development and acceptance tests are conducted, we shall turn our attention to the Naval Command Support Activity, Washington, D.C. This organization is a software development house for Naval commands. Its responsibilities include (1) development of systems of applications programs, and, (2) the production phase, the maintenance and operation of these systems of programs for the users.

---

[1]Thiess, H.E., Mathematical Programming Techniques for Optimal Computer Use, Proceedings of the Twentieth National Conference of ACM, pp. 501-512.

ACCEPTANCE TESTING FOR APPLICATIONS PROGRAMS

The development phase can be viewed as a sequence of
stages: system analysis, system design, program coding,
debugging, testing, documenting, and user training. The developer's first concern is that he produce a program or system of programs that can read inputs of prescribed formats
and produce meaningful and valid outputs. Secondly, he must
be assured that his program does not exceed certain resource
utilization restrictions which are imposed upon him by the
availability of facilities. He is limited to the amount of
core memory, mass storage, and run time his program can utilize. He must also consider the logistics of how the inputs
will be transported from the user's desk to the core memory,
and how the output will be transported from the core memory
to the user's desk. The developer is interested in optimizing user satisfaction.

The production phase consists of acceptance testing of
a system of applications programs, and operation of the program for the user in a production status. An independent
group has recently been established to conduct acceptance
tests for completed applications programs, and to determine
whether the program is operational in a production environment. If the program is accepted, the group member assigned
to it monitors its operation to ensure user satisfaction and
to handle any problems which arise. There are numerous
development groups, but there is only one acceptance testing
group. During the acceptance testing state, members of the
testing group review the following for efficiency, validity,
or conformity to standards, as the case may be: documentation for the program, program design, hardware/software utilization, backup procedures, and user interface. And, of course,
the first requirement the acceptance tester demands of the
program is that it yield correct responses to inputs. Acceptance testing is conducted in three phases: the on—site
acceptance test, the remote terminal acceptance test, and
the user test.

Operational guidelines have been issued to members of
the testing group, but no techniques have been standardized
for acceptance testing principally because no literature can
be found which addresses itself to the topic. Experience
has shown that some programs about which the testers were
confident often fail to perform with consistency in their
production status. If adequate acceptance testing procedures
could be formulated, testers could have more confidence in
programs which they accept.

Observations.

Let us make some observations about the operation at the Naval Command Systems Support Activity. firstly, both the developer and the acceptance tester scrutinize many attributes of programs other than validity, such as optimum use of hardware and support software, and optimum use of service functions such as EAM support and transportation of output from computer site to user. The tester views the program as more than a software package. Rather, it is conceived by him as a flow of information originating and ending with the user. This macroscopic view is shared by the developer and the acceptance tester alike.

Secondly, members of the acceptance testing group do not have time or resources to learn the internal logic of the programs they test. The tester learns the general flow of information within the program; but, for him to learn the precise internal logic of every program he tests, would be prohibitively expensive and time-consuming.

Implications.

There is more to testing a program than checking to see if the program is valid. Of interest also is optimization of hardware/software utilization, effective program documentation, and user interface.

Developer testing and acceptance testing are qualitatively different. Since the developer is precisely aware of the logic of the program, he can attack the problem of a program from a flowchart approach. For any "branching point" (node) in the logic of the program, he can partition the set of all possible inputs to that branching point with respect to which branch (arc) would be taken as determined by the value of the input. He can then reason which operation would be executed for any branch taken, and deduce what the outcome of any data cell will be upon entering the next "branching point". His approach is characterized by deductive logic.

The review of the literature revealed that substantial work has been done along these lines to deductively prove programs to be correct. While these techniques are quite adequate for the developer, they do not satisfy the needs of the acceptance tester. The reason for this is because, in order for one to utilize these techniques, he must possess

a complete knowledge of the logic internal to the program.
While the acceptance tester may have a good deal of knowledge of the program logic, there is some point at which it
becomes a mystery to him (by the definition of an acceptance
tester). At this point, his testing will consist of selecting samples of inputs and observing the ensuing outputs. His
testing method will be empirical. Insofar as testing the
validity of a program is concerned, the acceptance tester
needs to know how to select his data in such a way that he
can attain some arbitrary percentage of certainty that the
program is valid. For example, he may wish to be ninety-five
percent certain that the program is valid. How should he
choose his sample data in order to ensure that level of confidence? He is interested in similar information regarding
other program attributes such as hardware/software utilization.

SOME CONSIDERATIONS The intent here is not to present a model
TOWARD A MODEL FOR for acceptance testing. In the first
ACCEPTANCE TESTING   place, as has been pointed out, any ap-
                     plications program has several attributes
which the tester is interested in scrutinizing, and this implies a possible need for several models. Secondly, the author has no model for any of these attributes to propose, at
this time.

This is an attempt to stimulate conversation about models
for acceptance testing. The considerations which shall be
presented here are designed for this purpose.

A case for approaching acceptance testing from an empirical stand has been made. Terminology such as "ninety-five
percent confident that the program is valid" has been used
in an effort to present the view that statistical rather than
analytical models are those by which acceptance testing will
be best described. With this assumption, it is necessary to
state the problem of modeling in a language amenable to statistical description. Specifically, stating the problem of
modeling a computer program empirically, for the purpose of
validating it, will be emphasized.

As has been pointed out, there has been substantial work
accomplished toward the development of a deductive model for
proving programs correct (valid). In particular, D.I. Good

has developed an analytical model for computer programs which
he calls the a-process. It is suspected that the mathematics
of the a-process is strong enough to imply a mathematical description of computer programs which is amenable to statistical formulation. This suspicion will be exploited after the
a-process has been presented.

The a-process.

The a-process is a mathematical model for algorithmic
processes, of which the computer program is a special case.
The a-process is defined in terms of a "directed graph" and
a "memory". The memory, M, is defined to be a finite ordered
n-tuple (vector) of "cells". That is, $M = (M_1, M_2, \ldots, M_p)$,
where the M_k's may be conceived as the locations of the data
area of a computer program. For every cell, M_k, there exists
a set R_k, such that for any time, t, exactly one element
$v_k \in R_k$ is associated with ("contained in") M_k. R_k is called
the range of M_k. Consequently, the Range of M is
$R = R_1 \times R_2 \times \ldots R_n$, or the Cartesian product of the R_k's. And
for any time, t, exactly one vector in R, $M(t)$, is associated
with ("contained in") M. $M(t)$ is the state vector of M at
time t.

In an a-process, a sequence of "operations" is performed
on M resulting in a sequence of state vectors in M for times
t_s, where s is a non-negative integer. However, for different values of the initial state vector $M(t_0)$ the sequence of
operations may vary. This is because the determination as to
which operation will be performed on the memory at time t is
determined by $M(t)$, the state-vector of M at time t. To describe these relations, D.I. Good defines the concept of a
directed graph. Let $N = \{N_1, N_2, \ldots, N_n\}$ be finite and
non-empty. Let A be a subset of $N \times N$. Then the ordered
pair (N,A) is called a directed graph. $(N_i, N_j) \in A$ is said to
be an arc of (N,A) and $N_i \in N$ is called a node of (N,A).

Now, with each node, N_i of (N,A), is associated a function w_i: $R \to R$ called a node operation. An executable instruction in a computer program may be conceived of as a node
operation. Let $N' = \{(N_i, w_i) \mid i \text{ is a nonnegative integer}\}$.

Also, with each arc $A_{uv} = (N_u, N_v)$ in the directed graph
(N,A) associate a predicate (open sentence) V_{uv} whose uni-
verse is R. V_{uv} is called the traversal condition for A_{uv}.
The following property is true for all traversal conditions

of a directed graph. Let N_n be a node. Let V_n be the set of all predicates whose arcs have N_n as their first entry. Then for any state vector in R exactly one predicate in V_n is true for that state vector. In other words, the collection of "truth sets" of the predicates in V_n is a partition of the range R of memory M. Define $A'=\{(A_{uv},V_{uv})\mid u, v \text{ are nonnegative integers}\}$.

Also true, for any node of the graph (N,A) is that its associated node operation is the identity function or that it is the first entry of no more than one arc.

Thus far, we have N', a set of ordered pairs of nodes with their associated node operations, and A', a set of ordered pairs of arcs with their associated predicates. Also, a graph must have at least one node with no "preceding" arcs, called E, and exactly one node with no "succeeding" arcs, called X. The ordered set $L = (E, X, N', A')$ is called an a-process with memory M and range R.

Note that for any initial input state vector $v = M(t_0) \epsilon R$, the relationship between nodes and node operations, arcs and predicates determines a sequence of node operations to be performed. Recalling that a node operation is a function from R into R, obtain the function L_v by composing (functional composition) the sequence of node operations which is determined by inputting v into the a-process L. If, for some v, the sequence of functions is not finite, then composing the w_i's will be undefined. If, for any $v \epsilon R$, the sequence of functions generated for it by L is a finite sequence, the last of whose node is X, then L is called an algorithm. In an algorithm for example, there are no "infinite loops". Let $L:R \rightarrow R$ be defined by $L = \{(v, L(v)) \mid v \text{ is an initial state vector } N(t_0) \text{ of the algorithm } L\}$. L is a subset of what D.I. Good defines as the "Memory function". L describes M at execution termination time regardless of $v \epsilon R$. Any pair in L shall be called an <u>execution</u> of L.

IMPLICATIONS OF GOOD'S MODEL TOWARD AN EMPIRICAL MODEL FOR ACCEPTANCE TESTING

Since our interest is in viewing an algorithm as a function from R into R (where R is the range of the memory M), attention is focused on L rather than on the a-process (algorithm) L. L is called an algorithmic <u>operator</u> on R. Every algorithm on M with range R induces exactly one algorithmic operator on R.

It was mentioned earlier that a computer program which we shall call P' can be viewed as a representation of some information process, P. This can be stated by saying that both P and P' are algorithms. And to say that P' "represents" P means that in some sense, P and P' are "alike". By looking at the <u>algorithmic operators</u> induced by P and P', it is intended at this point to define precisely in what sense P and P' are similar.

Let P and P' be algorithms on M and M' over ranges R and R', respectively. Let L and L' be the respective algorithmic operators induced by P and P'.

Recall that L is a function from R into R and L' is a function from R' into R'. Let us consider the pairs (R,L) and (R',L'). We shall call such pairs <u>algorithmic systems</u>. In much the same manner that <u>algebraic systems</u>, such as groups, rings, etc., are defined to be homomorphic, algorithmic systems will be defined as "homomorphic". Let H be a map from R into R'. H is said to be a homomorphism if $L'(H(a)) = H(L(a))$ for any $a \epsilon R$. If there exists a homomorphism from R into R', it is said that (R,L) is homomorphic to (R',L').

Suppose for example, that we have written a computer program to read three floating point values a', b', and c' (significant to three decimal places), and to replace the value of c' by the value of c' to the a' power added to the value of b'. (These operations of "addition" and "power" are hardware operators as defined by circuitry within the computer, and are qualitatively distinct from abstract mathematical operations.) We can treat this program as an algorithmic system (R',L'), where R' is the set of ordered triples of floating point values such as (.500, 3.000, 2.000) and L' is a function from R' into R', and in particular $L'(.500, 3.000, 2.000) = (.500, 3.000, 4.4.4)$.

Now, there is an information process that we hope our computer program has successfully "represented". This process involves associating ordered triples of real numbers (a, b, c) with ordered triples of the form (a, b, c^a + b). We can treat this process an an algorithmic system (R, L), where $R = \{(a, b, c) \mid a, b,$ *and* c *are real numbers, and* a *and* c *are not both zero* $\}$ and L is a function from R into R,

-272-

and in particular $L(\frac{1}{2}, 3, 2) = (\frac{1}{2}, 3, 3 + \sqrt{2})$.

Obviously, we wish to make an association between elements of R and elements of R', in an effort to say that they are "alike". This is accomplished by the mapping of H. For example,

$$H(\frac{1}{2}, 3, 3 + \sqrt{2}) = (.500, 3.000, 4.414).$$ Notice that H is not , in general, one-to-one (injective). For example, $H(\sqrt{2}) = 1.414$ and $H(\sqrt{2} + 10^{-117}) = 1.414$.

Notice that the relation $L'(H(a)) = H(L(a))$ holds for $a = (\frac{1}{2}, 3, 2)$:

$$L'(H(a)) = L'(.500, 3.000, 2.000) = (.500, 3.000, 4.414)$$
and
$$H(L(a)) = H(\frac{1}{2}, 3, 3 + \sqrt{2}) = (.500, 3.000, 4.414)$$

Having been given the algorithmic systems (R,L) and (R',L'), if $L'(H(a)) = H(L(a))$ for every $a \epsilon R$, then (R,L) is homomorphic to (R',L').

Now, to say that a computer program P' represents an information process is meant that (R,L) is homomorphic to (R',L') where L and L' are the algorithmic operators induced by P and P' respectively. To say that a computer program is valid for P means that there is an information process, P which P' represents.

Consequently, in order to determine whether P' is valid for P it must be proved that one algorithmic system is homomorphic to another.

Since each of the algorithmic systems is completely determined by the a-processes L and L' respectively, it is possible to logically deduce that one is homomorphic to the other, if indeed, it is. But, to do so, one must assume a complete knowledge of L. As has been pointed out, the developer has access to such knowledge; but, in general, the acceptance tester does not. He must be content with proving that L and L' are "alike" by observations. He must randomly choose some pairs from L and from L' and check to see if they are "alike". How does he know when he had made sufficient numbers of inspections to be "95% confident", that P' is valid for P?

J.G. HOLLAND

CONCLUSION   The preceding is a statement of the prob-
                    lems of acceptance testing as seen present-
ly. It is not maintained that this problem statement is the
best possible. Certainly, no theoretical model for acceptance testing has come out of it at this time. But it has
been presented in an effort to provoke thought on the subject.

        In the introduction to D.I. Good's thesis [14], he stat-
ed that the object of his research was to move toward the
goal of proving programs correct for "nontrivial, real-life
programs". Admittedly, this paper's statement of the problem of acceptance testing is quite distant from that end.
But to get to the end, one must start at the beginning and
travel in the right direction.

Acknowledgements

        The author would like to thank Commander Jan Prokop,
U.S. Navy, for his criticism, his recommendations, and his
time.

Through and through the world is infested with quantity: to talk sense is to talk quantities. It is no use saying the nation is large - How large? It is no use saying radium is scarce - How scarce? You cannot evade quantity.

- Alfred North Whitehead

In the space of one hundred and seventy-six years the Lower Mississippi has shortened itself two hundred and forty-two miles. That is an average of a trifle over one mile and a third per year. Therefore, any calm person, who is not blind or idiotic, can see that in the old Oolitic Silurian Period, just a million years ago next November, the Lower Mississippi River was upward of one million three hundred thousand miles long, and stuck out over the Gulf of Mexico like a fishing-rod. And by the same token any person can see that seven hundred and forty-two years from now the Lower Mississippi will be only a mile and three quarters long, and Cairo and New Orleans will have joined their streets together, and be plodding comfortably along under a single mayor and a mutual board of aldermen. There is something fascinating about science. One gets such wholesale returns of conjecture out of such a trifling investment of fact.

- Mark Twain (Life on the Mississippi)

A UNIFIED STANDARDS APPROACH TO ALGORITHM TESTING

21

W. L. Sadowski and D. W. Lozier
National Bureau of Standards, Washington, D. C.

INTRODUCTION   As more and more computing power becomes
                 available, and the mathematical models em-
ployed in engineering and science grow more complex and realistic, scientific computation is confronted with more difficult problems. These problems call for sophisticated mathematical and computing techniques. In particular, the need
for more and more accurate special function calculation is
rising steadily, and the mathematics community has responded
by developing new routines for such calculations. The algorithms developed by NATS [K1] and by the NBS Algorithm Project [K44] are only a few examples of the work being done in
this area at many institutions. By an algorithm we mean in
this paper a specific computer implementation of a mathematical method for computing a function.

Development of high-quality mathematical function routines is a long and difficult process. Experience of the
people working on the Bell Telephone Laboratories Numerical
Mathematics Program Library Project has shown that testing,
certification and documentation of a high-quality routine
requires over six man-months of work [K45]. Testing, in
fact, is a major component in the truly "professional" development of any mathematical function routine. Algorithm
authors frequently develop techniques to test the performance of their own products, but the effectiveness of these
techniques depends on the time available for developing them
and on the author's competence in the field of testing. All
too often the testing is less thorough and incisive, is more
time consuming, and finds its results less readily and widely
accepted than would be the case if a unified approach to
testing were to be adopted.

We propose below a systematic approach to algorithm
testing that derives from the experience of the National
Bureau of Standards in calibration and standards work. The

problems in performing such work for the national measurement
system and in software testing are analogous despite their
apparent dissimilarity. In each case the job is to ensure
that a tool, be it a measuring instrument or a mathematical
function subroutine, performs according to certain accepted
standards, and furthermore to ensure that these standards
are complied with in the long run. In metrology, periodic
calibration gives information on how the environment has affected a standard. In algorithm testing, periodic checks
give information on how changes in the computer operating
environment affect the precision of an algorithm. The language in which the testing system will be described in this
paper is the language of standards. Its use will emphasize
the basic unity between instrument calibration and algorithm
certification.

PROPOSED ALGORITHM TESTING SYSTEM	The proposed algorithm testing system will consist of a standards chain i.e., a primary standard, a transfer standard and a working standard.

The functions that each of these standards is to fulfill
is described below. Some of the uses to which a standards
system such as this can be put will be enumerated following
the description of the system.

Primary Standard

The *primary standard* is a tape that contains a set of
arguments and corresponding function values. Such a tape is
created for each major computer system on the market. The
set of arguments is chosen on the basis of the mathematical
properties of the function plus computer considerations such
as number base, word length and normalization. It also includes a subset designed to test the transfer standard, a
description of which appears later in the chapter. Note that
no question of tape compatibility between different computers arises, since primary standards for a particular machine
will be generated on a machine of the same type.

The cotangent function on the UNIVAC 1108 provides an
illustration. Based on hardware considerations, our test
methods require that a certain number of special mantissas
be supplied for each value of the floating point characteristic.

This means that the density of special arguments is logarith-
mically distributed. This density is indicated in Figure 1
by the dashed curve of the graph.

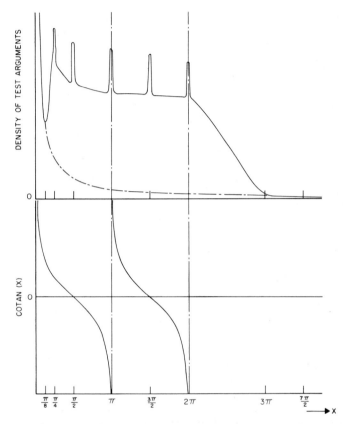

FIGURE 1. Density of Test Arguments for the Primary Standard
for the Cotangent Function

The region from 0 to 2π is supplied with additional arguments to test the behavior of the function in its first two
periods where most tabulated values are published. The peaks
at $\pi/2$, π, $3\pi/2$ and 2π are placed to test passage through
zeros and poles. Placement of similar peaks at large zeros
and poles is done but is off the scale of the graph. The
peak at $\pi/4$ is based purely on an algorithmic feature of the
transfer standard. The transfer algorithm for the cotangent,
given as an example at the end of the chapter has a crossover
point at $\pi/4$.

The choice of arguments for the primary standard is to
be fixed in consultation with the members of the testing
community. The correctness of the function values will be
established on the basis both of tabular checks and of independent tests by the members of the testing community. The
primary standard will thus be a consensus standard.

Transfer Standard

The *transfer standard* is a general algorithm, written
in standard FORTRAN, so as to be portable, for computing
function values. It is capable of computing these values to
arbitrary precision, i.e., with an arbitrary small truncation
error. In addition, of course, the chosen method must be
such that roundoff errors can be kept under control. A simple mathematical approach, such as a power series, allows
this to be achieved most easily. Simplicity is important in
an algorithm such as this because it builds confidence in the
checking and the use of the algorithm. To illustrate the
principles involved in constructing a transfer standard, a
FORTRAN subroutine from our transfer standard library is presented as an example at the end of the chapter. It computes
the sine and cosine functions.

The transfer algorithm must be used in conjunction with
a multiple precision arithmetic package such as that developed
by Maximon [K34]. Since its work will always be performed in
a specific computer environment, the use of a local multiple
precision package may offer the advantage of familiarity and
greater efficiency. The use of multiple precision in the
transfer algorithm is necessary because function values for
testing must be computed in a precision higher than that of
the computer, to eliminate the effects of roundoff.

One use for the transfer standard is to generate function values for the primary standard. Although this appears
to contradict the connotation of a "primary" standard, since
the transfer standard is apparently primary if it is used for
this purpose, such is not the case. As a primary standard
for mathematical functions, we feel that a set of argument-
function value pairs is the only acceptable entity. These
can be verified independently, whereas an algorithm can
never be tested for all possible inputs. Furthermore, since
the argument-function value pairs are stored on tape, they
are less susceptible to changes in the operating environment
than is a computer algorithm.

A UNIFIED STANDARDS APPROACH TO ALGORITHM TESTING

Working Standard

The *working standard* is a set of arguments chosen specifically for the subroutine to be tested, and of function values for these arguments as generated by the transfer standard. The set of arguments and function values is put onto a storage device such as magnetic tape, drum or disc, and is used when testing is required.

As an example of some of the features in which the primary and working standards can differ, consider an algorithm for the calculation of double precision tan(x) based on a Taylor series for x in $(0, \epsilon)$ and the rational function approximation TAN 4205   for x in $(\epsilon, \pi/8)$. Assume argument reduction is done in quadruple precision.

The working standard for this algorithm should include a large number of arguments straddling the crossover points at ϵ and $\pi/8$. Note that the density peak around $\pi/4$ in Figure 1 is of no particular interest and so need not be included in the working standard, although the peaks at zeros and poles would be retained. Since the main working region of the test algorithm is $(0, \pi/8)$ the bulk of testing arguments would be concentrated there, whereas the primary standard maintained a high density over the interval $(0, 2\pi)$. Because the precision of the argument reduction is limited, arguments larger than a certain maximum should return an error message. Arguments to test for the triggering of this error return will affect the density in the region of large x.

Calibration

The *calibration process* is performed as follows. The primary standard is used to "calibrate" the transfer algorithm as compiled on a specific computer with a specific multiple precision package. The calibration is done by an automatic comparison program such as our Bit Comparison Program [K31]. The calibration routine calls the primary tape and the transfer standard, applies the latter to the arguments on the tape, and compares function values. If the environment, i.e., the software and hardware, is in order, the transfer algorithm will generate values identical to those on the master tape. At this point the primary standard can be used directly for a rough calibration of the subroutine to be tested.

The second step in the calibration chain is to generate a set of arguments designed to test a particular mathematical function algorithm. Since the choice of arguments for the working standard is dictated by crossover points between the component algorithms of which the algorithm to be tested is made, and by the region of difficulty for each component algorithm, the preparation of the working standard is best left to the author of the algorithm to be tested. The transfer standard then generates function values for the selected arguments. Since a calibration routine, such as ours, will have a table of statistics that characterizes the performance of the algorithm, no retesting of the algorithm by an independent service is necessary for validation. From the study of the documentation describing the algorithm an expert in testing will see whether the choice and density of arguments are proper to test the algorithm. If so, a look at the statistics table will show whether the performance of the algorithm is in accordance with the specifications stated by the author of the algorithm.

Figure 2 shows a table of statistics from our Bit Comparison Program for the cotangent function.

NUMBER OF FUNCTION VALUES TESTED IS 8180

ARG   1 TO 8180 IN STEPS OF   1

BIT DEVIATION STATISTICS (FOR ARGUMENTS IN ALLOWABLE RANGE):

NUMBER OF FUNCTION VALUES WITH BIT DEVIATION OF 0 4620
NUMBER OF FUNCTION VALUES WITH BIT DEVIATION OF 1 2995
NUMBER OF FUNCTION VALUES WITH BIT DEVIATION OF 2 426
NUMBER OF FUNCTION VALUES WITH BIT DEVIATION OF 3 100
NUMBER OF FUNCTION VALUES WITH BIT DEVIATION OF 4 17
NUMBER OF FUNCTION VALUES WITH BIT DEVIATION OF 5 1
NUMBER OF FUNCTION VALUES WITH BIT DEVIATION OF 6 0
NUMBER OF FUNCTION VALUES WITH BIT DEVIATION OF 7 0
NUMBER OF FUNCTION VALUES WITH BIT DEVIATION OF MORE THAN 7 0

MAXIMUM BIT DEVIATION IS   000000000005

MAX BIT DEVIATION OCCURS AT   1   ARGUMENTS, THE FIRST HAVING SEQUENCE NUMBER   6918

NUMBER OF ERRORS NOT TRACED 13

NUMBER OF ERRORS TRACED 8

FIGURE 2

The "Bit Deviation" is the difference between the tested
function value and the standard function value, expressed in
units of the last bit position of the floating point mantissa.
The "Number of Errors Not Traced" is the number of error conditions not detected by the subroutine undergoing testing
that should have been detected. In this example, the subroutine failed to inform the user that certain very small arguments were invalid because the function values overflow the
range of the computer. The "Number of Errors Traced" is the
number of arguments that led to such error conditions that
were properly handled by the subroutine.

POSSIBLE USES   It is estimated that more than 90% of re-
OF THE STANDARDS   search and development work on mathematical
SYSTEM   software is duplication [K43]. Communica-
                    tions of the ACM lists 9 routines for Bes-
sel functions published between 1960 and 1971.[1] This number
is a small fraction of the routines available in various organizations. For instance, the contributed subroutine library of NBS has 11 subroutines for Bessel functions. The
proposed standards system will assist in the testing and
choosing of the best special function subroutines for certification.

By applying consensus standards to the testing of mathematical function subroutines, dissemination and acceptance of
certified subroutines will be aided. This work has to proceed in parallel with work on standardized documentation to
be fully effective. Reference [K32] is an example of an attempt to provide standardized testing documentation.

By requiring that a contributor to an algorithm journal
test his routines at least against the primary standard tape,
and preferably against a fully documented working standard
of his own making, the work of the editor will be reduced and
the reliability of published algorithms will improve.

It is known that an algorithm developed on one computer
will have an unknown error on a computer with either a different normalization or different word length, unless extended precision arithmetic is used. The errors are due to

[1]Communications of the ACM, 11 p.827, 12 p.693, 12 p.751.

differences in roundoff and truncation. The proposed system, if used in the development of an algorithm, makes it possible to test for errors due to transfer with only a small amount of effort.

The standards system is of use to the testing community as well. Frequently, performance testing of a mathematical function library is done by comparing test values to reference function values generated by the library on a computer with a greater word length [K18]. This means that before the test can be evaluated, any large discrepancy between a test value and a reference value must be resolved by eliminating the possibility of error in the reference algorithm. The standards system, with its high reliability, will make this unnecessary. By using a highly automated system such as the one proposed here, the testing community can devote more attention to the mathematical and programming analysis of the algorithms to be tested.

Finally, the ultimate customer, the physical scientist who employs or writes a great many routines for his own work, will have a simple tool for checking special function algorithms that he relies on, either individually or as part of a large program.

CONCLUSION The *technological base* for the system exists today. The NATS project is using reference tapes on various computer systems to check their special function algorithms. These tapes, in the language of this chapter, are working standards. The algorithm testing and verification project at NBS has developed both primary standard tapes and transfer algorithms as well as a highly automated package [K31] to perform the tests themselves. Thus the system is here today in components and it is just a matter of putting it all together.

An Example of a Transfer Algorithm

The FORTRAN subroutine SINE listed at the end of this section is an example of a transfer algorithm for computing sines and cosines. Transfer standards for other trigonometric functions are readily obtained from it. Since it is a multiple precision routine it makes calls to subroutines that perform arithmetic and various other operations. For the purposes of SINE all multiple precision numbers are represented according to a format to be described below. This format may not correspond to the format used by the multiple precision subroutines actually being employed. Therefore, these subroutine calls may be viewed as connections to interface routines which convert between formats.

Numbers are stored in one-dimensional integer arrays in a floating point format. For example, the array

NX(1) = 12345
NX(2) = 67890
NX(3) = 12345
NX(4) = 7
NX(5) = -1

stands for the number $-0.123456789012345(10)^7$. Here three cells are used for the fraction, but this is not a restriction since any number of cells may be used for this purpose. Furthermore, the number of digits stored in each cell is variable (here it is 5), subject to the limitation that the word size of the computer is not exceeded. Also, the number base need not be 10 but may be specified by the user.

These parameters are held in the COMMON block

COMMON/DGS/ND,ND1,ND2,NDW,NBRT,NBASE.

Here ND is the number of cells devoted to the fraction, ND1 = ND+1 is the exponent cell, ND2 = ND+2 is the sign cell, NDW is the number of digits per word, NBRT is the number base and $NBASE = NBRT^{NDW}$.

A list follows of external references to multiple precision coding in the SINE subroutine and their purposes. The symbols NA,NB,NC stand for integer arrays at least of the length ND2.

PRM2(NDG,NDW,NBRT)	Initiate COMMON/DGS/ and set up for calculation with NDG digits, of base NBRT, stored NDW per cell;
INT(I,NA)	Store integer I in array NA;
PI(NA)	Store π in NA;
MULT(NA,NB,NC)	Multiply NA by NB, store in NC;

DIV(NA,NB,NC)	Divide NA by NB, store in NC;
SUB(NA,NB,NC)	Subtract NB from NA, store in NC;
SEP(NA,NB,NC)	Store integer part of NA in NB, fractional part in NC;
ICMP(NA,NB)	FORTRAN Function setting ICMP negative, zero or positive according to whether NA is less than, equal to, or greater than NB.

Note that PRM2 is assumed to have been called prior to entry into SINE. The parameters it initializes remain until the next time it is called.

Now we can give a description of the method used to compute $\sin(x)$ and $\cos(x)$. Given an argument x, the first step is to reduce it to the interval $(0, 2\pi)$. Here x, which is stored in the array NX to D digits, let us say, is assumed exact. The argument reduction is done in a precision higher than D, say D + E, in order to retain the precision D in the reduced argument. Determination of E and reduction of x is done in Coding Section 1 of the subroutine.

Let w be the result of reducing x to $(0, 2\pi)$. The values of $\sin(w)$ or $\cos(w)$ are computed from a Taylor series in $(0, \pi/4)$ by using appropriate identities, e.g.,

$$\sin(w) = - \cos(3\pi/2 - w)$$

when $5\pi/4 \leq w \leq 3\pi/2$. Hence there is a further reduction of the argument here, namely, the determination of

$$a = 3\pi/2 - w \ .$$

This calculation is done with the precision D + E, as before. The determination of a and setting of switches to determine which Taylor series to use, i.e., the one for $\sin(a)$ or the one for $\cos(a)$, is done in Coding Section 2.

From this point on the originally specified precision D is used. Coding Section 3 ascertains the number of terms needed in the Taylor series to provide the required truncation. This is done by Newton iteration to solve the equation

$$\frac{a^{2n}}{(2n)!} = 10^{-q}$$

-286-

for n, where $q = D \log_{10}$ (NBRT). Finally, Coding Section 4 is where the actual computation of the function values from Taylor series is performed.

```
000001                    SUBROUTINE SINE(NX,NFX)
000002                    COMMON/DGS/ND,ND1,ND2,NDW,NBRT,NBASE
000003                    DIMENSION NX(ND2),NFX(ND2)
000004                    DIMENSION NA(102),NB(102),NC(102),N2PI(102)
000005           C        SINE ENTRY
000006                    IND=0
000007                    GO TO 1
000008                    ENTRY COSINE(NX,NFX)
000009           C        COSINE ENTRY
000010                    IND=1
000011                  1 CONTINUE
000012                    IF (NX(1).GT.0) GO TO 2
000013                    CALL INT(IND,NFX)
000014                    RETURN
000015           C        ARGUMENT REDUCTION...ARGUMENT IS WRITTEN AS  X=(2*PI)*N+
000016           C        (PI/4)*M+A  WHERE N.GE.0, 0.LE.M.LE.7 AND 0.LT.A.LT.(PI/4).
000017           C        EITHER SIN(A) OR COS(A) WILL BE COMPUTED FROM TAYLOR SERIES AND
000018           C        PROPER ALGEBRAIC SIGN SUPPLIED.
000019           C           IMPORTANT NOTE...PRECISION IS EXTENDED TO ENSURE THAT THE
000020           C        REDUCED ARGUMENT  A  HAS FULL PRECISION EVEN WHEN THE SUPPLIED
000021           C        ARGUMENT  X  IS NEAR A LARGE ZERO OF THE FUNCTION. THE RELATIVE
000022           C        ERROR IN THE FUNCTION VALUE IS ALWAYS OF THE ORDER OF THE LAST
000023           C        SIGNIFICANT DIGIT IN THE CALCULATION.
000024           C
000025           C *** BEGIN CODING SECTION 1 ***
000026           C        DETERMINATION OF NUMBER OF FIGURES TO BE USED FOR ARGUMENT
000027           C        REDUCTION, FOLLOWED BY REDUCTION TO (0,2*PI). I.E., W=X-(2*PI)*N
000028           C        IS CALCULATED.
000029                  2 NEXTRA=ND
000030                    IF (NX(ND1).GT.0) NEXTRA=NEXTRA+1+(NX(ND1)-1)/NDW
000031                  3 NDSAV=ND
000032                    ND1SAV=ND1
000033                    ND2SAV=ND2
000034                    ND=ND+NEXTRA
000035                    CALL PRM2(ND*NDW,NDW,NBRT)
000036                    CALL PI(NA)
000037                    CALL INT(2,NB)
000038                    CALL MULT(NB,NA,N2PI)
000039                    DO 4 I=1,NDSAV
000040                  4 NB(I)=NX(I)
000041                    DO 5 I=ND1SAV,ND2
000042                  5 NB(I)=0
000043                    NB(ND1)=NX(ND1SAV)
000044                    NB(ND2)=+1
000045                    CALL DIV(NB,N2PI,NA)
000046                    CALL SEP(NA,NB,NC)
000047           C *** END CODING SECTION 1 ***
000048           C
000049           C *** BEGIN CODING SECTION 2 ***
000050           C        USE OF IDENTITIES TO DETERMINE FURTHER REDUCTION OF ARGUMENT
000051           C        TO (0,PI/4) AND SETTING OF SWITCHES FOR TAYLOR SERIES. I.E.,
000052           C        A=W-(PI/4)*M IS CALCULATED.
000053                    CALL INT(8,NB)
000054                    CALL MULT(NC,NB,NA)
000055                    DO 20 I=1,7
000056                    CALL INT(I,NB)
000057                    IF (ICMP(NA,NB).LT.0) GO TO 21
000058                 20 CONTINUE
000059                    CALL INT(1,NA)
000060                    CALL SUB(NA,NC,NB)
000061                    CALL MULT(NB,N2PI,NA)
000062                    ISGN=-NX(ND2SAV)
000063                    ASSIGN 100 TO LABEL
000064                    IF (IND.EQ.0) GO TO 50
```

```
000065                      ISGN=+1
000066                      ASSIGN 200 TO LABEL
000067                      GO TO 50
000068                   21 GO TO (17,16,15,14,13,12,11),I
000069                   11 CALL INT(6,NC)
000070                      CALL SUB(NA,NC,NB)
000071                      CALL INT(8,NA)
000072                      CALL DIV(NB,NA,NC)
000073                      CALL MULT(NC,N2PI,NA)
000074                      ISGN=-NX(ND2SAV)
000075                      ASSIGN 200 TO LABEL
000076                      IF (IND.EQ.0) GO TO 50
000077                      ISGN=+1
000078                      ASSIGN 100 TO LABEL
000079                      GO TO 50
000080                   12 CALL INT(6,NC)
000081                      CALL SUB(NC,NA,NB)
000082                      CALL INT(8,NA)
000083                      CALL DIV(NB,NA,NC)
000084                      CALL MULT(NC,N2PI,NA)
000085                      ISGN=-NX(ND2SAV)
000086                      ASSIGN 200 TO LABEL
000087                      IF (IND.EQ.0) GO TO 50
000088                      ISGN=-1
000089                      ASSIGN 100 TO LABEL
000090                      GO TO 50
000091                   13 CALL INT(4,NC)
000092                      CALL SUB(NA,NC,NB)
000093                      CALL INT(8,NA)
000094                      CALL DIV(NB,NA,NC)
000095                      CALL MULT(NC,N2PI,NA)
000096                      ISGN=-NX(ND2SAV)
000097                      ASSIGN 100 TO LABEL
000098                      IF (IND.EQ.0) GO TO 50
000099                      ISGN=-1
000100                      ASSIGN 200 TO LABEL
000101                      GO TO 50
000102                   14 CALL INT(4,NC)
000103                      CALL SUB(NC,NA,NB)
000104                      CALL INT(8,NA)
000105                      CALL DIV(NB,NA,NC)
000106                      CALL MULT(NC,N2PI,NA)
000107                      ISGN=NX(ND2SAV)
000108                      ASSIGN 100 TO LABEL
000109                      IF (IND.EQ.0) GO TO 50
000110                      ISGN=-1
000111                      ASSIGN 200 TO LABEL
000112                      GO TO 50
000113                   15 CALL INT(2,NC)
000114                      CALL SUB(NA,NC,NB)
000115                      CALL INT(8,NA)
000116                      CALL DIV(NB,NA,NC)
000117                      CALL MULT(NC,N2PI,NA)
000118                      ISGN=NX(ND2SAV)
000119                      ASSIGN 200 TO LABEL
000120                      IF (IND.EQ.0) GO TO 50
000121                      ISGN=-1
000122                      ASSIGN 100 TO LABEL
000123                      GO TO 50
000124                   16 CALL INT(2,NC)
000125                      CALL SUB(NC,NA,NB)
000126                      CALL INT(8,NA)
000127                      CALL DIV(NB,NA,NC)
000128                      CALL MULT(NC,N2PI,NA)
000129                      ISGN=NX(ND2SAV)
000130                      ASSIGN 200 TO LABEL
000131                      IF (IND.EQ.0) GO TO 50
000132                      ISGN=+1
000133                      ASSIGN 100 TO LABEL
000134                      GO TO 50
000135                   17 CALL INT(8,NB)
000136                      CALL DIV(NA,NB,NC)
000137                      CALL MULT(NC,N2PI,NA)
000138                      ISGN=NX(ND2SAV)
000139                      ASSIGN 100 TO LABEL
```

```
000140              IF (IND.EQ.0) GO TO 50
000141              ISGN=+1
000142              ASSIGN 200 TO LABEL
000143           50 CONTINUE
000144              NA(ND1SAV)=NA(ND1)
000145              NA(ND2SAV)=NA(ND2)
000146              ND=NDSAV
000147              CALL PRM2(ND*NDW,NDW,NBRT)
000148        C *** END CODING SECTION 2 ***
000149        C
000150        C *** BEGIN CODING SECTION 3 ***
000151        C      DETERMINE NUMBER OF TERMS NEEDED TO GIVE SPECIFIED TRUNCATION.
000152           60 U=ALOG10(FLOAT(NBRT))
000153              A=0.43429+ALOG10(FLOAT(NA(1))/FLOAT(NBASE))+FLOAT(NA(ND1))*U
000154              B=FLOAT(ND*NDW)*U-0.39909-0.5*A
000155              X=5.0
000156              IX=5
000157              DO 51 I=1,5
000158              E1=2.0*X
000159              E2=ALOG10(E1)-A
000160              E3=E1+0.5
000161              FX=E3*E2-B
000162              FPX=E3/X+2.0*E2
000163              X1=X-FX/FPX
000164              IX1=X1
000165              IF (IX1.EQ.IX) GO TO 55
000166              X=X1
000167           51 IX=IX1
000168              WRITE (6,52)
000169           52 FORMAT('0TERMINATION IN  SINE  SUBROUTINE...NEWTON ITERATION FAILE
000170             1D TO CONVERGE IN FIVE STEPS')
000171              STOP
000172           55 N3=2*IX+3
000173              N2=N3+1
000174              N1=N2+1
000175        C *** END CODING SECTION 3 ***
000176              GO TO LABEL,(100,200)
000177          100 CONTINUE
000178        C
000179        C *** BEGIN CODING SECTION 4 ***
000180        C      TAYLOR SERIES CALCULATION OF THE FUNCTION VALUES .
000181        C      TAYLOR SERIES FOR SIN(A)
000182              DO 110 I=1,ND2
000183          110 NFX(I)=NA(I)
000184              CALL MULT(NA,NA,NB)
000185              K1=N1
000186              K2=N2
000187          120 CALL MULT(NB,NFX,NC)
000188              CALL INT(K1*K2,NFX)
000189              CALL DIV(NC,NFX,N2PI)
000190              CALL SUB(NA,N2PI,NFX)
000191              K1=K1-2
000192              K2=K2-2
000193              IF (K2.NE.0) GO TO 120
000194              NFX(ND2)=ISGN
000195              RETURN
000196          200 CONTINUE
000197        C      TAYLOR SERIES FOR COS(A)
000198              CALL INT(1,NFX)
000199              CALL MULT(NA,NA,NB)
000200              CALL INT(1,NA)
000201              K2=N2
000202              K3=N3
000203          220 CALL MULT(NB,NFX,NC)
000204              CALL INT(K2*K3,NFX)
000205              CALL DIV(NC,NFX,N2PI)
000206              CALL SUB(NA,N2PI,NFX)
000207              K2=K2-2
000208              K3=K3-2
000209              IF (K2.NE.0) GO TO 220
000210              NFX(ND2)=ISGN
000211        C *** END CODING SECTION 4 ***
000212              RETURN
000213              END
```

Acknowledgements

The systematic approach to algorithm testing proposed in this paper evolved over the course of nearly two years, during which time the authors, with Dr. L.C. Maximon of NBS, were engaged in testing the FORTRAN library on the NBS computer. The work was performed with the support of the Center for Computer Sciences and Technology of NBS. The authors gratefully acknowledge the aid and support of both the Center and Dr. Maximon.

ON THE FEASIBILITY OF FORMAL CERTIFICATION

22

Ralph E. Keirstead and Donn B. Parker
Stanford Research Institute, Menlo Park, California

INTRODUCTION   This paper considers the feasibility of establishing certification and validation
services to ascertain the reliability of software products.
Two steps are required to do this. The first is to develop
the technology required to certify software. Software system certification should be based on reliability measures
that must be developed for the components of the system.
The determination of component reliability should be done in
such a way as to account for the effects on reliability of
supporting software such as the operating system, the input-
output system and the file management system.

Secondly, the feasibility of developing independent
mechanisms in the private sector must be determined to ascertain that the methodology available is being used and
that software products reflect this in adequacy of specifications, performance, and reliability.

The mechanisms requiring investigation are software product certification and the certification of the producers'
quality assurance methods. Proper implementation of these
mechanisms could result in better software products at lower
cost to both producers and users, increased software development productivity and greater user confidence in software
products and their specifications. The overall result will
be a rational software marketplace. Better mechanisms also
give meaning, value and purpose to efforts in the software
field to document knowledge and practices and to establish
voluntary standards. Formal certification mechanisms could
become the vehicle for making these efforts practical and
useful. Similar mechanisms have proven successful in the
lumber, gas heating, and electrical products industries. For

example, Underwriters Laboratories has been highly successful in electrical and materials testing for safety since
1894.

SOFTWARE
RELIABILITY AND
CERTIFICATION

To provide a rational basis for software
system certification, we must:

1. Develop means for determining the adequacy of software specifications
2. Develop methods for calculating a reliability measure
   for a component software module
3. Develop procedures for combining component measures
   to derive a measure of software system reliability.

The following approach is suggested. One major step
toward certification would be to measure software system
performance in a realistic and believable way. For some aspects of software performance there are such measurements.
We can determine how much memory a computer program occupies.
We can measure how a program uses input-output channels. We
can measure print speed, file capacity and file access rate
for a computer program. And we can measure processing speed
for a program.

There is, however, no equivalent measure of software
system reliability. Yet, without a way to measure software
reliability other measures of software performance are often
misleading. A software system may have been measured and
found to have a processing rate of 1000 input records per
second. If this system is so unreliable as to occasion a
rerun every five runs, this measured processing rate should be
modified. Taking into consideration the rerun effort, the
expected processing rate is more nearly eight hundred cards
per second. Similarly, if a file handling system misallo-
cates space under some conditions, the measured file capacity
of the system must be modified to account for this possibility. Some way to quantify software system reliability is
needed so that measured software performance can be used to
predict future use with confidence.

Software systems are usually developed in a modular way.
An appropriate approach for determining the reliability of

a software system, therefore, is to develop ways to calculate the reliability of the individual software modules and from these measures derive a measure for system reliability.

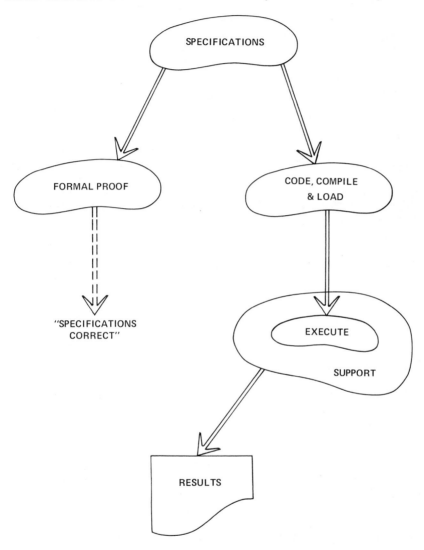

IF SPECIFICATIONS ARE PROVED CORRECT, WILL
RESULTS BE CORRECT?

FIGURE 1

The use of formal proof techniques leads in many cases, to the conviction that an algorithm will perform as planned. However, such techniques operate on the source language in which the algorithm is written. Before an algorithm is executed it must be compiled, loaded, interact with the operating system, the input-output system and so on, as indicated in Figure 1. Because of this, there can be no guarantee that what was true of the source program will hold during execution. It can be argued that by proving the correctness of the compiler, the loader, the operating system, the input-output system and so on, one may be assured that algorithms proved correct from the source text will indeed be correct when executed.

Given the current state of compilers, loaders, operating systems and other support software, however, an approach involving the intelligent selection of test cases appears to be more fruitful. The use of test cases permits a program to be examined during execution where the effects of the support software systems on program performance can also be examined.

The correct execution of a single test case cannot guarantee that a program is correct, although it may demonstrate that it is not. However, a systematically chosen set of test cases, together with appropriate supporting arguments that show how each test is representative of a class of inputs can produce results that approach the completeness of formal proof. Test cases will be selected by examination of the specifications against which product performance is to be tested. The key role of program specifications in testing is evident in Figure 1. Let us consider the requirements on specifications that make testing effective.

SPECIFICATIONS   Specifications should be complete, consistent and coherent, for they form the basis for testing. Program specifications determine the way the program will separate the input domain into subdomains each of which will be treated by particular parts of the program. The methods of formal proof can be used to identify the subdomains of the input domain.

Completeness refers to the degree to which specifications state explicitly the expected behavior of a computer program over its entire input domain. During the completeness analysis one seeks missing specifications, gaps in the specifications, and so forth. In particular, the analysis must not only assess the completeness of specification in the area of what the product is designed to do, but must also place equal emphasis on product specification in the area of product behavior when presented with data it is not designed to deal with.

Consistency analysis seeks to determine whether or not the specifications describe program behavior in a totally unambiguous way. Systematic means to uncover ambiguities, and contradictions must be developed.

The methods of formal algorithmic proof can be used to determine specification completeness and consistency. Although formal manual procedures could be developed to carry out such analyses based on formal proof techniques, computer assisted procedures will ultimately prove necessary.

Product specifications are written in many languages: narrative English, Backus normal form, data dependency tables, flow charts, diagrams, decision tables, algebraic formulae, etc. The degree to which the analyses can be computer assisted depends strongly on the language in which the product description is written. We must establish the requirements that the specification language must meet so that completeness and consistency analyses can be accomplished effectively with computer assisted techniques.

COMPONENT
RELIABILITY
As shown in Figure 2 , each subdomain of the input space corresponds to a part of the program. Test cases must be selected from each subdomain, so that the entire set of test cases will test the whole input domain and, as a consequence, the entire program. The methods of formal proof can be used to indicate the test cases that should be employed to test the program. From the results of the individual tests, methods to calculate a measure of the testedness of the program are to be developed. This measure intuitively seems to be a function of the ratio of the number of tested subdomains to the total number of subdomains. This measure is the reliability of the program module.

The level of effort required to test each part of a program will not be the same for all parts. The inherent

INPUT DOMAIN

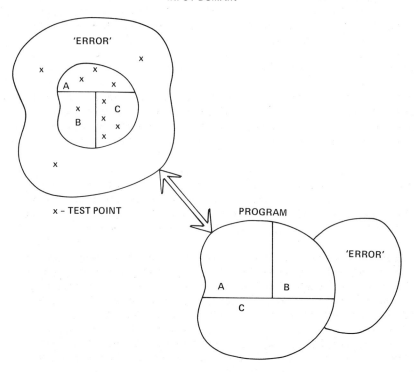

- SPECIFICATIONS IMPLY INPUT DOMAIN STRUCTURE AND CORRESPONDENCE WITH PROGRAM PARTS

- PROGRAM PART COMPLEXITY DETERMINES DENSITY OF TEST CASES

FIGURE 2

complexity of a program part differs from part to part, and the effect of this difference must be taken into account in calculating reliability.

Two program parts may deal with similar input subdomains, yet the number of test cases required to test the two parts adequately may vary due to the nature of the calculations involved. A numerical approximation, for example, may require the use of many more test cases than would a payroll calculation in order to demonstrate that the program behavior is correct for the subdomain under study.

One way to derive a measure of program complexity is to

assume that program complexity is proportional to the cost of producing the program. The characteristics of a program which affect the cost of its production have been studied. Some key characteristics are, for example, the total program size, the complication of program logic, and the dimensionality of the input domain. A previous study by R.A. Nelson of Systems Development Corporation developed some measures of these characteristics. We should refine and update the Nelson work to develop ways to estimate program complexity. These measures would then be used to develop estimates of the number and distribution of test cases required to examine a program exhaustively.

SYSTEM RELIABILITY   A software system is composed of many individual software modules. When each module of a system has been tested and a reliability measure calculated for it, it remains to combine these measures to derive system reliability. The way that the component measures could be combined depends on: (1) Criticality of the Component in the System Structure, and (2) the Popularity of the Component in the Use of the System.

Criticality is both system dependent and user oriented. For example, certain components may be of little direct interest to a user, but by their central position in the system must be thoroughly tested to ensure system reliability. Conversely, other components may not play a central role in the system, but produce results of great use. User determined criticality cannot be derived solely from a system description. However, inherent component criticality appears intuitively to be proportional to the number of computational paths of which the component is a part. This notion needs refinement and further development to produce means for calculating inherent component criticality from system specifications.

The popularity of a component refers to the probability that a given input lies in the subdomain corresponding to the component. This is dependent on a knowledge of the expected distribution of inputs. Ways of associating expected input distributions with component usage should be derived to develop measures of component popularity.

Component reliabilities, weighted in proportion to

criticality and popularity, combine to calculate system reliability. System reliability calculated in this way indicates the probability that an arbitrary input will be correctly dealt with by the system.

This measure, when combined with other performance measures, serves to provide a certification level for a software
product.

CERTIFICATION   The following tasks need to be undertaken
SERVICE   to establish the feasibility of an indepen-
                   dent certification service.

Technology feasibility. The feasibility of the techniques developed in the first part of the study should be
demonstrated in a practical case using an operational program
as an experimental vehicle. Measurements of the effort ex-
pended to apply the methodology, the degree of success and
the acceptance of the methods by those affected by certification form the basis for technological feasibility.

COBOL is suggested as a vehicle for proving the efficacy
of the test methods to be developed. The COBOL language is
accepted and used by a large number of business data processing organizations. The wide audience for COBOL techniques
means that useful information resulting from a study can be
communicated to many users. There is a definite need in this
community for improved methods of determining the reliability
of a program.

The form of the COBOL language requires a detailed definition for every data element to be used in a program. When
each variable is defined, the value range of every input variable is specified. This means that the entire input domain
can be known from the specifications. Decision tables are
widely accepted in the COBOL programming community. The use
of decision tables separates the logic that directs the computation from the computations themselves. This separation
facilitates the determination of the input subdomains. Intuitively, each logical condition does not imply that the condition will hold, it does imply that whenever an input point
satisfies the condition, a particular sequence of actions will
be executed in the program. This permits us to determine,
from program specifications, those subdomains that are treated

separately by the program.

A specification analysis would "sum" the conditions on each variable and compare it with the range of the variable determined by its definition. Formal analysis appears possible here and it should lead directly to identification of the subdomain structure of the program. Further, such analysis can determine how completely the subdomains cover the entire input domain.

An examination of the actions associated with each set of conditions enables determination of the complexity of the actions associated with each subdomain. These complexity measures can then be used to determine how test cases should be distributed within a subdomain.

To establish the effort involved to test a program, an existing program should be used. One would write new specifications for it using the language and methodology discussed earlier . These specifications are then compared to the original specifications to analyze the effectiveness and cost of preparation of the new specifications. Testing should be based on the new specifications. The COBOL program should be isolated from any other application programs with which it functions and then tested according to the plan and methodology developed. Independent evaluation based on the new and old specifications, the tests performed and production experience should be conducted to find weaknesses, inconsistencies and incompleteness of the work done using the new methodology. Finally, a reliability measure would be calculated and compared with actual performance.

Types of Service. Various types of services should be described and scenarios developed showing how they would work. Certification and testing services in the U.S.A., Canada and Europe should be studied to form the basis for determining types of services possible in the U.S. computer field.

Two types of services appear useful at this time. One type of service would certify that the quality assurance activities and self-certification methods of a software producer are adequate to produce reliable products. The other type of service would act as an independent certifier and validator of finished products.

Ancillary services such as contract testing, consulting

and publication of various types of information should also
be considered.

Franchisement. A certification service to be effective
must receive endorsement by those affected by certification.
Such endorsement might take the form of licensing by ANSI or
other recognized standards organizations. Trade associations,
professional societies and governments might support and en-
dorse it. The ownership status of a certification service
should be determined in such a way as to encourage endorsement.

Market. A market study should be performed to determine
how many software producers could be customers for a certification service. This might be done by studying advertise-
ments over a period of several months and by making surveys
of software producers. The major computer manufacturers and
software manufacturers should also be examined. The opinions
of producers and product users should be sought to further
determine the marketability of a certification service.

Cost and allocation of resources. The cost of a certification service must be determined taking into account start-
up costs, the kinds of services offered, the number and variety of products tested, the capital investment, marketing
costs, and expected volume of business.

The cost of various services should be compared to the
cost of a product. The value added to a product as a result
of certification is difficult to measure. However, ranges of
reasonable cost ratios could be determined to estimate the
probable financial soundness of various services.

Impact. A widely accepted certification service would
establish de facto standards. Proper and fair representation
of software producers affected must be established. The
possible effect of such a service on restraint of trade and
competition should be considered. For a service to be accepted, a net positive advantage should accrue to each segment of the software community.

The U.S. Department of Commerce and other regulating
agencies should be asked for opinions. The impact of similar
services in other fields should be studied to complete the
feasibility study.

CONCLUSION   Programming practice can be significantly
                    enhanced and software products improved by
developing quantitative measures for software reliability and
by developing specification and testing techniques that employ these measures. Formal certification based on this
methodology would provide a mechanism where by software users
and software producers could gain additional benefit from an
independent assurance that the products they use or produce
reached acceptable levels of certification.

QUALITY SOFTWARE CAN CHANGE THE COMPUTER INDUSTRY

23

Ruth M. Davis

National Bureau of Standards, Washington, D. C.

INTRODUCTION   One of the keys to success in the complex
world of today is the ability to be vicar-
ious—to put yourself in someone else's place and then suffer
as he does. This is a particularly important attribute for
anyone who is attempting either to formulate a technical
program to overcome a set of operational problems or to
transfer technology to resolve a different set of problems
than that for which it was originally intended.

Software epitomizes a product which demands tremendous
vicariousness from all of us who profess to tend it. For
software presents an entirely different facade depending u-
pon whether we view it as recipients of computer services,
as customers for computer applications, as producers of software or as suppliers of software services. To us, at the
National Bureau of Standards whose mission is to promote the
humane use of technology as well as equity in the marketplace, vicariousness requires simultaneous association with
both sides of the marketplace. We suffer both with the suppliers and the customer and we desire to simultaneously serve
both.

SOFTWARE   We believe that, today, software management
MANAGEMENT   encompasses in its scope most of the problems besetting the computer world as well
as most of the solutions.

To us, software management includes the various functions of:
            production
            measurement
            testing
            validation

documentation or specification
control (patents, taxing, etc.)
transferability
standards
maintenance
costing
pricing
contractual obligations
and software industry productivity enhancement.

In particular, when considering software products in a marketplace setting, it is immediately apparent that some of these software management procedures are applicable in the software production process while others are applicable in the marketplace when the software product is offered to customers.

For example, management procedures effective during software production include: Quality control, Testing, and Documentation or specification. Management procedures applicable in the marketplace setting include: Certification, Documentation or Specification, Validation, and Performance measurement.

Standards can be applied during the software production phase as well as in their more traditional marketplace role. In addition, we believe that the basic tenet for any program in software management is that the greatest increase in productivity within the software industry can be achieved by demanding:

1. Quality control procedures during software production.
2. Specification or documentation of software products against prescribed standards.
3. Testing the software product against quality control and documentation standards.

"Demanding" in this context implies making as mandatory components of a software product its documentation against prescribed standards and a statement of the quality control procedures invoked during its production as prescribed in terms of minimum allowable sets.

IDENTIFYING THE PROBLEMS   In general, the determination of what constitutes a crippling problem in computer utilization has been a haphazard process. Decisions as to those problems needing research and development for their resolution rarely took into account the problems that plague recipients of computer services. Neither did they adequately take into account the problems that manifest themselves in wrong or inaccurate substantive material flowing from computer systems. An even more fundamental omission was that set of problems traceable to poor performance and which result in poor productivity and unjustifiable system costs.

We have recently enlarged the traditional sources of computer problems to include those reported during Congressional hearings, those reported to consumer protection groups around the country, those cited in anti-trust suits filed within the computer industry and those implicit from reports of unduly expensive service costs.

This problem identification effort, which we believe to be the first of its kind is still in its formative stages. Nevertheless, it is already pointing out some highly significant findings which experience tends to validate. The crippling problems are lining up in the software rather than in the hardware field. In particular, they fall under what we call the application-independent problem category. These are software problems which are common to many applications.

To illustrate, the problem of handling changes to information contained in computer data bases is common to health insurance applications, air-traffic control, criminal records, credit bureaus and military systems that come in randomly from non-controlled sources and on any type of media. This occurs, for example, in billing systems where individual citizens attempt, mostly with no success, to correct errors in their bills by writing to "the computer."

A grouping of these crucial computer problems which we believe acceptable is as follows:

1. Poor quality software
2. Lack of controlled accessibility to computer data banks

3. Lack of consumer information on applications software (software documentation)
4. Malperformance of computing systems (credit, billing complaints)
5. Difficulties in producing applications software
6. Lack of marketplace software standards and specifications.

Responsibility for resolving these application-independent problems has been ineffectively diffused throughout most of the first quarter century of computer history, for although the problems arise in many applications, the solutions are application-independent and appear to be the responsibility of no one in particular.

THE
CUSTOMER
NEEDS

As we look at the needs for quality software management from the perspective of the customer's side of the marketplace, it is critically important for us to recognize the distinction between recipients of computer services and customers for computer services. The recipient of computer services differs from the customer for computer services in that the recipient has generally not made a conscious choice to be served by computers. Most of us, as private citizens, are such recipients. We have not made a conscious choice to have our social security records, employment records, criminal records, credit records, and medical records maintained by computers. Neither have we made the conscious decision that the checkless-cashless society, a truly computer-dependent society, is in our best interest. Recipients of computer services are not willing to adapt to the computer as were the early users of computers. Nor should they be asked to. Recipients of computer services are not totally forgiving of the mistakes made by the computer or by its managing organization. They are demanding both information on and assurance of quality and performance. As recipients we have every right to demand that. With 88,000 computers in our national inventory, we have one computer for every 2300 citizens or one computer for every 730 families. The distribution of these computers tells us that at least half these computers could reasonably affect us in our daily life or occupation. There is thus a large constituency of concerned citizens hoping for more humane application of computer

technology. We believe that quality software is the response
to that hope.

THE
INDUSTRY
NEEDS
When we now look at the industry side of the
marketplace, we must first state that we are
convinced that the computer industry has
changed so rapidly that many people dealing
with it have an out-dated impression of it. The association
of the industry with its eight major mainframe manufacturers
can charitably be called a myopic mythology. The computer
industry today can be best described not as a single entity
but as a set of interrelated sub-industries.

Admittedly, any decision on what to include in the set
is to some degree arbitrary. However, we have attempted to
identify as computer sub-industries those industries which
derive their primary source of income from the production
and use of the computer or in which the computer is fundamental to the existence of their product or service. Using
this approach, seventeen sub-industries with some 4900 member companies have been identified. The table at the end of
the paper lists these sub-industries along with estimates of
member companies and sales volume.

The problems we must tackle if we are to best serve the
public interest will impact directly on the operations of
those approximately 1100 (including eight mainframe manufacturers) companies having software products and services as
a major source of income. The principal technical capability
which we must use our funding to procure to work with us on
our critical computer problems will probably also come from
some 1100 of these 4900 companies. The overwhelming majority
of these companies are too young and struggling to have the
internal resources available for sponsoring any development
activities. And yet, they surely possess excellent technical innovative capabilities. They must become partners with
the Federal government if we are to launch any "computers in
the public interest" program.

It is apparent that demands for good software management are a key to a healthy marketplace and will affect significantly the structure and the growth of the computer industry as a set of interrelated sub-industries. Any such
demand will need the support of customers, industry and the

R. DAVIS

government in their allowable roles.

DEMANDS
FOR QUALITY
SOFTWARE

It is somewhat discouraging to realize therefore that demands for marketplace testing and for quality software are just beginning to materialize. No group has yet emerged as the recognized spokesman for the computer software world. In fact, I believe that today the major thrusts for change in the computer world are coming from:

1. Anti-trust suits
2. Shifts in the distribution of computer ownership
3. Shifts in sales policies
4. Congressional legislation
5. Changes in direction and amount of Federal research and development support to computers

In addition, we, at the National Bureau of Standards, are attempting to add to these major thrusts:

1. A push for quality software, and
2. A push for sharing of computer resources through computer networking.

We are still operating, however, in a computer world in which customers for software have not in any measureable way demanded any "guarantee" by software producers of error-free or error-limited software: further, very few buyers have contracts that "hold" software producers to certain products. Customer dissatisfaction is customarily expressed through contract termination or through non-extension of contracts to cover later phases of system development, implementation or operation.

REASONS
FOR TODAY'S
SOFT MARKET
PRACTICES

There are a number of historically-based reasons for the apparent soft market practices existing in software transactions. One is the familiar dispersion of responsibility between software companies and the customer organizations. Although this practice has been deemed essential for successful software production, it does effectively preclude any real assignment of responsibility for quality of software products to the producer. Contracts based on cooperative efforts between buyer and seller do not lend themselves to liability or malpractice establishment.

A second reason for present software marketplace practices is the non-existence of product performance or design specifications for software. Other than benchmark tests and simulations, both of which still lack any widespread acceptance, there are no uniformly useful market tests for software. Individual customers, left to their own devices, have difficulty evaluating delivered software soon enough to request modification under terms of the covering contract.

Another reason for today's market deficiencies is the lack of acceptable business procedures for estimating the extent of the software package to be produced, either in terms of number of instructions, man-hours to produce, time to run or complexity of design. Neither the buyer nor seller of software has devised such widely useful estimation procedures common to other service areas. For example, home-developers estimate rather accurately, the labor and material needed for a given size house, typing services estimate accurately the time and labor costs for producing manuscript copy and motors can be designed to meet stated performance specifications.

Still another problem in our software marketplace is the general disuse of quality control procedures during software generation and the lack of insistence on their use by customers. It is common practice when product performance cannot be specified or tested to use quality control procedures during production to insure that product components meet certain standards, are within allowable error tolerances or are produced using prescribed techniques. Quality control procedures can be demanded and invoked even when more complex design or performance specifications cannot be developed.

CONCLUSIONS   Today we are forced to face a situation
                where quality control practices, design and
performance specifications, cost estimation techniques and
productivity measures all still await development and acceptance in the computer field.

It is unfortunate that customers for computer software,
although dissatisfied, have not expressed their dissatisfaction as specific demands for the types of accepted marketplace practices discussed in previous paragraphs. Instead, the dissatisfaction manifests itself as general in-
dictments of computer technology in its entirety. As Wallace B. Riley aptly phrased it in the September 13, 1971 is-
sue of Electronics (pg. 62) "of all the problem areas in
computer technology of the '60s, software was far and away
the worst. And of all the solutions prophesied for the '70s,
those involving software are the most far-reaching, and could
even alter the structure of the industry. Everyone is agreed
on the need to turn programming from something 'handcrafted
by elves in the Black Forest' ... into a systematic, engineering discipline built around a core of basic principles
... But no one is agreed on how near this situation is."

We feel most encouraged by meetings such as this one
sponsored by ACM and directed towards Computer Program Test
Methods. When its recommendations become accepted practices
and when we have marketplace standards for quality control,
software validation procedures and adequate software documentation then, and only then, will we have a computer software world in which we can take pride.

Indeed, imaginative use of computers may well hold the
key to necessary improved productivity in our domestic economy. Already, our skill in computer technology is one of
the most valuable economic and technical assets we possess
as a nation. The timing is right, the needs are apparent
and the national leadership is ready to employ computers to
aid our economy and to assist in improving the lot of each
of us individually. Quality software could be the means to
the humane application of computer technology in the best
public interest.

QUALITY SOFTWARE CAN CHANGE THE COMPUTER INDUSTRY

THE COMPUTER INDUSTRY

SUB-INDUSTRY MEMBER POPULATION AND SALES VOLUME

MAJOR SUB-INDUSTRIES	NUMBER OF MEMBER COMPANIES	1970 SALES VOLUME ($ MILLIONS)
Equipment		
Mainframe (CPU) Manufacturing	8	4100
Peripherals Manufacturing	400-450	1620
Mini-Computer Manufacturing	50-75	250
Equipment Leasing Services (Third Party Services and OEM)	175	600
Software		
Independent Software Producers	1100	340
Mainframe, Users, Universities	25	240
Computer Services		
Regular Service Bureaus	800	600
Time-Sharing	225-235	490
Libraries	12	–
Facilities Management Services (Computer Resource Management- CRM)	12	180
Computer Network Services	5	N/A
Major Support Sub-Industries		
Electronics Components	65	600
Computer Technology (Research)	10-15	–
Education and Training Services	750	170
Media Suppliers	84	1170
Minor Sub-Industries		
Automated Reading Equipment Manufacturing	40	60
Process Control Device Manufacturing	1100	180
Soft Automation Manufacturing	5	40-50

BIBLIOGRAPHY

The following bibliography represents the results of a
literature survey on computer program testing and related
activities. Approximately 375 references have been selected
and grouped into sixteen topical areas lettered A through P
as follows:

A General Testing Concepts and Principles
B Program Design and Structure to Facilitate Testing
C Program Flow Analysis and Graph Models
D Automatic Testing Aids and Tools
E Formal Logic and Proof Methodology
F Program Specification Techniques and Specification Lan-
   guages
G Measuring and Estimating Program Reliability
H Test Data Generation
I Proof of Correctness Applications
J Testing As a Development Process
K Mathematical and Numerical Software Testing
L Testing Monitors and Simulators
M Debugging
N Hardware Testing Concepts
O Performance Testing
P Other Program Description and Analysis Models

Like all classification schemes, this one has its difficulties with overlap and ambiguity, however the editor feels
that some clarity and understanding of the breadth of the
literature on testing is obtained from the grouping. Several
of the groups are quite closely related. Groups D, H and L
collectively cover various automated testing tools with H and
L covering two of the common tools and D the remaining mis-
cellaneous ones. Groups B, F and J emphasize the idea of
considering the needs of testing throughout program design and
development. In the literature this is seen to focus on three
separate ideas: structuring programs to improve logical comprehension and testability, a concern for program specification methods and specification languages, and a view of testing as a staged process over the entire program development
cycle. One group of references covers each of these three
areas. Groups E and I are concerned with proof of correctness. Group E includes references on proof methodology and
formal logic systems while I covers the applications and

examples of the various proof techniques. Groups C, G and P collectively cover the use of various models to analyze programs. C is concerned with flow analysis and graph theory, G covers models and techniques for measuring and estimating reliability and P covers the remaining models for describing and analyzing programs.

References within a topical section are alphabetical by author but somewhat unconventionally have been listed with the title underlined and first. This was done to make the titles stand out so that a scan could provide a quick overview of the relavant literature. Late additions to the bibliography resulted in some of the reference numbers falling out of sequence.

No effort for completeness in groups E, I, M, N, O and P was attempted. References in these groups were collected as a byproduct of a thorough search for references in the other groups. Bibliographies by London on proof of correctness, Kocher and Evans on debugging and Miller on performance testing are available and rather than duplicate these we have included references only if they are highly pertinent to program testing per se or referred to by any of the chapters in this book. References were collected from a wide variety of sources and span dates up through June 1972. Several computer searches of government and university literature files were run as well as manual searches through Computing Reviews and resulting bibliography chains. Working as the editor for this book and Chairman of the Computer Program Test Methods Symposium uncovered the remaining references.

The editor is indebted to many for their help and in particular to Don Kosy at Rand for getting together a small scale bibliography last year, to Jim Cody at Argonne National Laboratories for collecting almost all of the Mathematical and Numerical Software Testing references, and to Ed Miller at General Research Corporation for putting together a large bibliography independently and letting me include a number of its references in the collection.[1] The work on the bibliography was funded by the National Science Foundation grant GJ-30410 to the University of North Carolina Computation Center.

[1]GRC plans to maintain their bibliography on software validation and readers are invited to submit new references or request updated issues by writing to E.F. Miller, General Research Corporation, 5383 Hollister Ave., Santa Barbara, California, 93105.

General Testing Concepts and Principles

[A9] Techniques for Program Error Diagnosis on EDSAC2, D. Barron and D. Hartley, Computer Journal, April 1963.
Criticizes the notion that with an operating system the tendency is to restrict diagnostic and testing facilities to keep jobs flowing. Calls for a system to provide elaborate checking procedures and for software to allow the user to specify the diagnostic information he requires.

[A1] Programming Language/One, F. Bates and M.L. Douglas, Prentice-Hall, Englewood Cliffs, New Jersey, 1967, Chapter 9.
Contains a discussion of PL/1 testing facilities including SIGNAL and CHECK and how they are used to assist in testing and debugging of PL/1 programs.

[A2] Some Information Processing Implications of Air Force Space Missions: 1970-1980, B.W. Boehm, RM 6213-PR, Rand Corporation, January 1970.
Comments on the cost of testing and debugging and calls for better testing techniques and facilities. Considers simulation languages, measuring techniques, interactive program execution and a dedicated software testing group.

[A3] Computer Results Questionned, Ruth Davis, Computerworld, December 1, 1971, p.4.
Short article describing the poor results of validation tests on 27 computer programs for calculating least squares representations of data.

[A4] Aids in the Production of Maintainable Software, H.R. Gillette, Software Engineering, NATO Science Affairs Division, pp.39-40, January 1969.
Emphasizes the design concepts of modularity, specification and generality.

[A5] Toward Better Software, J. Goldberg, Electronics Vol.44 #19, p.63, Sept. 1971.
A short article covering some of the possible methods for validating software.

[A7] Program Testing and Validation, F. Gruenberger, Datamation, Vol.14#7, July 1968, pp.39-47.
A general discussion of the principles of program testing, including some examples in constructing test procedures for simple routines.

[A8] Computer Programming: Debugging Epoch Opens, M. Halpern, Computers and Automation, November 1965.
A humorous but pertinent discussion of the problems of testing and debugging and their implications.

[A10] Testing Real Time Systems Part I, R.V. Head, Datamation, Vol.10, July 1964, pp.42-48.
Review of various aspects of real time systems which add to the test problem with emphasis on the lack of repeatability.

[A6] The Adequacy and Efficiency of Program Testing, J.B. Heard, Proc. Computers and Data Proc. Society of Canada, University of Toronto Press, pp.118-126, 1962.
General discussion of the problem of testing.

[A12] The Art of Computer Programming, D.E. Knuth, Vol. 1, Fundamental Algorithms, Addison Wesley, Reading, Mass. 1968.

[A13] An Empirical Study of FORTRAN Programs, D.E. Knuth, Stanford University, Computer Science Department, Report CS-186, 1971.

[A14] Annotated Bibliography of Debugging, Testing and Validation Techniques For Computer Programs, D. Kosy, Rand Corporation, Santa Monica, California, WN-7271-PR, January 1971.
A well organized short bibliography of articles relevant to various aspects of program testing.

[A15] Computer Programming Fundamentals, H.D. Leeds and G.M. Weinberg, McGraw Hill, 2nd edition, New York, 1966, pp.358-394.
General discussion of program testing especially in Fortran and the philosophy of segmentation.

[A11] The Testing of Computer Software, A.I. Llewelyn and R.F. Wickens, Software Engineering, NATO Science Affairs Division, January 1969, pp.189-199.
Discusses acceptance testing.

[A16] Design of Real Time Computer Systems, J. Martin, Prentice-Hall, 1967, Chapter 37, System Testing.
An overall discussion of the testing process as applied to large real time systems. Problems inherent in testing and existing techniques such as overload simulators, interrupt recorders, macro exercisers, and test output processors are covered.

[A17] Program Transferability Study, G.H. Mealy, D.J. Farber, E. Morenoff, and K. Sattley, Rome Air Development Center, Griffith Air Force Base, November 1968.
Study made to determine how to reduce software problems associated with transferring computer programs. Emphasized the lack of language facilities for explicit specification, representational bindings, lack of constraints on programmers and limited programming technology as the cause. Included here because the same problems seem to be at the root of our testing difficulties.

[A18] Methodology For Software Validation--A Survey of the Literature, M.R. Paige and E.F. Miller General Research Co. RM 1549, March 1972.
Surveys the tools for extended debugging, program testing, graph-theoretic treatments of source code structure, program proving, simulation and source code analysis.

[A19] Automatic Program Testing, G.F. Renfer, Proc. 3rd Conf. Comput. Data Process, Society of Canada, June 1962, 127-135, University of Toronto Press, Toronto, Ontario, Canada.
A limited article comparing some early methods of program testing.

[A20] Diagnosis of Software Faults, J.P. Roth, IEEE Int. Computer Society Conference 1971, p.83.
A broad discussion relating hardware diagnosis techniques to the testing of software.

[A21] Comparative Evaluation of PL/I, R.I. Rubey, Guide to PL/I Vol.I, American Data Processing, Detroit, Michigan, 1969.
A study to empirically compare PL/I, FORTRAN, COBOL and JOVIAL through the coding and checkout of benchmark programs. Provides quantitative information on various aspects of the debugging and testing of programs.

[A22] An Overview of Bugs, J.T. Schwartz in Debugging Techniques in Large Systems, edited by R. Rustin, Prentice-Hall, 1971, pp.1-16.
Surveys the type and habitat of bugs and discusses debugging and testing tools presently available along with suggestions for their development. The role of "proofs of program correctness: and the debugging process itself are discussed. Illustrates nicely the relationship between debugging and testing.

[A24] Symbolic Mathematical Computation - Introduction and Overview, R.G. Tobey, SIGSYM Conference Proceedings, 1968.
The paper although offered to a different audience nicely models the abstract development process and emphasizes the lack of feedback in programming technology. Emphasizes the idea of the uncertainty principle whereby no meaningful measurement can be made that does not affect the system being measured.

[A25] Systems Testing--A Taboo Subject?, T.J. Vander Noot, Datamation, November 1971, pp.60-64.

[A2 3] Advanced Program Testing Concepts, T.J. Wright, IBM Form Z77-6391, November 1966.

[A2 6] Towards Machine Independent Processors, J.K. Yarwood, Computer Bulletin, Vol 14 #7, pp.219-221, July 1970.

Program Design and Structure to Facilitate Testing

[B27] The Translation of GO TO Programs to WHILE Programs, E. Ashcroft and Z. Manna, Stanford AI Memo AIM-138, Stan CS-71-88, January 1971.

[B19] Evolutive Modelling and Evaluation of Operating and Computer Systems, R. Aslanian and M. Bennett 1971, Research Report CA-016, Compagnie International pour l'Informatique, France.

[B1] Chief Programmer Team Management of Production Programming, F.T. Baker, IBM Systems Journal, Vol 11 #1, 1972.
    Proposes new programming organization and relates it to ideas of structured programming.

[B29] System Quality Through Structural Programming, F.T. Baker, FJCC (to appear) April 1972.

[B4] Flow Diagrams, Turing Machines and Languages With Only Two Formation Rules, C. Böhm and G. Jacopini, CACM 9, #3, pp.366-371, May 1966.
    Proves structure theorem that any proper program (one entry and exit) can be written using only the progressions of sequence, IF THEN ELSE and DO WHILE.

[B2] A Constructive Approach to the Problem of Program Correctness, Edgar W. Dijkstra, Basic Information Technology, Vol.8 #3, 1968, pp.174-186.
    Development of the structured formalism applied to the problem of handling the programming of the cooperation of parallel dependent processes. An attempt to control the process of program generation such as to prove a priori the logical correctness of programs.

[B3] GO TO STATEMENT CONSIDERED HARMFUL , E.W. Dijkstra, letter to the editor, CACM 11 #3, March 1968, pp.147-148.
    Discusses the structural difficulties that arise from the use of GO TO .

[B5] Structured Programming, E.W. Dijkstra, Software Engineering Techniques, Report on a Conference sponsored by the NATO Science Committee, Rome, Italy, (April 1970), pp.84-88.

[B6] The Structure of "THE" - Multiprogramming System, E.W. Dijkstra, CACM, Vol 11 #5, May 1968, pp.341-346.
    Introduction of a structured logical system development for a real system with the idea of verification by induction from a steadily enlarged set of verified concepts or primitives.

[B20] Notes on Structured Programming, E.W. Dijkstra, TH-Report 70-WSK-03, Dept. of Mathematics, Technological University Eindhoven, The Netherlands, April 1970.

[B21] Programming Considered as a Human Activity, E.W. Dijkstra, Proc. of the IFIP Congress, 1965, Spartan Books, Washington, D.C.

[B7] A Model of Functional Reasoning in Design, P. Freeman and A. Newell, 2nd Int. Joint Conference on Artificial Intelligence, London, 1971.
    Considers the possibility of program design using functions and their interconnections as the representations of the objects being created.

[B15] An Experiment in Structured Programming, P. Henderson and R. Snowdon, 1971, Technical Report 18, Computing Laboratory, University of Newcastle Upon Tyne, 1971.

[B8] Segmented Level Programming, M. Jackson and A. Swanwick, Datamation, February 1969, pp.23-26.
    Suggests use of macros to provide standard module interfaces with working storage set up as a stack. Standard testbed permits testing of interfaces and provides facilities for symbolic definition of test data.

[B22] Software Design Techniques for Automatic Checkout, D.H. Jirauch, IEEE Trans. on Aerospace and Electronic Systems, pp.934-940, November 1967.
Concerns some software design techniques to facilitate checkout.

[B23] Formal Development of Correct Algorithms - An Example Based on Earley's Recognizer, C.B. Jones, Proc. of Conf. on Proving Assertions About Programs, January 1972, pp.150-169.
Considers the formal development of a correct algorithm from an implicit definition of the task to be performed.

[B24] Notes on Avoiding GO TO Statements, D.E. Knuth and R.W. Floyd, Computer Science Technical Report CS148, Stanford University, January 1970.

[B25] Extensions to Fortran and Structured Programming -- An Experiment, E.F. Miller, General Research Corporation, RM-1608, March 1972.

[B26] Chief Programmer Teams -- Principles and Procedures, H.D. Mills, Report # FSC 71-5108, IBM Federal Systems Division, Gaithersburg, Maryland, 1971.

[B10] Mathematical Foundations for Structured Programming, H.D. Mills, IBM Report FSC 72-6012, May 1972.

[B9] Top Down Programming In Large Systems, H. Mills in Debugging Techniques in Large Systems, edited by R. Rustin, Prentice-Hall, 1971, pp.43-55.
Proposes structured programming to develop a large system in an evolving tree structure of nested modules, with no control branching between modules except for module calls defined in the tree structure. By limiting the size and complexity of modules, unit testing can be done by systematic reading, and the modules executed directly in the evolving system in a top down testing process.

[B11] Programming By Action Clusters, P. Naur, B.I.T. Vol.9, 1969, pp.250-258.
Structure idea of program actions in clusters.

[B12] The Kernel Approach to Building Software Systems, A. Newell, P. Freeman, D. McCracken and G. Robertson, Computer Science Research Review, Carnegie-Mellon University, 1970-1971.

[B14] Analytic Design of a Dynamic Look Ahead and Program Segmentation System for Multi-Programmed Computers, C.V. Ramamoorthy, Proc. ACM National Conference, 1966, pp.229-239.

[B18] Iterative Multi-Level Modelling - A Methodology for Computer System Design, B. Randell and F. Yurcher, Proc. IFIP Congress 1968 pp.D138-D142.

[B28] Towards a Methodology of Computing System Design, B. Randell, Software Engineering, NATO Science Affairs Division, Brussels, 1968, pp.204-208.
Considers various strategies for program design.

[B13] The GO TO Statement Reconsidered, J.R. Rice, CACM, Vol 11 #8, August 1968.

[B16] Modularity: The Key to System Growth Potential, W.M. Taliaferro, Software Practice and Experience, July-September 1971, pp.245-247.
Suggests building software modularity with well defined interfaces just as hardware is built. Proposes independent module test procedures with programmers constrained in implementation technique so that the test can be prepared in parallel with the program.

[B17] Program Development by Stepwise Refinement, N. Wirth, CACM 14, 4, April 1971, pp.221-227.

Program Flow Analysis and Graph Models

[C1] A Comparative Sampling of the Systems for Producing Computer Drawn Flow Charts, M.D. Abrams
      Proc. 1968 ACM Nat. Conference, pp.745-750.
      Surveys and compares a number of flowchart programs.

[C6] A Computational Model with Data Flow Sequencing, D.A. Adams, Stanford University Technical
      Report CS-117, December 1968.

[C16] An "Atlas" for the Visual Comparison of COBOL Flowcharting Software, Bonneville Power Ad-
      ministration, Portland, Oregon, 1971.

[C9] Graph Models of Computations in Computer Systems, J.L. Baer, UCLA Engineering Report
      68-46, 1968.

[C2] Legality and Other Properties of Graph Models of Computations, J.L. Baer, D.P. Bovet and
      G. Estrin, JACM Vol 17 #3, July 1970, pp.543-554.
      Briefly reviews the properties of directed graph models of computations. Procedures for
      counting the number of possible executions and evaluating the probability of reaching a
      given vertex are considered.

[C10] Transformation of Program Schemes to Standard Forms, S.K. Basu , IEEE Proc. of Ninth Annual
      Symposium on Switching and Automata Theory, 1968, pp.99-105.
      Discusses the transformation of flow graph program schemes to block forms for easier
      analysis.

[C18] Theory of Graphs and Its Applications, C. Berge, Wiley, New York, 1962.
      A text on graph theory and its application to program modelling and flow analysis.

[C20] Multiprocessors, Semaphores, and a Graph Model of Computation, V.G. Cerf, UCLA Computer
      Science Report ENG-7223, April 1972.
      Considers the limitations of a graph model of parallel computation and the capabilities
      for representing the flow of control.

[C23] Some Properties of Cycle Free Directed Graphs and the Identification of the Longest Path,
      Y.C. Chen and O. Wing, Journal of the Franklin Institute, Vol 281 #4, April 1966, pp.293-
      301.
      Reviews some of the elementary graph theory material.

[C3] Automatic Simplification of Source Language Programs E.Clark, Proc. ACM 21st National Con-
      ference, 1966, pp.313-319.
      Considers simplification methods based on flow analysis that can be applied in a single
      scan to keep processing time reasonable.

[C24] Some Transformations and Standard Forms of Graphs, with Applications to Computer Programs,
      D.C. Cooper, Machine Intelligence 2, American Elsevier, pp.21-32, 1968.
      Considers transformations of programs to normalized directed graphs.

[C4] Flow Analysis for Program Correctness, J.J. Florentin, CSRR 2054 Research Report, Univer-
      sity of Waterloo, 1970.
      Provides an algorithm for constructing intervals which are subcomponents of a program
      having single entries, several exits and with all back loops coming into the entry point.
      Points out that the intervals provide a systematic way of segmenting a program and enable
      simpler proofs .

[C25] The Production of Better Mathematical Software, L.D. Fosdick, Dept. of Computer Science, University of Colorado, draft not yet published.
A general discussion of problems of software validation along with an overview of some elementary flow analysis considerations.

[C26] Automated Program Documentation, M.A. Goetz, Applied Data Research Inc., Princeton, New Jersey, 1965.
Description of flow charting program AUTOFLOW.

[C27] Flow of Control, Resource Allocation and the Proper Termination of Programs, UCLA Computer Science Report ENG-7179, K.P. Gostelow, December 1971.
Defines termination using the graph model of flow control.

[C5] A Problem in Man Computer Communication, J. Green, Harvard PHD thesis, 1969.
Describes the GRAPE system for graphical analysis of program execution.

[C28] A Program to Draw Multilevel Flow Charts, L.M. Haibt, IBM Yorktown Heights, N.Y., Research Report-89, April 1959.

[C29] Structural Models - An Introduction to the Theory of Directed Graphs, F. Haraby, R.Z. Norman and D. Cartwright, Wiley and Sons, 1965.
A thorough introduction of the application of directed graph theory.

[C30] Efficient Algorithms for Graph Manipulation, J. Hopcroft and R. Tarjan, Stanford University CS-71-207, AD72 6169 March 1971.
Discusses algorithms for partitioning a graph into connected components, biconnected components and simple paths.

[C7] A Note on the Application of Graph Theory to Digital Computer Programming, Information and Control, Vol 3, 1960, pp.179-190, R.M. Karp.
Introduces a graph model for programs.

[C8] A Global Flow Analysis Algorithm, K. Kennedy, Int. Journal of Computer Math., Section A, Vol.3, pp.5-15, 1971.

[C31] Computer Drawn Flow Charts, D.E. Knuth, CACM, September 1963, pp.555-563.

[C32] Automatic Segmentation of Cyclic Program Structures Based on Connectivity and Processor Timing, T.C. Lowe, January 1970, CACM PP.3-9.
Refines the segmentation techniques of Ramamoorthy to identify strongly connected subgraphs.

[C33] Models of Computational Systems--Cyclic to Acyclic Graph Transformations, D.F. Martin and G. Estrin, IEEE Trans. on Computers, February 1967, pp.70-79.
Considers graph model to study cyclic to acyclic conversion.

[C34] Experiments on Models of Computations and Systems, D.F. Martin and G. Estrin, IEEE Trans. on Computers, February 1967, pp.59-69.
Use of graph model to study sensitivity of system to input parameter vanation.

[C11] Models of Computations and Systems--Evaluation of Vertex Probabilities in Graph Models of Computation, D.F. Martin and G. Estrin, JACM, Vol 14 #4, April 1967, pp281-289.
Discusses methods for determining the probability of reaching vertices in a graph model.

[C35] Applications of Graphs and Boolean Matrices to Computer Programming, R.B. Marimont, SIAM Review, Vol 2 #4, October 1960, pp.259-268.
Elementary graph theory concepts.

[C12] Distinguishability Criteria in Oriented Graphs and Their Application to Computer Diagnosis,
W. Mayeda and C.V. Ramamoorthy, IEEE Trans. on Circuit Theory, Vol CT-16, November 1969
pp.448-454.

[C13] Systematic Mistake Analysis of Digital Computer Programs, Miller and Maloney, CACM,
February 1963, pp.58-63.
A discussion of an automated procedure for the use of a logical tree as a means of estab-
lishing a complete test deck covering all input cases.

[C14] On the Automatic Simplification of Computer Programs, J. Nievergett, CACM June 1965,
pp.366-371.
Considers automatic simplifications which depend only on a programs flow analysis.
Models a program an an incomplete sequential machine and uses standard minimization techniques to arrive at a flowchart for an equivalent program.

[C15] A Technique for Computer Flowchart Generation, F. O'Brien and R.C. Beckwith, Computer
Journal 11 (1968), pp.138-140.

[C19] Applications of Boolean Matrices to the Analysis of Flow Diagrams, R.T. Prosser, Proc. of
the Eastern Joint Computer Conference, 1959, pp.133-138.
A general discussion of the use of boolean matrices to represent program graph corrections.

[C36] A Structural Theory of Machine Diagnosis, C.V. Ramamoorthy, Proc. SJCC, 1967, pp.743-756.
Considers graph theory application to partition a system in order to pick test point
locations and to find sequences in which system elements must be tested.

[C37] Connectivity Considerations of Graphs Representing Discrete Sequential Systems, C.V. Ramamoorthy, IEEE Trans. on Computers, October 1965, pp.724-727.
Another introduction to the graph model for programs.

[C17] Analysis of Graphs by Connectivity Considerations, C.V. Ramamoorthy, JACM, Vol 13, No.2,
April 1966, pp.211-222.
Another introduction to the graph model for programs.

[C38] Automated Checkout of Every Possible Logic Path In Very Large Computer Systems, W.W. Royce
TRW Interoffice Correspondence EBC G039, December 1969.
Outlines a proposed system to provide automatic testing of every logic path for correct-
ness of arithmetic computations, storage references and execution sequencing.

[C39] Automatic Program Analysis, E.C. Russell, UCLA Report 69-12, AD, pp.686-401, March 1969.
Uses the graph program model to study the structure for analysis of space and time resource requirements.

[C40] Measurement Based Automatic Analysis of Fortran Programs, E.C. Russell and G. Estrin, Proc
SJCC, pp.723-732.
Specification for the graph representation of Fortran statements.

[C41] Fortran Loop Detecting Trace, J.W. Simmons, Software Age, March 1970, pp.19-21.
Discusses routine to trace the execution of Fortran programs.

[C42] Flowtrace - A Computer Program for Flowcharting Programs, P.M. Sherman, CACM, December 196(
pp.845-854.
A system to flowchart programs in any well structured language.

[C43] On Finding the Paths Through a Network, N.J. Sloane, Bell System Technical Journal, Vol 51
No. 2, February 1972, pp.371-390.
Gives techniques for finding all paths through a graph.

[C44] Loops in Computer Programs, S.M. Taylor, Biological Computer Laboratory Report, University of Illinois, Urbana, Ill., October 1970.
   Describes a matrix methodology for extracting variable dependencies within a program segment and an approach to determining loop termination based on that computational dependence.

[C45] An Algorithm for Computing All Paths in a Graph, L.E. Thorelli, BIT Vol 6 , 1966, pp.347-349.

[C21] Properties Preserved Under Recursion Removal, H.R. Strong and S.A. Walker, Proc. of ACM SIGPLAN Conference on Proving Assertions About Programs, SIGPLAN Notices Vol 7 #1, Jan.1972
   Discusses an automated technique for removing recursion from programs by transformation to a flow chart.

[C22] Automatic Program Segmentation Based on Boolean Connectivity, E.W. Van Hoef, Proc. SJCC, 1971, pp.941-945.
   Gives an algorithm for partitioning a program into a number of pieces (called pages) such that each page is limited in size and the number of intersegment references is reduced

Automatic Testing Aids and Tools

[D4] Software Tools for Certifying Operational Flight Programs, B. Dulac and R. Rubey, National Space Navigation Meeting Proceedings, 1967, pp. 164-177.
Proposed techniques for improving the testing of aerospace programs. First occurance of the idea of analyzing which instructions are not executed on particular test runs.

[D5] Survey of Program Packages--Programming Aids, K. Fallor, Modern Data, March 1970, pp.62-72.
A list of commercially available programming aids, many of which can be classified in the testing aids area.

[D6] The Air Force Cobol Compiler Validation System, H.T. Hicks, Datamation, August 1969, pp.73-81.
Description of a system to test compilers against the Cobol standard. Reasonably unique test generating conventions are used. Biggest problem areas were in interfacing the generated tests to the host system and in interpreting the test results.

[D15] A New Technique For Testing Of Programs For Process Control Computers, IEEE Int. Convention Record, G.L. Hilgore and R.E. Hohmeyer, Vol 13 #3, pp.256-260, 1965.

[D8] FETE, a Fortran Execution Time Estimator, D.H. Ingals, Report 204, Department of Computer Science, Stanford University, 1971.

[D9] One Way of Estimating Frequencies of Jumps in a Program, J. Kral, Communications of the ACM, Vol.11, No.7, July 1968, pp.475-80.

[D16] Computer Source-Language Optimizing Utilizing A Visual Display, R.E. Love, University of California at Berkeley Thesis.
Reports on an early attempt at producing a graphical display of a virtual machine.

[D10] Syntax Directed Documentation, Harlan Mills, Communications of the ACM, Vol.13 #4, p.216.
Technique is proposed for asking documentation questions by syntactic analysis of the program. Questions are generated from pre-stored skeletons and presented to the originating programmer. In testing compilers the technique might be a useful option to consider to obtain specification information.

[D3] OUTPUT CHECKER, Computerworld, October 6, 1971, Announcement by Synergetics, page 6.
Parameter card driven program to analyze one file at a time and report in detail where file failed to meet users specifications. Is able to define control breaks and check appropriate action on print files.

[D2] MODTEST Module Testing System, Product brochure from Computer Services Corporation, Southfield, Michigan, 1971.
Product to simulate a mainline program to permit module testing. Facilities to set up input parameters are provided. Same company also markets a test file generator called TESTCUBE.

[D11] Spelling Correction in Systems Programs, H.L. Morgan, Communications of the ACM, Vol.13, No.2, pp.90-94, February 1970.
Discusses spelling error identification and correctness techniques.

[D13] Decision Table Structure as Input Format for Programming Automatic Test Equipment Systems, B. Scheff, IEEE Transactions EC-14, April 1965.
Suggests the idea of using a decision table as input so as to be able to perform automatically any sequence of tests and choose the new testing sequence on the basis of the results.

[D1] SIMSCRIPT II. Testing Methods Manual, C.A.C.I. Los Angeles, California, November 30, 1971.
Manual indicates the testing techniques used for testing and isolation of errors.

[D7] TDG-II Test Data Generator, Product brochure from Information Management, Inc. San
     Francisco, California, 1971.
          Generates test files based on COBOL data division record descriptions and supplied
     parameter cards. Not sensitive to program logic.

[D17] IBM System 360 TESTRAN, SRL C28-6648-1, 1967.
      Program facility to aid in finding faulty logic by giving assembler language facilities
      to change storage areas, control blocks and check control flows from one group of
      instructions to another.

[D18] Computer Aided Test Systems, J.A. Walters, Bendix Corporation BDX 613 275, December 1970.
      Considers the use of minicomputers in test system designs.

[D14] Experiment in Automatic Verification of Programs, G.M. Weinberg and G.L. Gresset,
      Communications of the ACM, October 1963, pp. 610-613.
      Reports on a study where an error profile of keypunch errors was inserted. Format
      errors were the only group that could not be detected successfully.

Formal Logic

[E5] Derivation of Axiomatic Definitions of Programming Languages from Algorithmic Definitions, C.D. Allen, Proc. of Proving Assertions About Programs Conf., January 1972, pp.15–26. Describes study to develop an axiomatic definition of a language.

[E6] The Application of Formal Logic to Programs and Programming, C.D. Allen, IBM Systems Journal, Vol 10 #1, 1971, pp.2–38. Introduces the use of formal logic in program analysis.

[E7] Program Correctness Methods and Language Definition, E.A. Ashcroft, Proc. of the Conf. on Proving Assertions About Programs, January 1972, pp.51–57. Methods for proving correctness are related to language definition methods.

[E8] Programs and Their Proofs--An Algebraic Approach, B.M. Burstall and P.J. Landin, Machine Intelligence 4, American Elsevier, pp.17–43, 1969. Discusses an algebraic treatment of the proof of correctness of a simpler compiler for expressions.

[E1] Proving Properties of Programs by Induction, R.M. Burstall, Computer Journal, Vol 12 #1, February 1969, pp.41–48.

[E9] Formal Description of Program Structure and Semantics in First Order Logic, R.M. Burstall, Machine Intell. 5, American Elsevier, New York, 1970. The semantics of a programming language (ALGOL) are described by a set of sentences in first order logic, which in turn is used to prove correctness and termination.

[E2] Mathematical Proofs About Computer Programs, D.C. Cooper, in Machine Intelligence 1, N.L. Collin and D. Michie (eds.), American Elsevier, New York, 1967. An introductory article reviewing the kinds of theorems one tries to prove about programs and offering simple examples on a number of different approaches.

[E10] Some Theorem Proving Strategies Based on the Resolution Principle, J.L. Darlington, Machine Intelligence 2, American Elsevier, 1968, pp.57–71. Use of the resolution principle to generate a contradiction from an initial set of claims Surveys a variety of heuristic methods.

[E11] Fidelity in Mathematical Discourse: Is One and One Really Two? P.J. Davis, Brown University. A clever article that tries to show that mathematical proofs are not definitive.

[E3] An Assessment of Techniques for Proving Program Correctness, B. Elspas, K.N. Levitt and J. Waldinger, Stanford Research Institute, Final Report Project 8398, 1971.

[E4] Assigning Meanings to Programs, R.W. Floyd in Mathematical Aspects of Computer Science, Vol.XIX, American Mathematical Society, Providence, Rhode Island, 1967, pp.19–32. Description of a proof method dependent on associating logical predicates with the arcs of a flowchart in order to deduce relations on the output from relations on the input.

[E35] An Axiomatic Basis for Computer Programming, C.A.R. Hoare, Comm. ACM October 1969. Proposes a language definition by a set of axioms so as to be able to establish rules of inference based on the language and the nature of programs. This would permit proving correctness provided that the implementation of the language conforms to the axioms and rules of inference that are used in the proof.

[E15] Procedures and Parameters: An Axiomatic Approach, C.A.R. Hoare, Symposium on Semantics of Algorithmic Languages, Springer-Verlag, 1970.

[E20] Recursion Induction Applied to Generalized Flowcharts, D.M. Kaplan, Proc. 24th National ACM Conf., 1969, pp.491-504.

[E24] Proving Programs to Be Correct, J.C. King, IEEE Trans. on Computers, November 1971, pp.1331 to 1336.
Use of an abstract program model to define correctness.

[E25] Mathematical Induction, D.E. Knuth, Fundamental Algorithms, Vol 1 of Art of Computer Programming, 1968, pp.11-18.
Discusses the use of mathematical induction for the proof of algorithms.

[E14] Computer Programs Can be Proved Correct, R.L. London, Proc. of Systems Symposium at Case Western Reserve University, New York, 1970, pp.281-303.

[E13] Bibliography on Proving the Correctness of Computer Programs, R.L. London, Machine Intelligence 5, Edinburgh, 1970, pp.569-580.
An often referenced bibliography on proofs of correctness.

[E26] Proof of Algorithms--A New Kind of Certification, R.L. London, CACM, June 1970, pp.371-373.
Considers certification in the form of a formal proof.

[E16] Experience with Inductive Assertions for Proving Programs Correct, R.L. London, Tech. report #92, Computer Sciences Dept., University of Wisconsin, 1970.

[E12] Proving Programs Correct: Some Techniques and Examples, R.L. London, BIT 10, 1970, pp.168 to 182.

[E27] The Proof of Correctness Approach to Reliable Systems, B.H. Liskov and E. Towster, MITRE Corporation MTR-2073, Bedford, Mass, July 1971.
Surveys the literature and discusses proof of correctness as the preferred method to achieve reliable software.

[E28] On Formalized Computer Programs, D.C. Luckham, D.M.R. Park, and M.S. Paterson, Journal of Computer and Systems Sciences, June 1970, pp.220-249.

[E18] Properties of Programs and the First-Order Predicate Calculus, F. Manna, JACM, Vol 16 #2, April 1969, pp.244-255.

[E29] Inductive Methods for Proving Properties of Programs, Z. Manna, S. Ness and J. Vuillen, Proc. of Conf. on Proving Assertions about Programs, January 1972, pp.27-50.
Considers various proof methods for recursive programs.

[E17] Formalization of Properties of Functional Programs, Z. Manna and A. Pnueli, JACM Vol 17 #3, July 1970, pp.555-569.
Use of first order predicate calculus to formalize the convergence, correctness and equivalence problems.

[E30] Properties of Programs and Partial Function Logic, Z. Manna and J. McCarthy, Machine Intelligence 5, American Elsevier Co., 1970, pp.27-37.
Considers IF-THEN-ELSE recursive expressions in an effort to formalize their properties of correctness and convergence.

[E19] The Correctness of Programs, Z. Manna, Journal of Computer and Systems Sciences, Vol 3, #2, May 1969, pp.119-127.
General discussion of the applicability of the predicate calculus.

[E21] Toward a Mathematical Science of Computation, J. McCarthy, IFIP 1962, pp.21-28.

[E22] An Inductive Proof Technique for Interpreter Equivalence, C.L. McGowan, Formal Semantics of Programming Languages, R. Rustin (ed.) Prentice-Hall, 1972.

[E31] Proof of Algorithms by General Snapshots, P. Naur, BIT 6, 1966, pp.310-316.
 Very readable description of the process of 'proof' by taking a dynamic algorithm specification in the form of a program and assigning to it general snapshot conditions (assertions) to be able to show equivalence to the static properties of the result of the algorithm. Included here as the general tone is closer to the testing orientation than are other proof papers.

[E32] Some Results Concerning Proofs of Statements About Programs, R.J. Orgass, Journal of Computer and Systems Sciences, Vol 4, 1970, pp.74-88.
 Use of a system of logic to prove a variety of statements about programs.

[E33] Fixpoint Induction and Proofs of Program Properties, D. Park, Machine Intelligence 5, American Elsevier, 1970, pp.59-78.
 Develops a theory for the formalization and proof of arbitrary properties of computer programs.

[E34] A Review of Automatic Theorem-Proving, J.A. Robinson, Proc. of Symposium in Applied Math., Vol. XIX, Math. Aspects of Computer Science, American Math. Society, Providence, Rhode Island, 1967, pp.1-18.

Program Specification Techniques and Specification Languages

[F1] A System for Automatic Program Generation, F.C. Bequaert, Proc. FJCC, 1968, pp.611-616.
Proposed system to use question answering and macro expansion to executable code.

[F3] On a Laboratory for the Study of Automatic Programming, T.E. Cheatham and B. Wegbrest, Proc. of the Conf. On Proving Assertions About Programs, January 1972, pp.208-211.
An overview of an effort to develop a laboratory to study automatic programming techniques.

[F4] A Formal Description of System/360, A.Falkoff and K. Iverson and E. Sussenguth, IBM System Journal, Vol.0, No.2-3, 1964, pp.198-263.
Use of APL for system description.

[F5] Criteria for a System Design Language, A.D. Falkoff, Software Engineering, NATO Science Committee, January 1969.

[F6] The Design of a Design Language, T. Freeman and H. Liu, Proc. National Electronics Conf., December 1970, pp.89-92.

[F7] A System Descriptive Language and Its Uses, D.F. Gorman, University of Penn , Thesis 1968.

[F2] Software Reliability, B. Elspas, M. Green and K. Levitt, Computer 4 # 1, Jan/Feb 1971, pp.21-27.
Proposes language constructs such as FILL and BUMP which are more descriptive of the intended actions so as to limit error possibilities and improve reliability.

[F8] Programming Notation in Systems Design, K. Iverson, IBM Systems Journal,June 1963, pp.117-128.
APL used for various levels of specifications.

[F11] SOL--A Symbolic Language for General Purpose Systems Simulation, D. Knuth and J. McNeley, IEEE Trans. on Comp., August 1964, pp.401-414.
Gives a general language for describing and simulating complex systems.

[F13] The Next 700 Programming Languages, P.J. Landin, CACM February 1966, pp.157-166.

[F10] Method and Notation for the Formal Definition of Programming Languages, P. Lucas, P. Lauer and H. Stigleitier, IBM Vienna Laboratory Report TR-25-087, June 1968.

[F19] The Test Language Dilemma, F. Liquori, Proc. ACM Nat. Conf. 1971, pp.388-396.
General discussion of test languages ELATE, DIMATE, ATLAS and PLACE.

[F9] Proposed Language Extensions to Aid Coding and Analysis of Large Programs, E. Lowry, IBM Corporation, Systems Development Division, Poughkeepsie, New York, 1969, TR 00.1934.
Outlines new PL/1 statements permitting semantic conditions and constraints to be specified. The statements permit more compile time error checking and more automatic levels of testing.

[F12] Toward Automatic Program Synthesis, F. Manna and R.J. Waldinger, CACM 14 #3, 1971, pp.151-165.

[F22] A Proposal for a Computer Compiler, G. Metzl and S. Seshu , SJCC, 1966, pp.253-263.
The workability of higher level languages for design systems is discussed and a Fortran like language is proposed.

[F26] A Paradigm for Software Module Specification with Examples, D.L. Parnes, Carnegie-Mellon Dept. of Computer Science, March 1971.
For each output variable or output function the range, domain, parameters affecting the calculation and side effects are given.

[F27] Information Distribution Aspects of Design Methodology, D.L. Parnas, Proc. IFIP Congress 7:
Proposes dividing a system into modules and making explicit statements about their complete context. Each module is described by a function to be performed, a set of inputs and a set of outputs.

[F28] A Language for Describing the Functions of Synchronous Systems, D.L. Parnas, CACM, February 1966, pp.72-76.
Describes inadequacies of current languages and gives a dialect of Algol suitable for synchronous system specification.

[F29] More on Simulation Languages and Design Methodology for Computer Systems, D.L. Parnas, Proc. SJCC 1969, pp.739-743.
A SODAS description language including facilities for describing operating systems is given.

[F30] A Technique for Software Module Specification with Examples, D.L. Parnas, CACM May 1972, pp.330-336.
Approach to writing specifications for software systems that are precise enough so that other pieces can be written to interface without additional information.

[F31] A Digital Control Design Language, H. Potash, Applied Science Report 69-21, May 1969.
Language formats for modelling the control in a digital machine.

[F32] A Calculus and an Algorithm for a Logic Minimization Problem Together with an Algorithm Notation, J.P. Roth and E.G. Wagner, IBM Research Report RC 2280, November 1968.

[F15] Abstract Algorithms and a Set-Theoretic Language for their Expression, J.T. Schwartz, Courant Institute of Mathematical Sciences, N.Y.U., Draft.

[F14] Limits of Programmability and the Design of Programming Languages, J.T. Schwartz, Int. Computer Society Conference, 1971, pp.159-160.

[F33] A Formal Language for Describing Machine Logic, Timing and Sequencing, H. Schlaeppi, IEEE Trans. on Computers, August 1964, pp.439-448.
A machine description language LOTIS is described including a hierarchical structure so segmentation can be accomplished.

[F34] Definition of Systems, G. Seegmuller, Software Engineering, NATO Science Committee, April 1970.

[F35] A Control System for Logical Block Diagnosis with Data Loading, M.E. Senko, CACM April 1960, pp.236-240.

[F16] A Language for Algorighms, R.H. Stark, Computer Journal, February 1971, pp.40-44.
Specifies an algorithm or specification language for a class of mathematical problems designed to facilitate proofs of equivalence as well as translation into efficient machine programs.

[F17] On Means to Record Algorithms to Facilitate Generation of Error Free Programs, R.H. Stark, WSU Computing Center Report 68-1, 1968.

[F36] A Language Design for Concurrent Processes, L. Tesler and H. Enea, Proc. SJCC 1969, pp.403-408.
Describes languages to allow parallelism and provide a means for tracing dependence during compilation.

[F18] Toward a Programming Laboratory, W. Teitelman, 1st Int. Joint Conf. on Art. Intell, Washington, D.C., 1969.
Discusses problems of providing "Do what I mean" facilities.

[F37] PROW--A Step Toward Automatic Program Writing, R.J. Waldinger and R.C.T. Lee, Proc. Int. Joint Conf. on Artificial Intelligence, 1969.
Considers construction of programs automatically using theorem proving.

[F24] The Vienna Definition Language, P. Wegner, Computing Surveys, March 1972, pp.5-63.

[F38] The Psychology of Computer Programming, G.M. Weinberg, Van Nostrand Reinhold Company, New York, 1971.
A beginning attempt to provide a scientific identification of language constructs that tend to cause errors.

[F21] Toward Automatic Debugging of Low Level Code, W. Worley,Jr., IBM Corporation, Systems Development Division, Poughkeepsie, New York, TR 002211, July 23, 1971.
Discusses the concept of redundantly coded (RC) languages consisting of a code language (CL) and a dual language (DL) to specify assertions, specifications and test criteria. Proposes a DL to work in conjunction with a reasonable subset of OS/360 Assembler language. Resulting compiler is capable of testing in static (from the source) dynamic (interpretively testing DL conditions) or monitor (execute and wait for trap) modes.

[F39] The Outer and Inner Syntax of a Programming Language, M.V. Wilkes, Computer Journal, Vol.11 1968, pp.260-263.

[F20] Programming and Programming Languages, N. Wirth, International Computing Symposium, Bonn, 1970.

[F23] BLISS: A Language for Systems Programming, W. Wulf, D. Russel, and A. Habermann, CACM 14 #12, December 1971, pp.780-790.
Discusses the first major language implemented without a GO TO statement and containing a number of other language considerations to facilitate testing.

[F25] Fuzzy Algorithms, L.A. Zadeh, Information and Control, Vol 12, 1963, pp.94-102.
Discusses fuzzy or imperfect languages, algorithms and environments.

Measuring and Estimating Program Reliability

[G 2] Standards for Software--What Is In the Future, R.M. Davis, ADAPSO Software Section Management Conference, Dallas, Texas, February 1972.
Discussion of quality assurance standards.

[G 5] Qualitative Analysis of Software Reliability, J.J. Dickson, J.L. Hesse, A.C. Krentz and M.L. Shooman, Proc. of the Annual Reliability and Maintainability Symposium, January 1972, pp.148-157.
The probabilistic methods of hardware reliability analysis are extended toward software testing and reliability.

[G 1] Historical Analysis of Computer Program Changes as a Guide to Establishing Quality Control Measures, O.E. Ellingson, TM 2887 Systems Development Corporation, Santa Monica, California March 17, 1966.
This paper is an extension of Tucker's paper with more data. Illustrates consistency of the exponential error plot where new code was involved but for modified code shows the magnitude of the exponential is not easily predicted.

[G 10] A Predictor Tool For Estimating the Confidence Level of a Computer Program Subsystem In the Space Programs Department, O.E. Ellingson, SDC Tech. Memo #L3335, January 1967.

[G 11] Complexity Measures for Programming Languages, L.I. Goodman, AD 729-011 , Project MAC, September 1971.
Equations are developed for measuring complexity as a function of the amount of resources used.

[G 3] Using the Computer for Program Conversion, M.H. Halstead, Datamation 16,5 May 1970, pp.125-129.
Although the paper is not directly related to testing, the usage of a figure of merit concept to evaluate the decompiler performance seemed to be a technique that could be applied similarly to measure the efficiency of the test process and evaluate how much to do by hand.

[G 12] Program Errors As a Birth and Death Process, G.R. Hudson, SDC Corp., Report SP 3011, December 1967.
Considers a large system of many modules where unit testing is mostly complete and develops equations for modelling the error detection process based on a Markovian birth and death scheme.

[G 13] Program Quality Assurance, A. Karush, Datamation, October 1968, pp. 61-66.
Article considers quality control in a large analytical or statistical program. Suggests including features in the design such as the ability to manipulate the input in a controlled manner to observe variations in the output and the inclusion of automated methods to judge reasonableness of final program values.

[G 4] On the Statistical Validation of Computer Programs, H.D. Mills, Draft not yet published available from author at IBM Corporation, Gaithersburg, Maryland, July 1970.
Proposes a statistical sampling test based on the introduction of intentional but random programming errors into a program before the testing process starts.

[G 14] Software Reliability, R.B. Mulock, Proc. Symposium on Reliability, Jan. 1969, p. 495.

[G 15] Software Reliability Engineering, R.B. Mulock, Proc. of the Annual Reliability and Maintainability Symposium pp. 586-593, January 1972.
Summarizes various aspects of software engineering from a reliability standpoint.

[G6] Quantitative Measurement of Program Quality, Raymond J. Rubey and R. Dean Hartwick,
      Proceedings, 23rd National Conference, ACM, 1968, pp.671-67.
        Proposes establishing metrics for various program attributes which are then
      normalized and combined in a weighted score in an overall quality model. The
      attributes still appear to be quite subjective.

[G7] Definition and Evaluation of Merit in Spaceborne Software, R.J. Rubey et al, Logicon
      Report # CS 6832-R0096, 1968.

[G8] Problems In, and a Pragmatic Approach to Programming Language Measurement, J.E. Sammet,
      Proceedings of FJCC, 1971.

[G16] Reliability in Computer Programs, J.L. Sauter, Mech. Engineering, Vol 91 #2, pp.24-27,
      February 1969.

[G17] Computer Reliability Bibliography #3, D. Siewiorek, Digital Systems Lab, Stanford,
      October, 1970.

[G9] Correlation of Computer Programming Quality with Testing Effort, A.E. Tucker, TM 2219
      Systems Development Corporation, Santa Monica, California, January 28, 1965.
        Investigates the possibility of defining the quality of a computer program as a
      function of the testing time expended. Based on a small amount of data, the author
      concludes that some confidence can be gained from the exponential slope of the error
      accumulation vs. testing plot and that many of the intuitive feelings on the factors
      that influence the curve are not supported. A technique of normalization to compute
      an index allows an estimation of how much testing remains before a system can be
      delivered.

[G18] A Software Reliability Program, O.L. Williamson, G.G. Dorris, A.J. Rybert and W.E.
      Straight, Federal Electric Corporation, Huntsville, Alabama, 1970.

[G19] Application of Decision Theory to the Testing of Large Systems, P.J. Wong, IEEE Trans.
      on Aerospace and Electronic Systems, March 1971, pp. 379-384.
        Model for the allocation of test resources based on a priority ranking of performance
      uncertainty and performance sensitivity based on a value structure over the test
      program.

Test Data Generation

[H1] Test Data Generation, M.R. Barrett, U.S. Army Computer Systems and Support and Evaluation Command, Systems Techniques and Analysis Directorate, Washington, D.C. , U.S. Army ADP Symposium, March 1972.
   Evaluates the current state and future for test data generation tools.

[H7] Generating Test Programs from Syntax, W.H. Burkhardt, Computing 2, 1(1967) pp.53-73.

[H3] Automatic Generation of Test Cases, K.V. Hanford, IBM Systems Journal, Vol.9#4, 1970, pp.242-257.
   Describes a syntax directed program for automatically generating syntactically correct PL/1 programs (test cases) for testing compiler front ends. Restricts BNF notation to specify the generation of only valid strings by adding context sensitive rules to form dynamic grammars.

[H2] Test Data Generators and Debugging Systems...Workable Quality Control, Part I and II, Data Processing Digest Vol 18, #2 and 3, February and March 1972, S.M. Naftaly and M.C. Cohen.
   Survey of various automated aids for test data generation.

[H5] Generalized Satellite Telemetry Data Simulation Program, B.G. Narrow and R.C. Lee, NASA Goddard Space Flight Center, Greenbelt, Maryland, November 1966.
   Description of a data simulation program which generates test tapes used for debugging and testing.

[H6] General Test Data Generator For Cobol, R.L. Sauder, AFIPS Conference Proceedings SJCC 1962, pp.317-323.
   Adds a Requirements division to Cobol programs with a Relation section to specify the logic of data relationships. Employs a network analysis program to generate test data for different branches. In general, the paper describes a system considerably ahead of its time.

[H4] Test Data Generation Study Report, Management and Computer Service Inc. Report, Philadelphia, Pennsylvania, 1971.

Proof of Correctness Applications

[I1] The Verifying Compiler, R.W. Floyd, Computer Science Research Review, Carnegie-Mellon University, pp.18-19, 1967.

[I2] Toward Interactive Design of Correct Programs, R.W. Floyd, Proc. IFIP Congress 1971, North Holland Publishing Company, Amsterdam, August 1971, pp.1-4.
Proposes an interactive language allowing the purpose of the program to be specified as well as the algorithm. The machine is expected to demonstrate the correctness of whatever program has been constructed to satisfy this specification.

[I3] Proof of a Recursive Program--Quicksort, M. Foley and C.A.R. Hoare, Computer Journal, Vol.14 pp. 391-395, November 1971.
A rigorous but informal proof of correctness.

[I4] Toward A Man Machine System for Proving Program Correctness, D.I. Good, Thesis University of Wisconsin, 1970.
Description of a man machine system automating various parts of the proof process.

[I5] Proof of Programs: Partition and Find, C.A.R. Hoare, Dept. of Computer Science, Queens University of Belfast, April 1969.

[I6] Proof of a Program: FIND, C.A.R. Hoare, CACM 14 #1, January 1971, pp.39-45.

[I7] Correctness of a Compiler for Algol Like Programs, D.M. Kaplan, Artificial Intelligence Memo #48, Stanford University, July 1967.

[I8] A Program Verifier, J.C. King, Thesis, Carnegie Mellon University, 1969.

[I9] A Verifying Compiler, J. King in Debugging Techniques in Large Systems, Edited by Randall Rustin, Prentice-Hall, 1971, pp.17-39.
Suggest annotating a program to be compiled with propositions about the relations among its variables. Consistency between these propositions and the actual program is then verified by the compiler. Once "verified" the program is guaranteed to compute correct results.

[I17] The Definition and Validation of the Radix Sorting Technique, J.A. Lee, Proceedings of the Conference on Proving Assertions About Programs, pp.142-149, January, 1972.
Proof of validity for radix sort.

[I10] Correctness of the Algol Procedure, ASFORHAND, R.L. London, University of Wisconson, 1968, Computer Sciences Technical Report #50.

[I12] Computer Interval Arithmetic: Definition and Proof of Correct Implementation, D.I. Good and R.L. London, JACM Vol 17 #4, October 1970.

[I13] Correctness of a Compiler for Arithmetic Expressions, J. McCarthy and J. Painter in Mathematical Aspects of Computer Science, Vol XIX, American Mathematical Society, Providence, Rhode Island, 1967, pp.33-41.
Proves the correctness of a compiler employing recursive functions.

[I14] Semantic Correctness of a Compiler for an Algol Like Language, J.A. Painter, Artificial Intelligence Memo #44, Stanford University, March 1967.

[I15] <u>A Mechanical Proof Procedure and Its Realization In an Electronic Computer</u>, D. Prawitz,
H. Prawitz and N. Voghera, JACM Vol 7 #2, 1960 pp.102-108.
Predicate calculus in a machine representable format.

[I16] <u>A Verified Program Verifier</u>,(Working title), L.C. Ragland, Ph.D Thesis University of Texas
at Austin, in preparation.
A proof of correctness for the verifier used in the Nucleus language of provable programs.

Testing As A Development Process

[J11] Checklist for Planning Software System Production, R.W. Bemer, Software Engineering, NATO
Science Committee, January 1969.
Includes a number of testing oriented ideas.

[J1] Controlling the Functional Testing of an Operating System, W.R. Elmendorf, IEEE Transactions on Systems Science and Cybernetics, Vol. SCC-5,No.4, October 1969, pp.284-290.
General definitions of testing concepts and lessons. Indicates testing is becoming
systematic and describes a test process of five steps - survey, identify, appraise, review
and monitor. Distinguishes between specification testing and program testing.

[J2] Notes on Testing Real-Time System Programs, M.C. Ginzberg, IBM System Journal, Vol.4#1,
1965, pp.58-72.
Considers the stages of testing from individual subsystem test in a simulated environment
up to entire system test in the real environment. Software needed at each stage is discussed.

[J12] The Design and Production of Real Time Software For an Electronic Switching System, J.A.
Harr, Software Engineering, NATO Science Committee, January 1970.

[J3] Program Validation, V.D. Henderson, Logican Inc., San Pedro, California, 1969.
A working paper describing the process of validation as applied to an onboard missile
computer. Tools of validation emphasized are various levels of simulation and auxiliary
programs such as path analysis codes, equation generators and flow charters. Success for
the techniques described depends quite a bit on the small machine programming assumptions
made.

[J4] Debugging and Assessment of Control Programs for an Automatic Radar, K. Jackson and J.R.
Prior, Computer Journal, November 1969.
Outlines a four stage debugging or test process for a real time radar system.

[J13] The Management and Organization of Large Scale Software Development Projects, R.H. Kay,
Proc. SJCC, pp.425-433.

[J14] The Test and Evaluation of Large Scale Information Processing Systems in the Army,R.M. Lilly
Info. System Science and Technology, D.E. Walker (editor) Washington, D.C., Thompson
Publishing Company, pp.35-38.

[J15] Operating Validation Testing, W.C. Mittwede and K.P. Choate, AD 724 717, January 1971.
Test procedures for use in validation testing of computer operating systems.

[J6] Management Control in Program Testing, A.M. Pietrasanta, TR 00.1474, Systems Development
Division, IBM Corporation, Poughkeepsie, New York, July 1966.
Discusses a methodology for managing the testing of large systems using a test case
library and plotting number of test cases coded, run and run successfully vs. time. Potentially the graphs could be generated automatically.

[J16] An Engineering Approach to Software Configuration Management, B.L. Ryle, IEEE Trans. on
Aerospace and Electrical Systems, November 1967, pp.947-951.
General Discussion of Development and testing problems.

[J8] Application of Disciplined Software Testing, P. Schlender in Debugging Practices in Large
Systems, edited by Randall Rustin, Prentice-Hall, 1971, pp.141-142.
Defines ideas of unit testing, interface testing and regression testing. Comments on the
need for an improved specification language and a testable design.

[J7] Verification of the Apollo Real Time Mission Program, J.V. Schnurbush, AIAA Aerospace
Computer Systems Conference Proceedings, September 1969.
  Description of the testing techniques used for a large real time system including test
case generation, test plans and management and validation procedures.

[J17] Testing the NORAD Command and Control System, R.T. Stevens, IEEE Trans. on Systems Science
and Cybernetics, March 1968, pp.47-51.

[J9] Program Quality Control, N.C. Willmorth, Rand Corporation, Santa Monica, California,
TM 2222/016/00, 1965.
  General description of program quality control techniques. Includes a table of common
program errors and their causes. Suggests a staged testing process of parameter testing,
assembly testing and system testing.

[J10] System Integration as a Programming Function, N.A. Zimmerman, TR 53.003-1, System Development Division, IBM Corporation, Yorktown Heights, New York, July 1969.
  General discussion of the problems of a large system of programs.

Mathematical and Numerical Software Testing

[K56] Unnormalized Floating Point Arithmetic, R.L. Ashenhurst , and N. Metropolis, Journal of the ACM, July 1959, Vol. 6/3, pp.415-428.

[K1] NATS, a Collaborative Effort to Certify and Disseminate Mathematical Software, J.M. Boyle, W.J. Cody, W.R. Cowell, B.S. Grabow, Y. Ikebe, C.B. Moler and B.T. Smith, submitted for ACM National Conference, 1972.

[K54] A Software System for Tracing Numerical Significance During Computer Program Execution, H.S. Bright, B.A. Colhoun, and F.B. Mallory, Proc. SJCC 1971, AFIPS Conference Proceedings, Vol 38, AFIPS Press, Montvale, New Jersey, 1971.

[K59] Error Analysis in Floating-point Arithmetic, J.W. Carr III, Comm. ACM 2/5 May 1959.

[K21] A Comparison of Some Numerical Integration Programs, J. Casaletto, M. Pickett and J.R. Rice Report CSD TR 37, Computer Science Department, Purdue University, 1969.

[K58] Binary Notations in Automatic Computer Algorithms and Operation Codes, B.F. Cheydleur, ACM Third Annual Conference (paper preprint only) Oak Ridge, Tennessee, 1949.

[K3] Performance Statistics of the Fortran IV(H) Library for the IBM System/360, N.A. Clark, W.J. Cody, K.E. Hillstrom and E.A. Thieleker, Argonne National Laboratory Report ANL-7321, Argonne, Illinois, 1967.

[K4] Preliminary Report on Study of Fortran Library Functions, Comput. Center Newsletter 6, #1, Lawrence Radiation Laboratory, Berkeley, California, 1969.

[K5] Performance Testing of Function Subroutines, W.J. Cody, AFIPS Conference Proceedings, SJCC, 1969, pp.759-763.
  Description of a method for testing function codes. To test the code on one machine a second machine with a longer word length is used to randomly generate a table of argument values and corresponding function values. The arguments and values are then rounded and converted to the internal format of the first and used as a test standard.

[K6] Software For the Elementary Functions, W.J. Cody in Mathematical Software by J. Rice, Academic Press, New York, 1971, pp.171-185.
  Review of activities and results of various certification projects aimed at validating elementary mathematical function codes.

[K9] Accuracy of Single Precision UNIVAC 1108 Subroutine Library Functions, C.J. Devine, and C.L. Lawson, JPL Space Programs Summary 37-56, Vol.II, pp.115-121, 1969.

[K10] CADRE: An Algorithm for Numerical Quadrature, C. de Boor, in Mathematical Software, J.R. Rice, Editor, Academic Press, New York, 1971.

[K11] An Evaluation of Five Polynomial Zero Finders, D.S. Dodson, P.A. Miller, W.C. Nylin and J.R. Rice, Report CSD TR24, Computer Science Department, Purdue University, 1968.

[K55] Pitfalls in Computation, or Why a Math Book Isn't Enough, G.E. Forsythe, Stanford University Technical Report CS-147, January 1970; also available from Commerce Clearinghouse as AD-699,897.

[K12] A Simple Set of Test Matrices for Eigenvalue Programs, C.W. Gear, Math Comp. 23, 1969, pp. 119-125.

[K60] Normalized Floating-point Arithmetic With an Index of Significance, H.L. Gray and C. Harrison, Jr., Proc. EJCC,'59, NJCC, New York, 1959.

[K13] <u>A Collection of Matrices for Testing Computational Algorithms</u>, R.T. Gregory and D.L. Karney, Wiley-Interscience, New York, 1969.

[K14] <u>Statistical Validation of Mathematical Computer Routines</u>, C. Hammer, SJCC, 1967, Thompson Book Company, Washington, D.C., 1967, pp.331-333.
Suggests a Monte Carlo approach to develop an estimator for a routines precision.

[K8] <u>Topics in Interval Analysis</u>, E. Hanson, Clarendon Press, 1969.

[K15] <u>Certifying Linear Equation Solvers</u>, R.J. Hanson, SIGNUM Newsletter, Vol.4, No.3, October, 1969, pp.21-29.

[K16] <u>Computer Approximations</u>, J. Hart, et al, J. Wiley, New York, 1968.

[K17] <u>Comparison of Several Adaptive Newton-Cotes Quadrature Routines in Evaluating Definite Integrals with Peaked Integrands</u>, K.E. Hillstrom, Comm. ACM 13, 1970, pp.362-365.

[K18] <u>Performance Statistics for the Fortran IV(H) and PL/I (Version 5) Libraries in IBM OS/360 Release 18</u>, K.E. Hillstrom, Report ANL-7666, Argonne National Laboratory, 1970.

[K9] <u>The Correctness of Numerical Algorithms</u>, T.E. Hull, W.H. Enright, and A.E. Sedgwick, Proc. of the Conf. on Proving Assertions About Programs, January 1972, pp.66-73.
Considers the use of structured programming and assertions for organizing proofs of numerical algorithm correctness.

[K19] <u>A Search for Optimum Methods for the Numerical Integration of Ordinary Differential Equations</u>, T.E. Hull, SIAM Review, 9, 1967, pp.647-654.

[K20] <u>Comparing Numerical Methods for Ordinary Differential Equations</u>, T.E. Hull, W.H. Enright, B.M. Fellen, A.E. Sedgwick, Report 29, Dept. of Computer Science, Univ. of Toronto, 1971.

[K21] <u>Comparison of Numerical Quadrature Formulas</u>, D.K. Kahaner, in Mathematical Software, J.R. Rice, Editor, Academic Press, New York, 1971.

[K22] <u>On Testing a Subroutine for the Numerical Integration of Ordinary Differential Equations</u>, F.T. Krogh, JPL Sect. 314 Tech. Memo No. 217, JPL, Pasadena, California, 1969.

[K23] <u>A Plea for Tolerance in the Evaluation of Numerical Methods and Mathematical Software</u>, F.T. Krough, SIGNUM Newsletter, vol.6, No.3, November, 1971, pp.7-8.

[K24] <u>Comments on the ANL Evaluation of OS/360 Fortran Math Function Library</u>, H. Kuki, SHARE Secretary Distribution 169, 1967, C-4773, pp.47-53.

[K25] <u>FORTRAN Extended-Precision Library</u>, H. Kuki and J. Ascoly, IBM Sys. J., 10, 1971, pp.39-61.

[K26] <u>A Statistical Study of the Accuracy of Floating Point Number Systems</u>, H. Kuki and W.J. Cody to appear Comm. ACM.

[K27] <u>Study of the Accuracy of the Double Precision Arithmetic Operations on the IBM 7094 Computer</u>, C.L. Lawson, JPL Tech. Mem. #33-142, Jet Propulsion Laboratory, Pasadena, 1963.

[K28] <u>Basic Q-Precision Arithmetic Subroutines Including Input and Output</u>, C.L. Lawson, JPL Section 314 Tech. Mem. #170, 1967.

[K29] <u>Q-Precision Subroutines for the Elementary Functions and Aids for Testing S.P. and D.P. Function Subroutines</u>, C.L. Lawson, JPL Section 314 Tech. Mem. #188, 1968.

[K30] <u>Summary of Q-Precision Subroutines as Revised in October 1968</u>, C.L. Lawson, JPL Section 314 Tech. Mem. #211, 1969.

[K31] <u>A Bit Comparison Program for Algorithm Testing</u>, D.W. Lozier, L.C.Maximon, and W.L. Sadowski, National Bureau of Standards Report #10-449, Washington, D.C., 1971.

[K32] <u>Report on NBS FORTRAN Single Precision Tangent and Cotangent</u>, D.W. Lozier, L.C. Maximon, and W.L. Sadowski. To appear as an NBS Technical Note.

[K33] <u>Guidelines for Automatic Quadrature Routines</u>, J.N. Lyness, to appear in Proc. IFIP Congress 1971.

[K34] <u>FORTRAN Program for Arbitrary Precision Arithmetic</u>, L.C. Maximon, NBS Tech. News Bulletin, October 1971, p.242.

[K35] <u>Accuracy Enhancement of the Fortran V Math Library</u>, T.H. Miller, Univac Product Development, Salt Lake City, Utah, 1970.

[K36] <u>Matricial Difference Schemes for Integrating Stiff Systems of Ordinary Differential Equations</u>, W.L. Miranker, Math. Comp. 25, 1971, pp.717-728.

[K62] <u>Automatic Estimates of Computational Errors</u>, G.J. Moshos, and L.R. Turner, IEEE Conference Paper CP-63-1474, October 1963.

[K37] <u>Consistency Tests for Elementary Functions</u>, A.C.R. Newbery and A.P. Leigh, AFIPS Conf. Proc. 39, 1971 FJCC, AFIPS Press, Montvale, New Jersey, 1971, pp.419-422.

[K38] <u>Accuracy of Double Precision Fortran Functions</u>, E.W. Ng, and C.L. Lawson, JPL Sect.314, Tech. Memo No. 214, JPL, Pasadena, California, 1969.

[K39] <u>Certification of Algorithm 385-Exponential Integral</u>, E.W. Ng, Comm. ACM Vol.13, pp.444-445, 1970.

[K40] <u>Unpublished referee's report on an algorithm for the complex gamma function</u>, E.W. Ng, 1971.

[K41] <u>Eigenvalue and Eigenvector Routines in the McMaster Program Library</u>, K.A. Redish, and W.A. Ward, Report 5.2.5, McMaster University, Hamilton, Ontario, 1970.

[K42] <u>A Set of 74 Test Functions for Nonlinear Equations Solvers</u>, J.R. Rice, Report CSD TR 34, Computer Science Department, Purdue University, 1969.

[K43] <u>Mathematical Software</u>, J.R. Rice Editor, Academic Press, New York, 1971.

[K44] <u>Automatic Computing Methods for Special Functions</u>, I.A. Stegun and R. Zucker, NBS Journal of Research, 74B, 1970, p.211.

[K46] <u>On the Equation of State of A Relativistic Fermi-Dirac Gas at High Temperatures</u>, R.F. Tooper, Astrophys. J. Vol. 156, pp.1075-1100, 1969.

[K45] <u>High Quality Portable Numerical Mathematics Software</u>, J.F. Traub, Mathematical Software, ACM Monograph Series, Academic Press, 1971, J.R. Rice, Editor, p.133.

[K47] <u>SIGNUM Subroutine Certification Committee Report</u>, K.H. Usow, SIGNUM Newsletter, vol.4, No.3 October 1969, pp.15-18.

[K48] Certification Bibliography, K.H. Usow, SIGNUM Newsletter, Vol.5, No.2, August 1970, pp.14-15.

[K57] Numerical Inverting of Matrices of High Order, J. von Neumann and H.H. Goldstine, Bull. American Math. Soc. 53, 1947, pp.1021-99.

[K52] Fortran V Library Functions Reference Manual for 1108, W. Wallace, University of Wisconsin, Madison, Wisconsin, 1969.

[K49] An Evaluation of Linear Least Squares Computer Programs, R.H. Wampler, J. Res. Nat. Bur. Standards, Sect. B, 1969, pp.59-90.

[K50] Rounding Errors in Algebraic Processes, J.H. Wilkinson, Prentice-Hall, Englewood Cliffs, New Jersey, 1963.

[K51] Comparative Tabulations of Test Problems and Test Results for Mathematical Computer Routines, SIGNUM Newsletter, Vol.2, No.3, December 1967.

[K53] Computer Programming for Accuracy, J.M. Yohe, Mathematical Research Center, University of Wisconsin, U.S. Army Report #866, April 1968.
      Fairly general discussion of accuracy problems in mathematical software. Discusses internal arithmetic, bounds analysis and testing on multiple computers. Very little content

Testing Monitors and Simulators

[L1] Software Validation of the TITAN Digital Flight Control System Utilizing a Hybrid Computer, R.S. Jackson and S.A. Bravdica, Proc. FJCC, pp. 225-232, 1971.
    Describes the simulation of a space vehicle to investigate the use of an airborne flight control system.

[L7] A Program Simulator By Partial Interpretation, K. Fuchi, H. Tanaha, and T. Yiba, Second Symposium on OS Principles, October 1969, pp. 105-111.

[L8] Hierarchical Control Programs for Systems Evaluation, D.D. Keefe, IBM Systems Journal, Vol. 7 #2, 1968.
    Reviews short history of systems testing and proposes testing with another level of monitor program so that regular control program can be run in problem state and be controlled and tested. This technique is contrasted with classical systems testing using specially built equipment or a second computer.

[L3] Testing Conversational Systems, N.J. King in Debugging Techniques in Large Systems, edited by Randall Rustin, Prentice-Hall, 1971, pp.143-146.
    Describes the support facilities used in the testing of TSS/360 including the HOOK facility to permit testing to proceed independently of other shared users.

[L4] Conceptual Design for an Automatic Test System Simulator, F. Liquori, Proc. National ACM, 1969.
    Describes a basic test simulator design.

[L5] MUSE: Tool for Testing and Debugging a Multi-Terminal Programming System, E.W. Pullen and D.F. Shuthee, AFIPS Conference Proceedings, SJCC 1968, pp.491-502.
    Describes a system to simulate the user and communications environment to permit exercising a multiterminal system independent of multiplexing or terminal hardware.

[L9] Debugging Under Simulation, R.M. Supnik, Debugging Techniques in Large Systems, edited by Randall Rustin, Prentice-Hall, 1971, pp.118-136.
    Argues for the extensive use of machine simulation as a test and debugging tool in the development of programming systems for small machines. Permits getting at the data items, controlling the test and repeating sequences.

[L2] Test/360 (360A-SE-24L), Version 3, Applications Description, IBM Corporation, White Plains, New York, Form Y20-000902.
    Describes a simulator for testing IBM teleprocessing systems. The simulator provides the specified environment and supplies system data.

[L6] The Validation Control System Functional Design Specification, E. Youngberg, D. Williams, J. Witlow and R. Schwartz, UNIVAC, July 1971.
    Describes the basic design of a validation oriented control system.

[L10] LOCS, An EDP Machine Logic and Control Simulator, M. Zucker, IEEE Trans. on Computers, June 1965, pp.403-416.
    Inputs are a machine description and set of test programs and outputs are performance statistics and data.

Debugging

[M12] The Use of An Auxiliary Computer With A Graphic Display As An On Line Debugging Aid,
E.T. Ashby, Naval Postgraduate School Thesis, AD 728 719, June 1971.
System to monitor a program running on another computer.

[M1] EXDAMS - Extendable Debugging and Monitoring System, R.M. Balzer, AFIPS Conference Proceedings SJCC 1969.
Describes a system EXDAMS, aimed at providing a single environment in which users can
easily add new on line debugging aids. Aids are classified as static and motion picture.
Program can analyze how information flowed to produce a specified value and print an in-
verted tree with nodes marked giving the history. Operates in four phases of program
analysis, compilation, run time, history gathering, and history play back.

[M2] Extendable Non-Interactive Debugging, J. Blair in Debugging Techniques in Large Systems,
edited by R. Rustin, Prentice-Hall, 1971, pp.94-115.
The basic construction of a debugging system and the interface used for extension are
described at a technical implementation level.

[M13] Debugging in a Time Sharing Environment, W.A. Bernstein and J.T. Owens, FJCC 1968, pp.7-14.
Time sharing system with supervisor calls for debugging support.

[M3] Operating Environment for Dynamic Recursive Computer Programming Systems, W.S. Brown,
Comm. of the ACM, June 1965.
Description of a control program OEDIPUS designed on the premise that debugging is a
central problem and providing features to assist in the process of debugging user programs.

[M14] A New Approach to On Line, Run Time Program Logic and Error Debugging Using Hardware Implementation, Vol 2 # 1, pp.33-37, 1970.

[M4] On Line Debugging Techniques: A Survey, T.G. Evans and D. Darley, Air Force Cambridge Research Methods and Instrumentation, Bedford, Massachusetts, AFIPS Conference Proceedings,
FJCC, 1966, Vol.29, pp.37-50.
A good survey of on line techniques used for both assembly language and higher level
languages. Examples of various techniques in each are given and a description of implementation methods is included.

[M15] Error Correction In CORC, D.N. Freeman, Proc. FJCC, 1964, Vol 26, Part I, Spartan Books,
pp.15-34.
Description of the error correction facilities in the CORC compiler.

[M5] The Debugging of Computer Programs, R.S. Gaines, CRD Working Paper No. 266, August 1969,
Institute for Defense Analysis, Princeton, N.J.
A thorough and general study of the tools and techniques for debugging computer programs
including the design of compilers and operating systems to facilitate debugging. Also
given is a good survey of the various types of plots of location counter vs. time to
facilitate program analyses.

[M16] The Debugging System--Aids, R. Grishman, Proc. SJCC 1970, pp.59-64.
System for debugging of compiler code emphasizing the use of location, event and expression or value tags.

[M17] Criteria For a Debugging Language, R. Grishman in Debugging Techniques in Large Systems,
edited by R. Rustin, Prentice-Hall, 1971, pp.58-75.
The features of a good debugging system language are described and compared with the
language of current systems. Offers idea of a microprogram modified to check loads, stores
and transfers against a table set up by a debugging system. Discusses the debugging system AIDS.

[M21] Automation of Program Debugging, K. Jacoby and H. Layton, Proceedings of 16th National ACM Conference, 1961.
   Very general discussion with little content of the types of testing problems.

[M6] A Survey of Current Debugging Concepts, W. Kocher, NASA Report CR-1397, August 1969.
   A fairly extensive survey of debugging techniques including discussions on dynamic testing, logical tree data case selection and the need to allow multiple versions of the same procedure to be tested in the same run. Emphasizes the need for developing a better method in obtaining test data. Included here because it contains a large bibliography of debugging related references.

[M7] A Combination Hardware-Software Debugging Aid, K.C. Knowlton, IEEE Trans. on Computers, Vol C17 #1, pp.84-86, January 1968.

[M8] Extending the Interactive Debugging System HELPER, H.E. Kulsrud, in Debugging Techniques in Large Systems, edited by R. Rustin, Prentice-Hall, 1971, pp.78-91.
   HELPER is a debugging system which is extensible so as to permit continual upgrading in its debugging capabilities. The structure of the system is given and an evaluation is made.

[M18] New Approaches to Documentation and Debugging, J.J. Marshall, Data Processing, Vol 14, pp. 425-435, 1970.

[M9] DITRAN - A Compiler Emphasizing Diagnostics, P.G. Moulton, and M.E. Muller, CACM 10, January 1967, pp.45-52.
   Emphasizes messages in source language terms, trace and audit routines and the detection of all non logical errors.

[M10] WATFOR ... Speedy FORTRAN Debugger, S. Siegel, Datamation 17, 22, November 1971, pp.22-26.

[M19] TALK -- A High Level Source Language Debugging Technique With Real-Time Data Extraction, R.L. Ver Steeg, CACM July 1964 , pp. 418-419.
   Source code is examined by context to allow patches and monitoring for data.

[M20] An Interactive Graphical Debugging System, A.W. Walker, AD 728 711, Naval P.G. School, June 1971.
   Describes a debugging system with a formal definition of a debug command language.

[M21] Three Criteria for Designing Systems to Facilitate Debugging, E. Van Horn, CACM Vol 11 #5.
   Criteria are input recordibility, input specifiability and asynchronous reproducibility of output.

Hardware Testing Concepts

[N11] **Fault Diagnosis of Digital Systems**, H.Y. Chang, E.G. Manning and G. Metze, Wiley Inter-science, 1970.
Introduces fault diagnosis and provides a guide to the latest references in the area.

[N1] **Logical Design to Improve Software Debugging - A Proposal**, Ned Chapin, Computers and Automation, February 1966.
Proposes adding an auto monitor and snapshot and dump instructions to the reportoire of machine hardware so as to facilitate a debug package. Included here because the same hardware seems needed in testing packages.

[N2] **Diagnostic Engineering Requirements**, J. Dent, AFIPS Conference Proceedings, SJCC, 1968, pp. 503-507.
General classification of diagnostic strategies into the start small, multiple clue where diagnosis is on the basis of a series of individual tests and the start big where a failure results in changing the sequence to a lower level.

[N3] **A Pragmatic First Look at Diagnostic Programming For Digital Computers**, Phillip Enslow, DDC Report AD 652 730, May 1967.
General discussion of problems and techniques used in software machine checkout. Concludes that most important factor is to consider the needs of the diagnostic program throughout the machine design stages. Also feels that testing oriented at the logic level has been much more successful than that aimed at the microinstruction or instruction level.

[N12] **Test and Diagnosis Procedures for Digital Networks**, E.J. McCluskey, IEEE Computer Society, Computer Vol 4 #1, Jan Feb 1971.

[N13] **A Logic Design Translator Experiment Demonstrating Relationships of Language to Systems and Logic Design**, R. Proctor, IEEE Trans. on Computers, August 1964, pp.422-430.
Machine description translation to hardware equations to allow analysis and testing of an intended hardware design.

[N7] **A Graph Theoretical and Probabilistic Approach to the Fault Detection of Digital Circuits**, J.C. Rault, Int. Symposium on Fault Tolerant Computing, March 1-3, 1971, pp.26-29.

[N6] **System Segmentation for the Parallel Diagnosis of Computers**, C.V. Ramamoorthy and L.C. Chang, IEEE Trans. on Computers, Vol. C20 #3, pp.261-270, March 1971.

[N4] **Computer Fault Diagnosis Using Graph Theory**, C.V. Ramamoorthy, Honeywell Computer Journal, Fall, 1967, p.91.

[N8] **Programmed Algorithms to Compute Tests to Detect and Distinguish Between Failures in Logic Circuits**, J.P. Roth and G. Bouricius and P.R. Schneider, IEEE Trans. on Elec. Computers, Vol EC-16 #5, October 1967, pp.567-580.

[N9] **Hybrid Diagnostic Techniques**, T.K.Seechus, FJCC 1968, pp.997-1009.

[N14] **On An Improved Diagnosis Program**, S. Seshu, IEEE Trans. on Computers, February 1965, pp.76-79.
Discusses a machine test program to simulate many simultaneous failures. Can be extended to graphical path sensitizing.

[N10] **Hardware Software Tradeoffs In Testing**, J.E. Stuehler, IEEE Spectrum, December 1968.
Gives a methodology in the framework of hardware testing for deciding what to test and whether by hardware or software.

Performance Testing

[01] A Classification and Survey of Computer System Performance Evaluation Techniques,
      P.R. Blevins and C.V. Ramamoorthy, University of Texas at Austin, ERC Report
      April 1970.
         Methodology for various performance evaluation schemes is discussed and compared.

[02] System Performance -- A Survey and Appraisal, P. Calingaert, CACM, January 1967, pp.12-18.
         Emphasizes simulation.

[03] Modelling the Performance of the OS/360 Time Sharing Option (TSO), E.R. Lassetre and
      A.L. Scherr, Symposium Brown University, November 1971.
         Discusses performance specification and performance testing for TSO.

Other Program Description and Analysis Models

[P1] A Matrix Approach to Program Description and Optimization, R.L. Basford, Columbia University Thesis, 1967.

[P2] A Survey of Models for Parallel Computing, T.H. Bredt, Stanford University, Electronics Lab Report TR-8, August 1970.

[P3] An Algebraic Description of Programs With Assertions, Verification and Simulation, R.M. Burstall, Proceedings of the Conference on Proving Assertions About Programs, January 1972, pp. 7-14.
   A program in flow diagram form is described by a functor from a free category
      to the category of sets and relations.

[P4] Working Set Model For Program Behavior, P.J. Denning, CACM, May 1968, pp. 323-333.

[P5] On the Logical Schemes of Algorithms, S. Igarashi, Information Proc. in Japan, Vol. 3, 1963, pp. 12-18.

[P6] Analysis of Boolean Program Models for Time Shared Paged Environments, T.C. Lowe, CACM, pp.205-199, April 1969.
   Extends the use of Boolean descriptive matrices to consider segmentation of instructions and data in a time shared environment.

[P7] Models for the Control of Errors In A Management Information System, M.G. Lindquist, G. Montelius, Lars Owe Stakeberg, IBM Nordiska Laboratories, Stockholm, Sweden, 1971.
   Considers models for the correction value of errors defined as the utility gain from a correction minus correction cost. Criteria for selection of correction processes are given.

[P8] A Theory of Computer Instructions, W.D. Maurer, JACM Vol. 13, 1966, pp.221-235.

[P9] A Theory of Programming Languages, R.J. Orgass and F.B. Fitch, IBM Research Paper RC-1979, 1967.

[P10] Decision Problems In Computational Models, M. Paterson, Proc. of Conference on Proving Assertions About Programs, January 1972, pp.74-82.
   Discusses program assertions of correctness, equivalence, accessibility of subroutines and guarantees of termination.

[P11] Calculating Properties of Programs By Valuations On Specific Models, M. Sintyoff, Proc. of the Conference on Proving Assertions About Programs, January 1972, pp. 203-207.
   Models used to prove that programs have various properties.

[P12] Operational Semantics of Programming Languages, P. Wegner, Proc. of Conference on Proving Assertions About Programs, January 1972, pp.128-141.
   Operational Model for the Characterization of the Semantics of Programming Languages.

[P13] Formal Models of Some Features of Programming Languages, H.P. Zeiger, Proceedings of the Third Annual Princeton Conference on Information Science and Systems, 1969, pp.425-429.

INDEX OF CONCEPTS

A-PROCESS 264,270

ASSERTIONS
    assert expressions 59,63,35
    assert statements 89

AUTOMATION 25

AXIOMS 9,111,112
    axiomatic approach 94

BOOSTRAPPING 94

CERTIFICATION
    certification activities 8,31,122,129,
    131,135,140,291,299
    certification service 298,300

COMPILER 116
    testing 23,31
    validation 31

COMPLEXITY
    of programs 225,296,297
    measuring 226,232
    of understanding 228,229

CONTROL
    validation control system 205,27
    hierarchical control program 21
    partition of a program 234

CORRECTNESS
    problem of 64,88,235
    checking for 68
    at points in time 30
    of programs 76
    See also PROOF

CRITICALITY 297
    critical section 243
    critical variables 247

DATA GENERATION - See TEST DATA GENERATION

DATA SENSITIVE 160

DEBUGGING 8,11,77
    tools 78
    aids 256

DECISION TABLES 25,298

DESIGN
    for testability 18,41
    errors 124
    of programming languages 75,77
    of testing 42,187

DESK CHECK 29

DEVELOPMENT PROCESS 168

DOCUMENTATION 122,125,168,179,229,266,282
    objectives document 169
    design change procedure 179
    build plan 170
    testing documentation 283
    synonomous with proof 229
    See also SPECIFICATIONS

DOMAIN ANALYSIS 126

EVNIRONMENT
    for programming 51,54
    for testing 177

ERRORS 76,139,173,227
    transmitted 125
    truncation 125,144,280,284
    roundoff 125,280,284
    generated 125,129,144,148
    forward error analysis 126
    backward error analysis 126,132
    input 144
    language causing constructions 83
    run time 67,80,90
    indicating arithmetic 145

EXPERIENCE INDEX 182,186

FLOWCHARTS 23,26
    automatic flow charting programs 29
    See also GRAPHS

FOLDING 241

FRANCHISEMENT 300

FUNCTIONAL PROGRAMMING - See STRUCTURED
    PROGRAMMING

GO TO FREE CODING 46

GRAPHS
    state 240-243
    directed 270